Screen Acting

Screen Acting
A Cognitive Approach

Dan Leberg

EDINBURGH
University Press

For Robin

Edinburgh University Press is one of the leading university presses in the UK. We publish academic books and journals in our selected subject areas across the humanities and social sciences, combining cutting-edge scholarship with high editorial and production values to produce academic works of lasting importance. For more information visit our website: edinburghuniversitypress.com

© Dan Leberg, 2022, 2024

Edinburgh University Press Ltd
The Tun—Holyrood Road
12 (2f) Jackson's Entry
Edinburgh EH8 8PJ

First published in hardback by Edinburgh University Press 2022

Typeset in Monotype Ehrhardt by
Manila Typesetting Company, and
printed and bound by CPI Group (UK) Ltd,
Croydon, CR0 4YY

A CIP record for this book is available from the British Library

ISBN 978 1 4744 8413 8 (hardback)
ISBN 978 1 4744 8414 5 (paperback)
ISBN 978 1 4744 8415 2 (webready PDF)
ISBN 978 1 4744 8416 9 (epub)

The right of Dan Leberg to be identified as author of this work has been asserted in accordance with the Copyright, Designs and Patents Act 1988 and the Copyright and Related Rights Regulations 2003 (SI No. 2498).

Contents

List of Figures vii
Acknowledgments ix

Introduction: The Missing Parts 1
1. The Moving Parts 9
   Cognitive Theater Studies and Acting 10
   Television Studies and Acting 21
2. All By Our Selves: Empathy and Acting 28
   Situational and Selfless Selfhood 29
   Empathy 32
   The Project Ahead: Screen Actors as Solicitors of Empathy 45
3. The Actor's Three Empathetic Connections 49
   Intrasubjective Empathy 51
   Intersubjective Empathy 63
   Performative Empathy 74
   Conclusion: "Camera rolling . . . and, action!" 80
4. Acting Culture and Audition Preparation 85
   Practice, Constraint, and Affordance 85
   "It's nice work if you can get it . . .": Auditions and Precarity 88
   Audition Logistics and Empathy 95
5. Empathetic Work Prior to Shooting 109
   From Guesswork to Scaffolding 109
   A Note on Terminology 110
   "Bottom-up Script Analysis": Extrapolating Specific Memories into Emotional Common Denominators 111
   "Top-down Script Analysis": Imagination, Abstraction, Archetype 117
   Cayonne's Minotaur: Balancing Memory and Imagination to Find the Character's Body Schema 125
   Conclusion: Arriving on Set 131

6. Empathy on Set	133
Actors and Production Culture: Inductive, Ecumenical, and Self-effacing Practices on Set	133
The Actor and the Camera: Habits, Techniques, and Technology	138
The Other Actor: Creative Labor and Intersubjective Empathy on Set	145
Real Fake Tears, and Talking to Tennis Balls: Incorporating Production Conditions into Acting Choices	158
Conclusion	166
7. Conclusion: "Ready for my Close-up"	171
Histories of Force and Eloquence	172
Collective Cognition and Production Studies	182
Sympathy for Kuleshov: (Re-)Introducing Acting to Film Form	185
Acting Studies and Resets	188
Bibliography	193
Index	203

Figures

2.1	Harvey Keitel and Robert de Niro in *Taxi Driver*	39
5.1	Natalie Lisinska and Tatiana Maslany in *Orphan Black*, season 1, episode 10, "Endless Forms Most Beautiful"	114
5.2	Kevin McGarry in *Heartland*, season 7, episode 10, "Riding Shotgun"	115
6.1	Lindsey Middleton in *Out With Dad*, season 3, episode 5, "Outed"	135
6.2	Sheila McCarthy and Eugene Robert Glazer in *Steppin' Out*	142
6.3	Joe Dinicol and Gil Bellows in *Passchendaele*	149
6.4	Kevin McGarry and Shaun Johnston in *Heartland*, season 7, episode 10, "Riding Shotgun"	165
7.1	Marlon Brando and Eva Marie Saint in *On The Waterfront*	173
7.2	Diane Keaton in *Annie Hall*	179

Acknowledgments

I am forever grateful to Patricia Pisters and Catherine Lord, whose regular support, criticism, and kindness were instrumental in helping me turn a long, strange rant into something legible. Thank you also to Maaike Bleeker, Agneta Fischer, Julian Kiverstein, Murray Pratt, Kati Röttger, Aaron Taylor, and Maryn Wilkinson for all of their insightful feedback. In particular, the Screen Acting and Embodied Cognition project led by Aaron Taylor at the University of Lethbridge is one that parallels my own, and his support for even the earliest versions of my plan was crucial to my feeling that it was worth seeing through.

Thank you to the reviewers who the Edinburgh University Press asked to assess the various stages of this book. My work is better because you pushed me to make it so.

The votes of professional confidence extended by Mariëtte Willemsen, Marcel Broersma, Susan Aasman, Julian Hanich, Miklós Kiss, and Erinç Salor have helped to keep my lights on, my coffee pot full, and my spirits high. Thank you also to the rest of Amsterdam University College's Humanities department, and the University of Groningen's Media Studies and Film Studies departments, who had to deal with all that optimism in all in those bright rooms after drinking all that coffee.

Thank you to the faculty and (former) graduate students of Concordia University's Mel Hoppenheim School of Cinema and Faculty of Humanities, for their friendship, guidance, and patience during the first stages of this project: Martin Lefebvre, Masha Salazkina, Luca Caminati, Tom Waugh, Kay Dickinson, Rosanna Maule, Dirk Gindt, Rachel Jekanowski, Antoine Damiens, Fulvia Massimi, Meredith Slifkin, and Viviane Saglier. I also have to thank Svetla Turnin, Ezra Winton, and the Cinema Politica team for making sure that I never lost sight of the present world while theorizing about imagined and remembered ones.

Thank you to the many mentors that I worked with during my years as a professional actor for sharing their craft, passion, and strength with me.

More immediately, the screen-specific and Method acting techniques that I learned from Bruce Clayton, Deb Mulholland, and Sebastian Gerold were invaluable firsthand experiences that informed considerable portions of this book.

I am deeply indebted to the wonderful actors who generously took the time to talk to me about their experiences: Chris Baker, Antonio Cayonne, Joe Dinicol, Julian De Zotti, Natalie Lisinska, Matt MacFadzean, Lauren MacKinlay, Sheila McCarthy, Kevin McGarry, Lindsey Middleton, Danelene O'Flynn, Jamie Spilchuk, and the innumerable others with whom I've discussed my ideas over the years. Jason Leaver and Meagan Allison-Hancock went out of their way to help connect me to as many of their favorite actor colleagues as they could.

This book's long strange journey would simply never have happened without the friendship, love, and support of Jamila Allidina, Sarah Joy Bennett, John Crawford, Gabriela and Steven Dale, and Robin Wright. I am blessed with the most supportive and loving family, and none of this would have been possible without them. Most of all, thank you to my wife, Sabrina Sauer, for being the most brilliant, thoughtful, and inspiring person that I could ever hope to share my life with.

Introduction
The Missing Parts

I had worked as a professional actor for nearly twenty years before enrolling in the Introduction to Cinema Studies course at the University of Toronto. As I flipped through the syllabus, I remember wondering where the lecture on acting would be: there were weeks on cinematography and *mise-en-scène*, a month on various genres, a week on experimental filmmaking, but where was the class on acting? The main discussion of acting came during the *mise-en-scène* week, where we discussed how everything put in front of the camera—including the actors—was part of a greater formal and narrational scheme. Needless to say, I was somewhat confused as to why everything I had learned as a professional storyteller was suddenly a glorified footnote in the study of a medium where stories are told (at least in part) through performances.

Later in my film studies career, we learned other ways of talking about actors and acting, especially in terms of what performances can signify in greater historical, cultural, theoretical, or industrial contexts. Even still, these new ways of talking about acting always felt distant from the acting work I had grown up doing: was all that time and energy I had spent acting actually just part of a catalyst for reawakening for the Lacanian mirror phases of my pacified consumer audiences? Were my professional performances of white North American Anglophonic heteronormative masculinity actually just another normalization of discursive tensions within late capitalist ideology under some dubious pretext of making art? Even though I am personally and politically sympathetic to those critiques, how was I to reconcile my experiences as a professional storyteller with the academic stories being told about my profession? After all, as cognitive theater scholar Rick Kemp notes, an actor's performance does not simply appear out of thin air: actors do an extensive amount of training, rehearsal, behind-the-scenes preparation, and creative experimentations of trial and error to make the verisimilitude of their final performances appear seamless.[1] Why didn't film studies appear to understand that?

In graduate school, I worked as a seminar leader on Introduction to Film Studies courses similar to the one I had taken. These courses inevitably omitted an analysis of film acting in favor of other important and accessible topics. One such course positioned actors as an afterthought during a lecture on filmic props, including a joke that the main difference between film actors and props is that actors are more likely to move of their own volition. I realized two things after this class. First, film studies lacks an accepted critical vocabulary for talking about the entirety of an actor's creative process; otherwise, the joke about actors being glorified props would not have landed. Second, and contrary to all of my experiences as a professional artist, the notion of performance in textual analysis had become an impediment to a serious critical study of what working actors actually do. Maybe there was a way to analyze film acting as a practice and process, rather than as only a performed result. Perhaps this could extend the joke's notion of "moving" beyond recorded physical gestures to include how actors emotionally "move" their audiences as skilled practitioners while also being internally and externally "moved" by the very act of performing? What would that motion look like, what trajectories would it travel, and what kind of critical framework would this motion need for film scholars and film practitioners alike to recognize themselves in my work?

The lack of an overarching critical framework for analyzing screen acting as a practice is hardly surprising. The most concerted effort in the history of film studies to analyze the creative output of a key production figure centered on the director, with auteurist criticism long outliving its 1950s–60s heyday. Some recent auteurist research has moved beyond analyzing individual directors as the sole creative agent on film sets to instead account for the film festival industry's commodification of creative genius[2] and the performances of directors who appear in their own films.[3] While the preoccupation with the director's contribution to the finished film does not completely vanish, however, nor does it share much of the spotlight.

The closest thing to an actor-centric discourse in modern mainstream film studies is performance studies, which positions an actor's performance as a finished object for spectatorial semiotic, cultural, and historical inquiry. With the greatest of respect for the fields of media history and cultural analysis, and the timely, important, and rigorous work of my many friends and colleagues who specialize in those fields, the predominantly spectatorial approach to performance analysis consistently runs into trouble when it tries to account for the totality of the actor's work, beyond what the actor's performance can signify and represent.

To explain what I mean, this book makes a necessary distinction between the two terms most frequently invoked when describing the work of an actor: "acting" and "performance." "*Acting*," for this book's purposes, will refer to the entire process of how an actor prepares to portray a character within the narrative at hand. The processes and practices of realist screen acting—this book's primary subject—therefore encompass a wide range of production circumstances, such as creative training, auditions, character preparation, rehearsal exploration, on-set habits for quickly immersing oneself in a scene during a fast-paced shoot, etc.[4] Following Sternagel, Levitt, and Mersch's distinction between the "force" of acting and its "eloquence" of performance,[5] this study treats that force of acting as the process that produces finished, filmed, lucid performances: the portrayals of the actor's character that are presented in front of the camera on set, some of which become part of the finished media text. In treating performance as eloquence, this study emphasizes *how* the actor's acting work facilitates her performance of the character. "*Performance*" here is therefore understood as the filmed end result of her creative work, regardless of what cultural paradigms that piece of acting demonstrates or the aesthetic merits (or lack thereof) of the actor's embodiment of her character. Performance is but one privileged aspect of the greater process of acting. The point of this distinction between acting and performance is to open up the academic tradition of analyzing actors and acting in purely spectatorial terms, which often reduce acting to performance—and actors to performers—without considering the creative work behind that on-screen performance.

Performance is a particularly loaded term—far beyond its capacity to label the "finished" version of an actor's enactment of a particular character—which is productively invoked across the humanities and social sciences. In film, television, and media studies, performance is often invoked to frame the cultural semiotics of an actor's representation of her character, such as, for example, Judith Butler's influential discursive model of gender as a performed identity,[6] or Richard Dyer's medium-specific analysis of how white ethnicity is normalized and made invisible within classical Hollywood.[7] I do not challenge Butler's notion that gender's social constructions can be rehearsed and renegotiated in media, nor do I challenge Dyer's assessment of Hollywood's implicit racial biases. I do, however, challenge the presumption that the semiotics of performance encompass all that can be said about screen acting.

Film studies traditions such as Dyer's star studies often analyze screen actors' performances for how they signify cultural paradigms such as race, class, and gender.[8] Indeed, this performance-centric approach positions actors as semiotic specimens ripe for dissection, rather than as creative agents who produce the performances in question:

> although [movie] stars signify in films by virtue of being an already-signifying image and by being given a character partly constructed by script, *mise en scene*, etc., [. . .] all of this is only there on the screen in its enactment or performance.[9]

Dyer's actor is a by-product of the texts in which she performs, a dead Barthesian author whose work exists only in the fodder it provides to the viewer's reassemblage and interpretation.[10] Insightful, influential, and productive as Dyer's approach has proven to be, its exclusively spectatorial approach to filmic performances struggles to account for the actor's work behind those performances, relegating all off-screen acting work to inconvenient ambiguity.

As just one example, Christina Adamou expresses frustration at the limited access that an actor's performance gives to the process of acting in her articulate analysis of post-feminist gender representations in *Mr. and Mrs. Smith* (Doug Liman, 2005). In this essay, Adamou claims that Angelina Jolie and Brad Pitt perform "imperfect" gender roles through their gestures, postures, and vocal intonations. Adamou's critical frustration manifests in trying to analyze acting at all because of the semiotic ambiguities of some performed moments:

> It is much easier and more objective to define, for instance, a particular shade of red in a set or costume, or a movement of the camera, than to define a particular smile. A close-up or medium close-up, a dark or light red are elements of the audiovisual text that can be identified and then interpreted whereas a broad smile or a cynical or crooked smile are notions "suspect" of containing subjectivity or already connoting a particular reading.[11]

Since a semiotic dissection of the performances cannot reveal the actors' creative intentions, motivations, and personal references behind the performance, Adamou cannot account for Jolie and Pitt's intentionalities, and therefore cannot disentangle acting from the performance of given narrative moments. I do not challenge Adamou's premise that Jolie and Pitt's performances are a compelling case study of post-feminist politics, nor do I suggest that Adamou's cultural approach is misinformed or unproductive. I do argue, however, that this performance-centric approach risks conflating performance with the entirety of acting by presuming that acting is nothing more than the cultural semiotics of an actor's gestures, postures, and speech patterns.

Adamou is far from alone in conflating the spectatorial experience of an actor's performance with the acting work and industrial collaborations behind that performance. James Naremore positions screen actors as the formally over-determined authors of performed texts about which scholars ask questions about historical styles, aesthetic movements, and production circumstances, and reception contexts. Although the ways in which actors signify those discursive codes can be informative, the "fuzzy, adjectival language"[12] used to describe how actors work, and the affective experience of acting as a whole, renders the actor's agency and practices as moot points.

In an inverse configuration, Andrew Klevan analyzes the pleasurable watchability of actors in classical Hollywood cinema by spatializing the actor's expressions of narrative subtext.[13] Klevan's analysis of Cary Grant's performances in *The Awful Truth* (Leo McCarey, 1937) and *The Philadelphia Story* (George Cukor, 1940) highlights how Grant skillfully incorporates his physical proximity to set pieces into his character's dramatic relationship with other characters in the scene.[14] In the last scene of *The Awful Truth*, for example, Grant's character's conversation with his soon-to-be ex-wife places Grant near bedroom doorframes and the bed itself. Klevan argues that Grant uses these doorframes and the bed to symbolically inform his dialogue's subtext about exiting the marriage or reigniting its intimacy. In this way, Grant's use of the film set anticipates his understanding of how he was being filmed, and his attempt to best align the raw materials of his performance with the anticipated final version of the film.

Despite the artistic agency that Klevan reads into a given actor's work in a particular film, his departure point is inherently spectatorial in that he implies directors skillfully capture whatever the actor does in front of the camera, which risks conflating actorly creative processes with their narrative results. That said, Klevan takes a major step towards accounting for the actor's creative agency by attributing the communicative nature of the actor's performance largely to the work of the actor herself. In this case, the screen actor's navigation of the film sets affordances and constraints—the perceived opportunities for action and the restrictions upon that action's results[15]—position the actor as a prominent collaborator in the film's meaning-making project, even if the point of access to this agency is whatever it makes visible to an inherently restricted spectatorial vantage point. To better account for this creative agency, a theory of screen acting must position intentionality as a productive force within acting practices, rather than as a hurdle for reception theory.

Aaron Taylor, for example, has argued persuasively that film actors can make complex philosophical assertions through their performances: the boyish sincerity of Jimmy Stewart's star persona in *Rear Window* (Alfred Hitchcock, 1954), for example, can be argued to undercut any easy equation of voyeurism with sadism.[16] An actor's performative indices—the enacted reification of a philosophical assertion through performed dramatic action—inevitably include the actor's individual articulation of that argument within the semiotic reading of the argument itself. When configured as a professional practice, actorly intentionality does not inherently aspire to present the actor's own creative inspirations as confessional, imaginary artifacts to be excavated by the spectator. Instead, the screen actor intends to communicate her participation within the narrative with as much verisimilar detail as possible.

In this line of thought, Taylor argues that the preoccupation with Dyer's star studies and the semiotic reading of actorly performances obscures the analysis of the process of acting within its performed results.[17] In a way, this is a question of scholarly access point: very few screen media scholars have also worked as professional screen actors, so studying acting by watching performances in finished films and television shows makes pragmatic sense. Like Taylor though, I suggest instead that performance is part of acting but not all of acting, and that an explicitly spectatorial critical framework—like the ones so keenly focused on star-studies-like performance analysis—cannot fully account for acting as a creative practice.

If acting generates "mediated performance[s] that lies at the intersection of art, technology, and culture",[18] then this book focuses on how the generation of a filmic performance combines creative expression, technological collaboration, and actorly practices for soliciting and sustaining a situational relationship with a fictitious lived world. In a sense, acting is a process of connecting lived intentionalities to the character's situational self[19] in a way that navigates the constraints and affordances of the character's world's mediation. The immersive practices that enable the actor's verisimilar communication need not demonstrate their inspirational or intentional content beyond that the actor compellingly communicates her part of the narrative. The actor's agency in communicating her part of the narrative, which generally comes down to her unseen creative work of realigning aspects of her quotidian[20] self to enact her character's situational self, is invisible to the audience of the finished film. This is therefore a far cry from arguing the actor's work that is never seen by the audience is inconsequential, accidental, or useless to an understanding of how acting practices generate performances. Performance is the end result of acting's process, but it not the entirety of that process.

Fortunately, recent developments in other fields with an understandable investment in realist acting, such as theater and television studies, have made great strides towards placing acting *as a practice* at the center of their critical conversations. This book aspires to connect the cognitive and phenomenological models of stage acting from theater studies with the ethnographic, historical, and production-centered approaches to acting in television studies, in order to develop a critical vocabulary for analyzing screen acting in terms of what the actor does creatively, industrially, and practically while filming. Just as Rhonda Blair and Amy Cook suggest that cognitive perspectives on theatrical acting can allow questions about creative process without discarding cultural concerns about performance,[21] so too does this book question what may have been overlooked in the study of film and television acting as a practice. This book seeks to map that bodymind movement from quotidian to situational self across acting's entire process through a broad model of bodymind self-organization and empathy, and then reinforcing these claims with interviews with actors about how they practice their craft. Beyond looking for performative indices as moments of actor-specific creative agency, this study looks to the instrumentality of the screen actor's bodymind to produce a critical methodology that accounts for performance *and* the acting work within it and behind it. This rhetorical move must necessarily start with the actor and work towards the audience, grounding this analysis in the common corporeal and cognitive resources that actors use while acting and that spectators use while viewing.

Notes

1. Kemp, "Devising—embodied creativity in distributed systems."
2. de Valck, "Film festivals, Bourdieu, and the economization of culture."
3. Sayad, *Performing Authorship: Self-Inscription and Corporeality in the Cinema*.
4. Cantrell and Hogg, "Returning to an old question: what do television actors do when they act?", p. 285.
5. Sternagel, Levitt, and Mersch, "Etymological uncoveries, creative displays: acting as force and performance as eloquence in moving image culture," p. 53.
6. Butler, "Gender Is burning: questions of appropriation and subversion"; Butler, "Performative acts and gender constitution: an essay in phenomenology and feminist theory."
7. Dyer, "White".
8. Dyer, *Stars*, pp. 1–2.
9. Ibid. p. 88.
10. Barthes, "The death of the author."

11. Adamou, "Postfeminist portrayals of masculinity and femininity in action films: *Mr. and Mrs. Smith*," pp. 105–6.
12. Naremore, *Acting in the Cinema*, pp. 2–3.
13. Klevan, *Film Performance: From Achievement to Appreciation*, 2005.
14. Klevan, *Film Performance*, pp. 32–46.
15. See Chapter 4 for a more thorough explanation of constraints and affordances.
16. Taylor, "Thinking through acting: performative indices and philosophical assertions", pp. 395–400.
17. Taylor, "Thinking through acting," pp. 408–9.
18. Baron, Carson, and Tomasulo, "More than the Method, more than one method," p. 1.
19. Kemp, *Embodied Acting: What Neuroscience Tells Us about Performance*, p. xviii.
20. Throughout this book, the term "quotidian" refers to the actor's selfhood when she is not acting. This categorization of selves will be explained more thoroughly throughout Chapters 1 and 2.
21. Blair and Cook, "Introduction," p. 1.

CHAPTER 1

The Moving Parts

The primary claim of this book is that post-1950s western realist film acting is a practice that solicits three complementary, simultaneous, and overlapping empathetic relationships: an intrasubjective relationship between the actor and her character; the intersubjective relationships among performing actors and among actors-as-characters; and, a performative relationship between the actor and her audience. While cognitive philosopher Shawn Gallagher and actor Julia Gallagher readily describe an actor's relationship with her character as empathetic,[1] this study expands the solicitation of this relationship to additional targets such as the other actors and the anticipated audience as part of creating acting's verisimilar illusion. Even if a complete empathetic connection is as much an ideal as it is a result of acting practices, the mental, corporeal, and emotional processes undertaken in the solicitation of each empathetic connection create the verisimilar illusion upon which realist acting depends. In other words, the actor's transformation into her character is the result of how she has aspired to connect—and often move herself imaginatively, physically, and emotionally closer—to her character, her fellow actors and their characters, and her anticipated audience.

This analysis of film actors as empathizers aspires to open a critical discussion about the creative agency of screen actors by theorizing from the actor outwards towards the spectator. The goal is no longer to consider screen acting as a mystical generator of semiotically dissectible performances, or an over-determined side effect of film production, nor does it possess a standardized benchmark for aesthetic merit. Instead, acting is a meaning-making practice wherein the actor reorganizes her quotidian self and its bodymind schema to enact the situational character's lived world, to align herself within the intentional pull of her fellow actors-as-characters, and to collaborate with camera as an access point to her anticipated audience. In short, the goal of this book is to account for the agency of the moving parts of the *mise-en-scène*, and the ways in which they move themselves and each other in order to move their audiences.

Cognitive Theater Studies and Acting

A major focal point with cognitive theater studies is the deductive—rather than empirical or inductive—application of neuroscience and theories of cognition to analyze the ways actors do creative work, and how audiences engage with that work.[2] This approach necessarily raises questions of selfhood, embodiment, emotion, and meaning-making in theatrical training and storytelling. This book seeks to synthesize recurring ideas within this branch of cognitive theater studies into a model of acting in which actors are on one hand, embodied cognizers who reorganize their bodyminds to enact the situational selves of their scripted characters and, on the other hand, key dynamic nodes in a network of creative cognition that is distributed across the environments and contexts in which acting takes place.

Neurophenomenology and Actors' Bodyminds

Cognitive and phenomenological models of theatrical acting often analyze the actor's deeply interconnected mind and body as an instrument of narrative communication. Rhonda Blair argues that the actor's core materials of creation are the interwoven and inseparable "body and the consciousness that rises out of it."[3] To this end, many actor-training techniques seek to train strong and versatile bodymind interconnections[4] to deeply enculture the actor's ability to act and react within the actor-as-character's social, historical, cultural, and aesthetic world and thereby give a verisimilar performance.[5] These interconnections enable the actor to not only learn through her body, but reimagine and apply that corporeal knowledge to her character's situation. The actor creates by unifying her body and her imagination through action, therefore emphasizing the communicative nature of intentionalized actions in fictitious and quotidian situations. Moreover, Blair's insistence that actors imagine with their bodies to generate source material for their performances[6] suggests that actors not only simulate their scripted character's but articulate that simulation in a communicative performance for an anticipated audience. The actor does not need to inscribe her personal memories directly within her character. The actor creates her role by *doing* and *playing* within the character's lived world, not by putting her quotidian self within the fictitious world,[7] but by empathizing with the character so as to imagine *as* someone else.[8] In arguing that western realist screen acting solicits multiple empathetic connections between the actor and a range of targets, this book provides a conceptual framework for the actor's bodymind movements—often in the solicitation of those connections—across her entire creative process.

Some theater scholars, for example, John Lutterbie and Philip Zarrilli, derive entire models of realist stage acting from the notion of mind and body interconnection by interpreting acting practices through neurophenomenology, a hybrid discourse which treats phenomenological philosophy and cognitive neuroscience as mutually informing bodies of literature. Neurophenomenologist Evan Thompson's model of selfhood revolves around the idea of the "bodymind,"[9] a holistic and non-compartmentalized integration of traditionally internal forces, such as memory, imagination, and emotion, with traditionally external forces, such as physical action, gesture, and posture. Reading neuroscientists such as Francisco Varela alongside phenomenologists such as Maurice Merleau-Ponty, Thompson presents mind and body as being inextricably linked in an autopoietic, self-organizing network of meaning-making systems and behaviors, such as action, perception, and emotion:

> Mental life is also bodily life and is situated in the world. The roots of mental life lie not simply in the brain, but ramify through the body and environment. Our mental lives involve our body and the world beyond the surface membrane of our organism, and therefore cannot be reduced simply to brain processes inside the head.[10]

This deep level of bodymind interconnectivity prompts Thompson to advocate for a model of cognition called embodied dynamicism, which insists that all levels of cognition and emotion are part of an iterative network of the mind, body, and "[the] material, social, and cultural environments in which the body is embedded".[11] The equal footing given to the body and its surrounding environment in cognition is a sharp break with earlier computational and connectionist models of cognition; embodied dynamicism's mind is no longer a central reception hub that collects and processes sensory information from a series of fixed nervous channels throughout the body.[12] Instead, embodied dynamicism replaces computational and connectionist models of mind–body relationships with dynamic systems theory (DST).

DST states that interactions among individuals, and between individuals and their environment, occur within a system of rules; however, in the iterative exchanges among individuals and their environments, the overarching rules begin to adjust themselves to align with the nature of those interactions. This inevitably changes the rules for all subsequent interactions, as well as the context for the next round of rule changes, thereby creating a dynamic and iterative loop of adjustments to actions and their boundaries alike.[13] Therefore, in applying DST to cognition's relationship to embodiment, Thompson's embodied dynamicism dissolves traditionally internal/cognitive-emotional and external/physical boundaries to explore how the bodymind changes and self-organizes over time.[14] Traditionally internal stimuli, for example, emotional fluctuations, and traditionally external changes, for example, sensory information, can both prompt changes throughout the bodymind system, depending on how those perturbations are sorted by the bodymind's ever-shifting intentional focus.[15]

The forces of intentionality that coordinate our bodymind self-organization delineate our autonomy within the external world, while also presenting our internal circumstances to us in a way that makes them as real to us as the world we perceive beyond our organism. Our sense of self within this intentionalized dynamic system often correlates with our perceptual experience of our own body, in terms of its appearance, abilities, affective states, and so on. The fluidity of exchange throughout the bodymind network of traditionally internal and traditionally external perturbations can inform the bodily self-representations. By focusing her intentionality on translating the character's situational intentionality into her quotidian bodymind, the actor begins to connect with how her character thinks, feels, and acts within the drama. The dynamic system of constant self-organization as the actor connects with her situational character is therefore largely coordinated through changes in intentional focus.

At least part of the appeal of embodied dynamicism for cognitive theater scholars is the notion that the iterative loop of perception, intention, action, and reaction at the core of western realist acting practices[16] is predicated on actors' minds and bodies communicating as a unified whole. Even if some prolific styles of actor training compartmentalize the actor's "interior" from her "exterior," or her conscious mind from her unconscious mind,[17] the actor's malleable bodymind ultimately reconfigures itself to "move" internally *and* externally as the performed character. In this regard, the functional storytelling goals of western realist acting across media are mostly the same: actors "become" their characters though the physical and imaginary transposition of their character's intentionality into the actor's own bodymind; they relate to their fictional surroundings as their characters; they communicate their characters' thoughts, intentions, actions, and feelings as part of their responsibility to performing the story; and so forth.

Both Zarrilli and Lutterbie interpret the theater actor's creative process through Thompson's notion of embodied dynamism to describe how theater actors integrate their bodies, imagination, and emotions into a single meaning-making system through performance.[18] The actor is in a constant state of reactive mental and physical change, "responding to internal and external cues, aware of changes in the performance (self-generated or an effect of the work of others), and in tune with the ebb and flow of audience involvement."[19] Lutterbie places an actor's work within this framework to argue that the actor and actor-as-character's constant reorganizations generate the situational world of the drama. In this model, the actor's imagination is a versatile and omnipresent force in the actor's capacity to create. Imagined events can trigger physical and emotional states that immerse the actor in the "Magic If"[20] of a crucial dramatic moment,[21] but these imagined events or recalled moments can themselves be triggered by physical actions and affective associations.[22] Zarrilli seconds Lutterbie's point that the application of Thompson's embodied dynamism to the study of acting productively shifts the conversation away from representational semiotics—a point that this study will return to in relation to film acting—and towards creative process through bodymind experience.[23] For Zarrilli, acting is a combination of opening one's bodymind to the tactile and non-tactile potentialities of the diegetic world and then, crucially, communicating those bodymind experiences on behalf of the anticipated audience.[24] Zarrilli and Lutterbie are preoccupied with the liveness of actor-to-actor and actor-to-audience exchanges, which are unsurprisingly more readily associated with live theater than a film set or television show without a live studio audience. One of the goals of this book—and in fact one of the rationales for framing screen acting as the solicitation of empathy—is to rework the richness of theatrical models of acting like those found in Lutterbie and Zarrilli for the creative and industrial circumstances of screen media production.

Most contemporary actors would argue that a common creativity at the core of realist acting transcends any medium-specific concerns. This study understands "creativity" as the actor's storytelling ingenuity that is produced and elucidated through her mastery of her bodymind instrument. This creativity manifests through performance in the continuity between the actor's source material and her engagement of these materials, all within an iterative loop of action and reaction. For example, and despite their vastly differing expectations and technical priorities for actors, even mutually opposed American Method acting practitioners such as Lee Strasberg, Stella Adler, and Sanford Meisner[25] would all agree that training actors for creativity entails all of the following: gathering potential source materials through observation, memory, action, and imagination; improving one's capacity for identifying those source materials, wherever they present themselves; relating to those source materials in a way that immerses the actor within the fictitious world of the character; and letting these resources inform the situational character's reactions within the iterative loop of the scene's social dynamics.[26] What makes neurophenomenological models of selfhood and empathy so applicable to the study of screen acting is the theory's deep investment in the component forces of actor's creativity: memory, imagination, intention, observation, action, malleability, enculturation, and—most of all—the capacity to make connections amongst it all. This common bodymind creativity suggests that realist acting's techniques, practices, and traditions—American Method or otherwise—for different media are essentially different mobilizations of the same bodymind resources of imagination, memory, action and reaction, and, as this book will proceed to argue, empathy.

One of the key benefits of neurophenomenological analyses of acting is a malleable model of selfhood, which is very helpful in accounting for the actor's bodymind reorganization as the actor-as-character in the contexts of embodied cognition, distributed cognition, and empathy. Theater scholar Rick Kemp disputes the commonplace notion that humans—including actors by extension—have an "essential self": a fixed and foundational personality which remains constant across all social contexts across one's whole life.[27] For example, I am a different person when I take my toddler son to the local playground than I am when I play on a city-league baseball team with friends, even if both scenarios involve enjoyable outdoor recreation with people I care about. The closest thing that I have to a constant self is my proprioception:[28] the sense of my own body which lets me walk without paying attention to how my legs and feet move, or to speak my first language without thinking about the coordination of my jaw, lip, and tongue movements. Otherwise, that which emerges from our bodyminds as our personality is a series of "situational selves"[29] which engage and embellish upon the proprioceptive self to function in different social contexts. The Dan-as-parent version of me at the playground and the Dan-as-centerfielder version of me are different situational selves which rely on the proprioceptive mastery of my bodymind, even if they engage it in different ways.

The ramifications of Kemp's distinction between proprioceptive and situational selves for how actors create their characters are significant, and will be unpacked in greater detail in Chapter 2. For now, I suggest a further level of terminology which I will use throughout this book to make a key distinction among an actor's many situational selves. If I were cast in a production of *Romeo and Juliet* as Mercutio, the situational selves of Dan-as-Mercutio, Dan-as-parent, Dan-as-centerfielder, and others all still engage with my proprioceptive self, and may have significant situational overlaps with each other. However, the imaginary circumstances which inform Dan-as-Mercutio only exist within the narrative framework of Shakespeare's play, which locates that situational self in a categorically different relationship to the world around him than my other situational selves, who exist primarily in my quotidian life. This book will therefore treat an actor's "quotidian self" as the accumulation of all situational selves which do not explicitly exist in fictional universes: Dan-as-parent, Dan-as-centerfielder, Dan-as-film-studies-researcher, and many more all fall under the label of my quotidian self. The situational self of the character, and of the actor-as-character, are free to engage with any aspects of the actor's proprioceptive and quotidian selves as the actor sees fit, but remain outside the category of quotidian self because they can only *act* within a fictional universe rather than my everyday one.

Conceptual Blending and Acting

Neurophenomenology is not the only overarching model of human mental life to inform recent cognitive studies of theater, nor is it inherently at odds with these other models. Gilles Fauconnier and Mark Turner argue for a common cognitive underpinning for how ideas occur across the human experience, regardless of the subject matter, the intelligence of the thinker who has the idea, the thinker's language or age, etc.[30] Conceptual blending is an unconscious, invisible, and pervasive mental process[31] by which the mind blends, extrapolates, and reconfigures the meanings bound to specific entities to produce new ideas. The meanings of these conceptual blends emerge through the deceptively complicated interactions of the identities that the mind binds to entities, the integrations of those identities, and the imagined frameworks which make sense of those integrated identities, such as metaphors, analogies, narratives, fantasies, and more. In their example, Zeus can be imagined as a bull, a swan, a king, and as an incestuous sibling without provoking a conflict with his godhood because of the mind's ability to blend concepts together in different narrative frameworks.[32]

Similarly, Fauconnier and Turner use the hypothetical example of pondering how Margaret Thatcher would have fared in negotiations with Midwest labor unions were she to have run for the American presidency rather than the office of British prime minister, to illustrate the forces of integration upon which the idea depends. To comprehend this hypothetical situation, one must draw multiple simultaneous parallels between the UK and the USA, Thatcher and her American ideological counterpart Ronald Reagan, the prime minister's office and the presidency, labor unions in the UK and in the American Midwest, and so on. Moreover, one would have to extrapolate, compress, and otherwise reconfigure other knowledge about Thatcher's personal history and political acumen to assess how she would have fared in the American political system, whether she would have used the same negotiating tactics with American unions as she did with British ones, and so on. This thought experiment offers a glimpse of the basic kinds of imaginary transpositions and narrative analogies which have proven foundational to cognitive theater scholars such as Rick Kemp, Bruce McConachie, Amy Cook, Rhonda Blair, and many more.

Within cognitive theater studies, conceptual blending becomes a way to account for the embodied cognition active on both sides of the stage's footlights. McConachie, for example, reads cognitive blending into acting-like activities, from childhood role-playing games to the suspension of disbelief through which the audience accepts the actors-as-characters and their actions as being simultaneously real and fictitious.[33] Within the conceptual blend of theatrical verisimilitude, audiences may come to empathize with the actors-as-characters they see on stage.[34] The same bodymind processes which allow audiences to experience empathy within a conceptual blend are sometimes targeted for development as part of an actor's professional training. Renowned theater practitioner Michael Chekhov, who also personally trained A-list movie stars in the Hollywood Studio era,[35] instructed actors to ask empathy-inducing questions about their characters to help the actors immerse themselves in the character's personality and worldview:

> "What is the difference between my way of thinking and the character's way of thinking? What are the differences between the feelings and emotions of the character and myself? What is the nature of my will and inclinations against those of the character."[36]

Rick Kemp argues persuasively that Chekhov's questions prompt the actor to create a conceptual blend around the character by investigating the differences between the actor's life and the scripted clues towards the character's personality.[37] Moreover, the prompts in Chekhov's questions for the observing actor to attend to and match the target character's disposition while still maintaining a distinct identity from the target align strikingly well with the models of empathy from researchers such as Jean Decety and Amy Coplan, which are unpacked in greater detail in the next chapter. In the later chapters of this book, I will extend the empathy-inducing conceptual blends that Kemp traces in Chekhov to the more individualized actorly habits that emerged in my interviews for this book with professional North American screen actors; actor Antonio Cayonne, for example, describes his process of creating characters as "making minotaurs" from "the body of one beast and the head of another," wherein the assembled body parts of his metaphor come from whatever remembered and imagery fodder he deems most productive for the role at hand.[38]

In any case, the questions about actorly empathy that McConachie and Kemp start to pose are the sort that this book strives to answer: what does the actor do encourage the audience's empathy?; how does the audience's experience of empathy for dramatic characters align with any potential empathetic connections among the actors?; and, crucially for this study, how can screen actors solicit an empathetic connection from audiences who are largely absent from the moment when the scene is filmed? Is empathy for a filmed character primarily attributable, as Carl Plantinga has argued, to a long-take close-up of the actor-as-character's face at an emotionally evocative moment in the narrative,[39] or do screen actors possess some personal agency in establishing empathetic connections with the anticipated audience?[40] This last question will be taken up more explicitly in Chapter 6's analysis of actorly strategies for making empathetic connections on set. This book will frequently frame this connection between actors and audiences as the solicitation of performative empathy,[41] emphasizing the ways in which the actor articulates their connections with her character and her fellow actors-as-characters for an audience which is largely absent from the set where the filming takes place.[42]

In the meantime, McConachie's interest in how conceptual blending participates in the actor's relationship with the audience dovetails with Amy Cook's cognitive analysis of dramatic casting. As a form of conceptual integration, Cook suggests that casting relies on compression to create fast, efficient, and potent meanings about characters, which optimally primes the audience's narrative engagement and comprehension.[43] Actors, their approaches to acting, and the range of roles within which they are typically cast, are compressed alongside the actor's appearance and personal history into groups of signifiers which lend themselves more readily to being cast in certain kinds of roles at the expense of others. For example, Richard Schiff was ultimately chosen for the role of Toby Ziegler on *The West Wing* (NBC, 1999–2006) over Eugene Levy. Although both actors possessed the depth of experience required for a major role on a primetime American television drama and were both considered solid fits within the studio's official character description, Levy was turned down for the role despite casting director's Jon Levey praise for Levy's audition as "the best reading of someone who didn't get the job" that Levey had ever seen.[44] Cook persuasively implies that the casting process for Toby Ziegler's character conceptually compressed the cumulative roles of each actor's careers to date: Levy's comedic persona as an awkward Jewish-American suburban bumbler from his roles in *Waiting for Guffman* (Christopher Guest, 1996) and *American Pie* (Paul Weitz, 1999) may have undercut his immediate social credibility as serious-minded White House communications director Toby Ziegler.[45]

The range of personal visibility within an actor's performances is often arranged on a spectrum of persona acting, in which the quotidian actor is productively visible within her characters, and transformative acting, wherein the actor seems to vanish into her character. Rick Kemp analyzes how Daniel Day-Lewis's transformative acting practices extend a tenaciously immersive conceptual blend of his characters outside the narrative, given that Day-Lewis often refuses to break out of character for the duration of a film shoot. On the set for *Gangs of New York* (Martin Scorsese, 2002), for example, Day-Lewis not only continued to present himself offset as Bill "the Butcher" but refused medication for the pneumonia that he contracted while shooting the film because Bill would not have had access to the twenty-first-century medication that the set doctors prescribed.[46] Similarly, Vladimir Zirodan, for example, suggests that Martin Freeman's persona roles as banal middle-class prudes such as Tim in the UK's *The Office* (BBC, 2001), *The Hobbit* films' Bilbo Baggins (Peter Jackson, 2012–14), and *Fargo*'s Lester Nygaard (FX Productions and MGM Television, 2014–21) always seem to traceable back to Martin Freeman.[47] For Cook, however, the actor's talents as a persona or transformational actor are not enough on their own to create a performance: the actor inevitability collaborates with directors, designers, technicians, and other skilled laborers who join the creation of the character.[48] Where this book picks up is the attempt to trace the bodymind movements within the actor's personal talent that reach out in search of creative connections with their collaborators; the self-reorganizations that reconfigure actors as actors-as-characters, whether or not some aspect of an actor's quotidian self and celebrity persona inform the performance of the actor-as-character.

Rhonda Blair combines conceptual blending with other neuroscientific research to analyze acting practices by stressing the importance of embodied imagination:

> [the actor] must pull apart the blends in a play in order to be able to mine the potentials in their constitutive parts, live in the blend, and make new blends to serve imagination for the purpose of embodiment and action.[49]

This "living in the blend" of the character's narrative world feels quite similar to what acclaimed Russian dramatist Konstantin Stanislavsky called the "Magic If." Stanislavsky discovered that an actor's emotions, imagination, and body could be quickly mobilized into action around the preposition *if*. The actor embraces a number of disbelief-suspending paradoxes to approach the story *as if* she were her character, *as if* her character's circumstances were real and therefore her own lived experiences happening for the first time, *as if* the other actors were their characters in the same dramatic world. Stanislavsky's Magic If is a tool for motivating actions and reactions to the character's circumstances, described mechanistically by Stanislavsky as "a lever to lift us out of the world of actuality into the realm of imagination."[50] This "lift" into the "realm of imagination" unifies the actor's physical, emotional, and mental activity as a cohesive whole, in that the realm of imagination should enable the actor to move and respond as her character. It stands entirely to reason that Stanislavsky's Magic If invites the actor to form a conceptual blend that encompasses the character's personality, life story, and opinions on other figures within the narrative. This book focuses on the forces of integration, attraction, compression, and extrapolation within that conceptual blend through which the actor solicits an immersive and empathetic connection with her character.

Blair also treats the Magic If as a conceptual blend that mobilizes the actor's bodymind into forming an empathetic connection with her character: "[the Magic If] engage[s] the character's experience imaginatively while at the same time maintaining a sense of self that is separate from the character."[51] The combined components of attending to another's experiences, sharing a qualitatively similarly affective state with that other, and all the while retaining a sense of one's own quotidian selfhood is consistent with many of the models of empathy that this book explores in Chapter 2. In fact, Blair's response to John Wesley Hill's criticism of the very possibility of actors empathizing with their characters is highly relevant to the types of actorly empathy for which this book advocates. Hill challenges Blair's assertion that actors can empathize with their characters because the character's selfhood is not entirely distinct from that of the actor who performs the role, since one logically cannot have empathy for oneself.[52] Blair responds to Hill in part by arguing for a fluid notion of self in which scripted characters are temporarily disembodied selves which become activated by the actor's bodymind.[53] Blair's conception of actorly empathy for a character clearly positions the actor as the empathetic observer and the character as the target: the actor is the one soliciting the empathetic connection, rather than the character going on a Pirandellian search for an actor. The overarching framework of realist acting provides enough support for extrapolating the conceptual blend of the character as a situational self that the actor can relate to her character like any other situational self.

In so doing, Blair begins making a case for a model of realist acting which is an instance of embodied cognition occurring within a distributed cognitive ecology—a space which facilitates and participates in thought processes which occur across a range[54] of "thinkers"—which enables the kind of thinking that can treat a fictional character as a coherent situational self.

Distributed Cognition and Cognitive Ecologies

The cognitive model of the extended mind examines how cognition moves beyond the traditional organism of the thinker into contact with other minds in the traditionally external world. The thoughts of the extended mind thinker are always relative to the central point of the thinker's own mind: the point from which the thought extends.[55] It is entirely reasonable to consider how, as Murray Smith does, an actor's performance of a character requires the actor to extend her imagination beyond the quotidian boundaries of her mind to place herself in her character's proverbial shoes.[56] While Smith is right to consider how the formal construction of a film actor's performance articulates and accentuates the performing actor's extended mind for an audience, a paradigm shift is required to go behind the scenes and examine how the social and material configuration of the film set shaped the acting work that generated the performance in question.

Expanding on the extended mind, distributed cognition analyzes how social systems and the nodes within in them think together through the interactions of those nodes, without exclusively privileging the human subjects within that social network.[57] Through the lens of distributed cognition, Evelyn Tribble invites cognitive theater scholars to: "see how a complex activity like performance is spread, smeared, and extended across mechanisms such as attention, perception and memory; the experience of training as it is sedimented in the body, social structures, and the material environment."[58] In other words, by situating cognition within a particular location or cultural framework, we can consider how the social and physical environments of that location become the cognitive ecology in which that thinking is situated.[59] Tribble's analyses of Shakespeare's Globe theater, for example, consider how the collective creative storytelling of Shakespeare's players was facilitated and co-created the physical construction of the theater and its stage, as well as the organization of the scripts, the social hierarchies of the actors' apprenticeship systems, the rehearsal processes, the memorization of dialogue, and so forth.[60] Shakespeare was certainly an important node within the cognitive ecology of the Globe; that said, the ways in which all the cognitive work required to produce his plays was distributed across the social, material, cultural, and economic structures of his company draws compelling attention to the historical processes of collective theatrical production.

In applying a similar logic to the cognitive ecologies of screen media production, such as a film set or a casting director's office during an audition, we can privilege actors as embodied thinkers as key nodes within the process of performing characters within the network of film and television production. This allows us to think about how acting occurs not only within and among actors, but how non-actor entities, such as the camera, the director, the shooting schedule, the make-up trailer, and so forth, form a cognitive ecology that facilitates acting work and, vicariously, creates the performed character. I suggest that, within this open-ended[61] framework of distributed cognition, the temporarily disembodied situational selves of the script which Rhonda Blair argued were viable targets for the actor's empathy are as much nodes of cognitive ecologies within which acting thrives as the director, the environmental conditions of the film set, the social hierarchies between a film's stars and its extras, the camera itself, and so forth. This book argues that film and television actors operate within a dynamic system of distributed cognition in which embodied cognizers—the actors—solicit different kinds of simultaneous empathetic connections across a range of targets. These solicitations demarcate and are demarcated by the ebbs and flows of cognition, which is distributed in shifting and often unpredictable ways from the actor's first reading of the audition script to the moment when the director calls "Cut!" at the end of the actor's last take.

How, though, is one supposed to study this within the film and television industries?

Television Studies and Acting

Recent work in television studies places the actor's experience of her own work and the intersection of industrial working conditions and creative labor at the center of the analysis of acting on television. This interview-based research largely positions the cultural significations of an actor's performance as secondary to her training, habits, and practices for preparing and producing that performance. Christopher Hogg and Tom Cantrell, for example, contend that the study of television acting should stem from interviews with actors about the entire process of professional acting, from preparation and auditions to their performances on set.[62] In this context, "television acting" refers to an actor's cumulative work process in portraying her character. Cantrell and Hogg relegate "television performance" to on-camera behaviors of persons in non-fiction broadcasts, such as reality television contestants and talk show hosts, and to non-actor performances within the *mise-en-scène*, such as an actor's costume or an important prop.[63] This distinction between *acting* and *performance* underlines a vehement interest in the work that actors do before and while shooting a scene and, since this work is largely invisible to audiences, the only point of access for scholars to a television actor's work is the actor's own description of that work.[64]

This book seeks to qualify what Hogg and Cantrell would explain as the "visible" and "invisible" parts of the screen actor's process with a common conceptual vocabulary. By analyzing the visible alongside the invisible aspects of screen acting—or what this book later calls the performative empathetic solicitation in comparison to the actor's invisible intrasubjective empathetic connection with her character, and the intersubjective connection to her fellow actors—from the reported experiences of actors themselves, I develop and apply a common critical vocabulary to screen acting practices that establishes a continuity between what actors do on- and off-set to make acting's verisimilar illusion possible.

Lucy Fife Donaldson and James Walters's study of the on-set habits of television actors shares this commitment to the analysis of the screen actor's creative work by examining how television actors include performance spaces and objects into their acting.[65] Actors with recurring roles on television shows often develop strategies for working around the often limited on-set rehearsal time. In some cases, mundane tasks—from Jennifer Aniston's throwaway dialogue on the set of *Friends* (1994–2004) to Charles Dance's meat-carving skills in *Game of Thrones* (2011–19)—can focus the actor's expression of the character's disposition.[66]

This engagement of on-set conditions, constraints, and affordances[67] is reframed here as part of the actor's performative empathetic solicitation to the audience, which, simply put, is her invitation to the audience to connect with her character through the act of performing. This performative tactic can also be studied in relation to how it engages the actor's other empathetic connections: her intrasubjective connection to her character and her intersubjective connection with her fellow actors. To that end, the tactic described later in this book as "Lisinska's Tears"[68] connects these on-set performative manipulations of *Orphan Black*'s shooting conditions directly to the actor's relationship with her character and her fellow actors. In the example case, actor Natalie Lisinska used the harsh environmental conditions of a cold drizzly Toronto winter night, tear-inducing eyedrops, and an off-set stash of affectively loaded personal artifacts to catalyze a livid, ferocious performance at the peak of her *Orphan Black* character's narrative arc.[69] Lisinska combined the performative on-set affordances of her personal discomfort and intrasubjective emotional reference points to "let the real tears unlock a realm of anger and sadness," all of which was aimed at co-star Tatia Maslany.

Television scholars Gary Cassidy and Simone Knox analyze the aesthetic dimensions of BBC actor Phil Davis's work, based upon Davis's particularly articulate and thoughtful self-reflection during a public interview.[70] For Cassidy and Knox, Davis's regular appearances in BBC television fiction in featured supporting roles, such as Smallweed in the miniseries adaptation of *Bleak House* (2005) and as the murderous taxi driver in the pilot episode of *Sherlock* (2010), fosters a "lamprotic" appreciation of a supporting actor's work. Whereas star acting is often celebrated for the Benjaminian aura of its originality and virtuosity,[71] the everyday unpretentiousness of Davis's work shines across his career of carefully crafted supporting roles, rather than the individual distinctiveness of a single role. Davis's remarkable capacity to communicate his characters and advance narratives through stillness, silence, and reaction to his co-stars' acting demonstrates his unpretentious and well-honed craftsmanship.

Cassidy and Knox's interview-driven approach is well-equipped to take the actor's work—and her experiences of her own work—as a starting place for a critical analysis of screen acting. My book echoes their approach to Davis's acting in that Cassidy and Knox apply a larger theoretical concept to interview-driven access to a professional actor's reflections on his career. Where this book differs from Cassidy and Knox's approach is in the trajectory of the theoretical framework. Rather than analyze the cumulative auteurist glimmer of Davis's supporting roles, this book approaches the cognitive and phenomenological process through which actors like Davis mobilize their bodymind resources to become their character, relate to other actors as characters, and present all of that work to the camera in a way that is as lucid, compelling, and communicative as possible. The portrait of Davis's work presented by Cassidy and Knox parallels a set of on-set tactics described later in this book as "Dinicol's Jazz,"[72] wherein screen actors like Joe Dinicol will deprioritize their own performance in favor of responding faithfully and spontaneously to their fellow actors-as-characters' work. Rather than worry about the artistic shine of his own performances, Dinicol draws on his training in Sanford Meisner's version of American Method acting to prioritize the intersubjective bonds with his fellow actors by letting his reactions to his scene partners demonstrate

Dinicol's character's disposition: "[the other actor and I] know the story we have to tell; the only question is how we're going to work together to tell it."[73] The assumption is that the camera will pick up on the sincere and verisimilar relationship between the actors-as-characters and vicariously produce a particularly compelling piece of storytelling. Therefore, the Dinicol's Jazz metaphor describes an on-set actorly tactic wherein the actor prioritizes an intersubjective connection that not only elucidates intrasubjective character choices but also solicits a performative connection from the anticipated spectator by being "real" with her fellow actors. Beyond the strong Meisnerian overtones, Dinicol's Jazz provides a compelling framework for how actors like Davis connect with their characters and also how those connections can inform the non-Meisnerian lamprotic performances that Cassidy and Knox rightly identify. By looking for broader causal associations between the visible aspects of an actor's work with the invisible, this book analyzes empathetic solicitation strategies such as Lisinska's Tears and Dinicol's Jazz as a means of simultaneously addressing the *acting* behind the *performance*, without losing sight of the performance itself.

Screen Acting: A Cognitive Approach embraces these contexts and approaches from theater and television studies to study how screen actors imagine, recall, and create with their bodyminds by soliciting the empathetic connections which move them, amidst the myriad of industrial constraints and affordances faced by actors during film and television production. This line of analysis approaches screen acting as a dynamically embodied transformation and an artistic expression *from the practitioner's perspective*. To preserve this practice-based perspective, the theoretical model of screen acting as a series of bodymind re-arrangements that solicit empathetic connections is supported by actors' descriptions of their own work. To that end, I draw upon published interviews with renowned screen actors, the results of fifteen semi-structured interviews with professional North American screen actors that I conducted throughout 2016 as part of this project, and my own experiences over twenty-five years as a professional actor. Some of my interviewees, such as Natalie Lisinska, Sheila McCarthy, Joe Dinicol, Jamie Spilchuk, and Antonio Cayonne, have well-established careers as North American film and television actors. Others, such as Matthew MacFadzean, Chris Baker, Lauren MacKinlay Danelene O'Flynn, and Julian De Zotti regularly work as directors, producers, and writers for film and television alongside their acting work. Although this study will periodically reference the practices and performances of well-known star actors in film and television, the greater hope is to show a continuity of screen acting practices with the testimonies of the often lesser-known actors who I interviewed. The goal of this book is to connect these findings and methods for studying realist acting to Film Studies and other screen media through a critical common denominator that can account for acting practices across media.

Notes

1. Gallagher and Gallagher, "Acting oneself as another: an actor's empathy for her character."
2. Blair and Cook, "Introduction."
3. Blair, *The Actor, Image, and Action: Acting and Cognitive Neuroscience*, pp. 2–3.
4. For example, Jacques Lecoq's highly physical training system demands that the actor creates through active physical experimentation that forces the actor to think with her body. Similarly, the Alexander Technique attempts to adjust the actor's posture so as to eliminate unnecessary bodymind tension, thereby improving the actor's access to her cognitive, emotional, and corporeal resources. See Varela, "Organism, cognitive science and the emergence of selfless selves," p. 192.
5. Jackman, "Training, Insight and Intuition in Creative Flow," p. 116.
6. Blair, *The Actor, Image, and Action: Acting and Cognitive Neuroscience*, p. 2.
7. Ibid. p. 33.
8. The degree to which these imagined materials are faithful reconstructions of the quotidian actor's memories, a complete fabrication of the actor, or a deliberate alteration of a memory to suit the dramatic moment at hand is a key point of difference among major Method acting gurus. These differences are taken up in greater detail in Chapter 3.
9. Thompson, *Mind In Life: Biology, Phenomenology, and the Sciences of the Mind*.
10. Ibid. p. ix.
11. Ibid. p. 12
12. Ibid. pp. 7–10.
13. Kelso, *Dynamic Patterns: The Self-Organizations of Brain and Behavior*.
14. Thompson, *Mind In Life: Biology, Phenomenology, and the Sciences of the Mind*, p. 11.
15. Ibid. p. 24.
16. Blair and Cook, "Bodies in performance," p. 76.
17. Mirodan, "Acting and emotion," pp. 104–5.
18. Lutterbie, *Toward a General Theory of Acting: Cognitive Science and Performance*, p. 22.
19. Ibid. p. 14
20. Stanislavsky's "Magic If," a key principle of how actors become their characters, will be explained in greater detail later in this chapter. This principle is also known as "the 'What If'". For internal consistency's sake, however, this book will use the term, "Magic If".

21. Lutterbie, *Toward a General Theory of Acting: Cognitive Science and Performance*, p. 67.
22. Ibid. p. 56.
23. Zarrilli, *(Toward) A Phenomenology of Acting*, p. 12.
24. Ibid. pp. 14–17.
25. See Chapter 3 for a detailed comparison of how these and other acting practitioners' ideas about acting prompt different configurations of the actor's bodymind.
26. Meisner and Longwell, *On Acting*, pp. 16, 37; Strasberg, *The Lee Strasberg Notes*, pp. 1–2; Adler, *The Art of Acting*, pp. 19–26, 50–1.
27. Kemp, *Embodied Acting: What Neuroscience Tells Us about Performance*, 104–8.
28. Ibid. p. 112.
29. Ibid. p. 108.
30. Fauconnier and Turner, *The Way We Think: Conceptual Blending and the Mind's Hidden Complexities*, p. 17.
31. Ibid. p. 18.
32. Ibid. p. 11.
33. McConachie, *Theatre and Mind*, pp. 20–4.
34. Ibid. p. 15.
35. Kemp, *Embodied Acting: What Neuroscience Tells Us about Performance*, p. 118.
36. Ibid. p. 119.
37. Ibid.
38. See Chapter 5 on "Cayonne's Minotaur."
39. Plantinga, "The scene of empathy and the human face on film."
40. Kemp, "Acting technique, Jacques Lecoq and embodied meaning," p. 177.
41. See Chapter 3.
42. See Chapter 6.
43. Cook, *Building Character: The Art and Science of Casting*, p. 35.
44. Ibid. p. 11.
45. Ibid. pp. 11–13.
46. Kemp, *Embodied Acting: What Neuroscience Tells Us about Performance*, pp. 150–2.
47. Mirodan, *The Actor and The Character*, 2.
48. Cook, *Building Character: The Art and Science of Casting*, pp. 79–80.
49. Blair, "Cognitive neuroscience and acting: imagination, conceptual blending, and empathy," p. 96.
50. Stanislavsky, *An Actor Prepares*, pp. 45–6.
51. Blair, "Cognitive neuroscience and acting: imagination, conceptual blending, and empathy," p. 100.
52. Hill and Blair, "Stanislavsky and cognitive science."
53. Ibid. pp. 10–11.
54. Blair and Cook, "Situated cognition and dynamic systems: cognitive ecologies," pp. 130–1.

55. Hutchins, "The cultural ecosystem of human cognition," p. 36.
56. Smith, "Empathy, expansionism, and the extended mind."
57. Blair and Cook, "Situated cognition and dynamic systems: cognitive ecologies," pp. 130–1; Tribble, "Distibuted cognition, mindful bodies, and the arts of acting"; Tribble and Dixon, "Distributed cognition: studying theatre in the wild."
58. Tribble, "Distributed cognition, mindful bodies, and the arts of acting," p. 134.
59. Tribble and Dixon, "Distributed cognition: studying theatre in the wild," p. 265.
60. Tribble, *Cognition in the Globe: Attention and Memory in Shakespeare's Theatre*; Tribble, "Distributing cognition in the Globe."
61. Tribble, "Distributed cognition, mindful bodies, and the arts of acting."
62. Cantrell and Hogg, "Returning to an old question: what do television actors do when they act?," p. 285.
63. Ibid. p. 285.
64. Ibid. p. 296.
65. Fife Donaldson and Walters, "Inter(acting): television , performance and synthesis."
66. Ibid. p. 355.
67. See Chapter 4 for a more thorough unpacking of Gibson's use of "affordances" and "constraints" in perceptual psychology, and how I connect this to how actors navigate their performance options within a given scene.
68. See Chapter 6 for a longer explanation of how Lisinska's Tears solicits and sustains the actor's three empathetic connections.
69. Natalie Lisinska (actor), in discussion with the author, October 2016.
70. Cassidy and Knox, "Phil Davis: the process of acting."
71. Ibid. p. 317.
72. See Chapter 6 for a prolonged discussion of how Dinicol's Jazz solicits and sustains its empathetic connections.
73. Joe Dinicol (actor), in discussion with the author, June 2016.

CHAPTER 2

All By Our Selves: Empathy and Acting

I argue throughout this book that the actor's role within acting's distributed cognition network is to solicit the empathetic connections upon which screen acting's verisimilar illusion depends, all the while adapting to the cognitive ecologies in which the acting in question takes place, such as the audition process or the actual filming on set. The goal of this chapter is to bridge the previous chapter's ideas from television studies and cognitive theater studies to the kinds of empathetic connections that screen actors make while acting, which is the focus of the next chapter and the overarching critical framework for the ensuing analyses various phases of acting work. To build this bridge, this chapter expands on the notions of fluid and situational selfhood to create conceptual space for the actor's many selves to create characters within the ever-shifting nature of screen acting's distributed cognition networks. This chapter concludes by synthesizing interdisciplinary research on empathy among flesh-and-blood humans and for fictional characters alike, to show how those situational selves can create empathetic relationships within acting's cognitive ecologies.

Empathy has become a subject of great interdisciplinary interest across the humanities, social sciences, and life sciences. In the absence of a universally accepted definition of empathy grounded in one critical domain, the hope here is to establish a common ground between some neuroscientific, anthropological, philosophical, and literary notions of empathy to contextualize how screen acting works as a dynamic system. In particular, Amy Coplan's interdisciplinary review of underlying criteria for empathetic relationships provides a valuable framework for assessing how screen acting practices solicit empathetic relationships through acting's creative strategies and tactics. Coplan's criteria shape the sprawling concept of phenomenological empathy into a pragmatic checklist for naming what various aspects of the empathetic solicitation actively do.

Situational and Selfless Selfhood

The core tenet of neurophenomenology is that cognitive science and phenomenological philosophy can be mutually informing discourses in a critical model of self, imagination, and intention which views the body and mind as inextricably interconnected.[1] The self which emerges is a constantly fluctuating reorganization of our bodymind resources in response to the iterative exchange between our intentions, motivations, and actions and the lived world in which they occur.

The key role of intentionality in our bodymind self-organization is the cornerstone of what cognitive theorist Francisco Varela calls the "selfless self." For Varela, the mind is a self-perpetuating system that uses its own self-perpetuations to distinguish itself as being autonomous from its environmental surroundings.[2] At the same time, the mind's meshwork of interconnected networks has no centralized governing entity to direct its activity.[3] Similar to Kemp's argument against actors possessing an essential self against which all their characters are relative, there is no monolithic "Self" at the center of our subjectivity: instead, the self is the current configuration of the bodymind's many malleable interconnected networks that adapt in relation to each other, rather than at the command of a centralized power.[4] In other words, we are the unity of our malleable meshwork of possible selves, arranged by goals and intention-based motivations.[5] The only constants in Varela's selfless self are the individual as a collection of possible bodymind configurations, and that these configurations will constantly self-organize as an assertion of their enworldment. In short, the quotidian self is just one possible "ongoing interpretive narrative"[6] about who we can be when we are not trying to be someone else.

This model of malleable selfhood carries great potential for describing an actor's ability to align with her character and to solicit connections with her fellow actors-as-characters and her audiences as an inhabitant of a situational, dramatic world. Varela's formation enables a clear differentiation between the actor's quotidian selves and the situational self of the character, who is the result of a deliberate rearrangement of intentional focus.[7] In this configuration, an actor does not ever become her character, but rather "wears" her character like imaginary clothes[8] to configure her body schema—her self-perception of her capacity for action[9]—for the performance. The actor-as-character is therefore a strategic rearrangement of the quotidian actor's bodymind resources and proprioceptive self in a way that is not immediately recognizable as the quotidian bodymind schema. Moreover, selfless selves allow for the character's situational self to self-organize in different ways throughout a story because of the decentralized status of the actor's quotidian self. A character's development across a narrative becomes the actor's embodiment of a malleable identity, predicated on the bodymind's capacity to reorganize itself to adapt to new circumstances. Actor Antonio Cayonne describes this situational self-reorganization as an imaginary cobbling together of personal references into a new self: "My character in a film might remind me of a guy I went to highschool with, Batman, and my aunt, all at the same time. My job is to bring them all together in the same body, like making a minotaur: a creature with the head of one beast and the body of another."[10] Cayonne's metaphor[11] demonstrates that the quotidian actor and the situational actor-as-character each contain realms of possible configurations, which positions the character to some extent as a derivative of the actor's ability to enact her.

A major part of the actor's creative work is to enworld her character within the dramatic circumstances of the script. This enworlding relies on a double functioning of the meshwork of selfless selves. First, the situational self of the actor-as-character is a product of the actor's self-perpetuating strategic re-arrangement of her quotidian bodymind schema. Second, the actor self-perpetuates her character in a way that vicariously creates the situational environment—the fictitious world of the drama— for her character to inhabit and from which to differentiate herself as an autonomous entity. For Rhonda Blair, Stanislavsky's system of acting is a creative application of Antonio Damasio's model of selfhood, in which selves emerge in the organism's relationship to the objects, events, and environments around them[12]:

> Stanislavsky's system [. . .] asks the actor to imagine and experience a fictive self engaged with issues of survival or thriving of one kind or another that ultimately involve, affect, and change the body. The actor plays out a variation on Damasio's organism-object relationship in order to embody a character: she takes on some form of the internal (mental) and external objects of the text and its given circumstances, integrates these with her own mental objects, derived from memory personal history, and devises a pattern of behavior. The result is typically a course of action related to the character's desire to acquire or avoid something.[13]

Through self-reorganizing to behave as her character, while also interacting as her character with objects and events in the narrative world as if they were real, and thereby reifying the character's intentions within that narrative world, the actor's meshwork of selfless selves begins to designate the ensuing situational selves as the actor-as-character. Put another way, the actor's simultaneous creation of and self-differentiation from the fictitious world becomes an iterative loop of stimuli and responses that sustain the verisimilar effect. This creative autopoiesis is neither passive nor accidental: the actor's situational self is the product of an intentionally motivated creative re-assemblage of her bodymind schema. The situational self is sustained by an equally intentional creative attention that responds to internal and external changes in a way that self-perpetuates the verisimilar illusion; in actorly terminology, by keeping one's intentionality "in the moment."

An actor who is "in the moment" may well be experiencing a "flow state" wherein the actor is fully immersed within the actor-as-character's world in an "almost automatic, effortless, yet highly focused state of consciousness."[14] John Vervaeke, Leo Ferraro, and Arianne Herrera-Bennett describe cognitive flow states as being "in the zone" where the subject loses self-consciousness through their effortless but vigorous attentiveness to the task at hand.[15] Crucially, a flow state is only possible when the challenge of the task at hand matches the upper end of the subject's proficiency with that task so that the subject must stretch their skill level to a peak level of proficiency. This "skill-stretching" helps to trigger an "insight cascade", the moment in which that peak of proficiency is sufficient to solve the challenge at hand and thereby produce new knowledge, experience, and expertise in the subject.[16] Therefore, the subject's creative breakthrough occurs when their problem-solving skills are initially insufficient but, through engaging strenuously with the seemingly impossible problem, their skill set grows to meet the challenge at hand, culminating in the "'aha!' moment"[17] of realization. This transformation of skill and insight then informs the subject's approach to the next seemingly impossible task. Vervaeke, Ferraro, and Arianne's "flow tunnel" is a clear application of dynamic systems theory (DST), wherein the process of adhering to the boundary rules of a system wind up changing the very boundaries of the system that first defined its rules, which is also key to the bodymind reorganization of Thompson's embodied dynamicism.

If intentionality guides the bodymind's self-organizing functions in relation to internal and external circumstances, it follows that intentionality is able to shift across targets as they present themselves. Thompson and Varela both argue that, although our mind is able to distinguish itself as a distinct entity within its environment, our consciousness is not a closed entity but is structurally open to experiences and intentionalities beyond itself.[18] Intentionality is therefore correlational, in that it starts in an observer's bodymind and extends towards her target. The observer and her intentional target co-inhabit the same world as fellow centers of intentionality,[19] and when the observer's attention fixates on the intentionality of her target, the observer is in the first stages of an empathetic relationship.

Given the importance of identifying, connecting with, and articulating the actor-as-character's intentions in realist acting practices, processes like empathy which can reorganize the actor's bodymind intentionality to act as the actor-as-character's situational self are clearly key to a cognitive understanding of acting.

Empathy

Thompson's broad definition of empathy as "a unique form of intentionality in which we are directed toward the other's experience"[20] acknowledges the importance of intentionality and the experience of others, two common features of many interdisciplinary models of empathy. For Thompson, empathy is an attempt at experiencing the world from the perspective of another, and the empathetic process therefore requires some way for the observer to reproduce the intentionality of her target for herself. Since the observer likely has no direct telepathic link to the mind of her target, and only so much can be learned through behavioral inference about why the target behaves as he does, empathy requires the observer to imaginarily reconstruct her target's situations to understand his behavior as if she were the target and living within her target's circumstances.[21]

Empathy, Stanislavsky, and Chekhov

The empathetic implications of, as Sanford Meisner described it, "living truthfully under imaginary circumstances"[22] speaks directly to the core ideas of many of twentieth-century realist acting's key practitioners. Michael Chekhov's questions for the actor, for example, encourage the actor to identify and contrast how her character's goals, desires, worldview, and more are distinct from her own, though no less plausible in the character's lived circumstances. It is also not difficult to consider Stanislavsky's Magic If as a theatrical instance of what Thompson, following Husserl, calls an appresentation: an imagined perception from the perspective of a different self.[23] Appresentations reveal the observer's best guess towards the intentionality and experiences of her target, which the observer must construct with her imagination.[24] The Magic If's prompt to the actor's imagination to start reorganizing her bodymind to accommodate the character's selfhood as she imaginatively extrapolates the character in the script into the actor-as-character's bodymind.

The appresentational Magic If has two primary functions in the reorganization of Varela's selfless selves. First, the Magic If explicates the conditions that differentiate the quotidian actor from the situational actor-as-character. In the previous example, the quotidian actor playing Juliet in that scene may have entirely different attitudes than Juliet towards her quotidian lover, government, and the world in general. The appresentational Magic If asserts the actor-as-character's autonomy from the quotidian actor since the actor-as-character's circumstances are fundamentally different from those of the quotidian actor. Although many traditions of realist acting insist upon some transference of quotidian memory and emotional experience to the actor-as-character, these transfers are predominately understood as verisimilitude-ensuring references rather than as direct confessions of the actor's quotidian self.

Second, the appresentational Magic If catalyzes the actor's renegotiation of her relationship with her character's situational environment. The autopoietic characteristics of the quotidian actor's autonomous organism carry over to her situational character, who is enworlded within the realm of the play and the real world that contains that realm of the play. The quotidian actor's creative choices, mobilized by the Magic If, create the situational world of the drama, which self-perpetuates through the actions of the actor-as-character, while also distinguishing the actor-as-character as an autonomous entity within it. In the Juliet example, the appresentational Magic Ifs of Tybalt's death and Romeo's banishment prompt a reaction from the actor-as-Juliet, which reciprocally creates the emotional stakes and socio-political context of the situational world within which Juliet is a distinct living entity.

In his comparison of styles of phenomenological investigation and Stanislavsky's training regimen, Daniel Johnston argues that the co-constitutive actor-as-character and her situational world are, for the actor, an embodied experiment in enworlding:

> In phenomenological terms, the [Magic If] is none other than the demand for the creation of a "world" in its rich, lived experience, not as actuality, but as possibility on stage. The truthfulness of the performance will be judged in the actor's capacity to flesh out the structures of the world that would be experienced by the character.[25]

This process of "fleshing out the structures of the world" means literally embodying one's character by aligning with the correlational structures of intentionality: to inhabit the actor-as-character's body schema as a realm of expressive possibilities; to relate to other actors-as-characters as similarly enworlded centers of intentionality[26]; to articulate one's situational enworlding to an anticipated audience. Stanislavsky's Magic If is firmly predicated on the potential for actors to develop empathetic appresentations to help them experience the world as their character; to help them see from a situational perspective similar to but not originally their quotidian own. Stanislavsky's Magic If therefore links physical, emotional, and cognitive activity through the intentional lens of the character, prompting the actor's bodymind meshwork to reorganize in order to accommodate the verisimilar dramatic world.

Despite the productive clarity of considering the Magic If as an appresentation, and the centrality of Thompson's version of neurophenomenology to cognitive models of acting for scholars such as John Lutterbie, appresentations on their own do not encompass the scope of modern interdisciplinary analyses of empathy. The term "appresentation" does not inherently account for other facets of empathy which can productively inform the analysis of the kinds of empathy and situational selves that emerge across screen acting's diverse cognitive ecologies, such as the rushed incompleteness of the casting process, the trial-and-error process of script preparation, and the multitude of distractions and inconveniences on a film or television set while filming. This chapter therefore expands its notion of actorly empathy to include Vittorio Gallese and Susan Feagin's insistence that an observer can experience empathy for fictional selves, Edith Stein's notion of the target's intentional pull, Amy Coplan's empathetic criteria, and Jean Decety's research on empathy's neurological and anthropological foundations.

Embodied simulation and cognitive scaffolding

Vittorio Gallese's theory of embodied simulation analyzes the importance of encultured intentionality within neural mirroring mechanisms in relation to visual and narrative art. Embodied simulation, in turn, provides a useful context for connecting neuroscientific notions of empathy to the arts, such as Susan Feagin's proposals for developing empathetic relationships with literary characters.

Gallese's recent neuroaesthetic work shifts the discussion of mirror neurons and aesthetics away from locating distinct emotional and intentional experiences in our neural anatomy.[27] Instead, Gallese's model of embodied simulation intertwines the biological foundations and social enactments of the mirror mechanism (MM), an umbrella term which includes the neural infrastructure for mapping an action's perception and its execution,[28] as well as the bodily interpretation of that which is mirrored. The MM avoids making the disputed claim that humans conclusively have mirror neurons[29] or advocating for a precarious one-to-one fixed connection between mirror neurons and empathy[30] by positioning mirroring as a simultaneously biological and encultured event; one can experience mirroring without needing to name the specifics of the neurological infrastructures which are participating in some way. As a model of selfhood based around action, intention, and communication, embodied simulation is useful for a neurophenomenological model of screen acting because of the parallel perceptual assemblages through which people relate to themselves, other people, and fictional narratives.

Embodied simulation presumes that the observer's MM interprets a target's perceived motor actions as intentionalized, motivated behaviors: for example, the observer watches the target extend his hand towards a glass of water, presumably to grasp the glass, potentially because he is thirsty. Beyond a basic motor identification, the observer makes inferences about the target's disposition and motivation, thereby simulating the target's intentionalized actions. This "intentional attunement"[31] is an essential component of the cognitive infrastructure that enables empathetic connections in that it engages the observer's body in mirroring the perceived intentionalities of other bodies as a means of navigating the lived world.[32]

This same intentional attunement prompts similar relationships between individuals as it does between an individual and an artwork because artworks are communicative acts laden with intentionalized content.[33] The observer ascribes intentionality to targeted images, actions, words, and objects by engaging the MM, reconstructing the presumed rationales behind the ascribed intentionality in a way that prompts the observer to simulate the target's presumed disposition.[34] While Gallese and Cuccio are primarily analyzing the spectatorial experience of artworks, they predicate this model of spectatorship on mirroring processes in human-to-human interactions. Gallese has recently reaffirmed the applicability of MM to cinematic communication in *The Empathetic Screen*, in which he and co-author Michele Guerra position embodied simulation as a communicative process that ascribes intentionality within others' actions, even if that means ascribing intentionality to shot scales and camera movements.[35] Therefore, embodied simulation can also function as a theoretical framework for collective artistic production among actors. Actors, like spectators, oscillate between the quotidian world and fictional, symbolic worlds of art and narrative[36]: if the bodymind experience of man-made images and narratives is inherently relational, the MM interprets man-made images and narratives as other subjects to whom we can intersubjectively and intercorporeally relate.[37]

Literary scholar Susan Feagin proposes that readers are able to form empathetic relationships with characters in realist novels because of the structural similarities between the reader and the character's mental processes.[38] Readers identify pertinent cues to the character's cognitive scaffolding, predicated on identifying the character's beliefs and desires, and imagining the character's body schema that accompanies those beliefs and desires. The act of reconstructing this cognitive scaffolding enables the reader to simulate and appresent the character's experiences, and thereby potentially form an empathetic connection.[39] The likelihood of empathetic connections with fictional characters is significantly higher when, as Matthjis Bal and Martijn Veltkamp argue, the reader is emotionally "transported" by the narrative into an immersive state in which the fiction's events feel real to the reader.[40] Put another way, if the reconstruction of the fictional character's cognitive scaffolding is sufficiently persuasive and resonant for the reader, the situational self of the character becomes as empathizable for the reader as any real-life quotidian self.

The ramifications of immersive fictions and reconstructing cognitive scaffolding for studying acting practices are significant. Broadly speaking, actors are trained to immerse themselves within fictional selves, at least in part through literary analysis. However, many styles of acting also encourage actors to observe human behaviors in the real world as companion texts inform their scripted characters.[41] Method acting guru Stella Adler, for example, demanded that her actors consume artworks and human behavior alike. Adler's hope was that actors would expand their imaginary and performative range by studying not only the characters of great literature, the form and style of fine art, etc., but also the actions and intentions of everyday people act in their daily lives. This stockpiling of performable reference points from all manner of readable situational selves, embodied or otherwise, could provide intention-laden construction materials for the cognitive scaffolding of any character the actor was then hired to play.

The actor's search for mimicable intentionalities in fictional and real-life performances reflects Gallese's argument that aesthetic texts are imbued with relational intentionalities that navigate their worlds in the same manner as the text's author and audiences.[42] Therefore, as an embodied simulation, the actor's process of reconstructing her character's psychological infrastructure from the script is a re-alignment of the actor's interpersonal relational processes, thereby reorganizing her quotidian self as the situational actor-as-character. Actors must not only reconstruct their characters' intentionality from the written script, but substitute this intentionality for their own by enacting the characters with the entirety of the bodymind schema. To propose that realist screen acting as a process of soliciting specific overlapping and complementary empathic relationships is therefore hardly an overstatement of an actor's work. Rather, the complexity of empathy as a theoretical framework is necessary to actually engage with the corporeal and emotional intensities of what sincere acting work actually entails.

The common mirroring functions associated that embodied simulation's associates with verbal and physical communicative actions have several major consequences for a neurophenomenological model of screen acting. First, an actor's pre-audition script analysis requires the actor to reconstruct her character's intentionality based on the limited information available from the sides[43] and thereby come to act as her character.[44] Second, if the mirroring in embodied simulation is always a response to a perceived state in one's target, relative to the observing self that perceives that state in the target,[45] then acting is a cultural construct for explicating through performance that which is mirrored. The Magic If, as a lever to propel the actor into the realm of the imagination, uses an intersubjective and intercorporeal connection to a target's intentions to trigger the actor's MM, and thereby simulate the lived experience of that character through a re-arrangement and reworking of the actor's quotidian memories, imaginations, and corporeality.

Phenomenological Empathy and Coplan's Criteria

Contemporary phenomenological models of empathy tend to focus on the forces of attraction between the observer and her target, and on the behavioral and experiential criteria for what experiences can be properly deemed empathetic. This section connects Dan Zahavi's reading of phenomenologist Edith Stein's ideas about empathy with Amy Coplan and Peter Goldie's criteria for empathetic connections, all as part of qualifying how my model of realist screen acting solicits empathetic relationships.

CONNECTIONS ARE MORE THAN IMITATIONS: STEIN'S INTENTIONAL PULL

Dan Zahavi's historical analysis of phenomenological empathy largely corroborates Coplan's criteria, while also concluding that Edith Stein's model of empathy is one of the most consistent predecessors of contemporary neurophenomenological research on the subject. Zahavi positions Stein's philosophy as being more consistent with contemporary research on empathy than the philosophy of Theodor Lipps. Stein herself rejected Lipps's ideas about empathy because of how Lipps downplays its imaginative dimensions, as well as empathy's capacity to create rather than only mirror.[46] Lipps argued that empathy is limited to an inner simulation of something that the observer has already experienced,[47] and therefore cannot generate new knowledge.[48] Lipps is effectively arguing for a theory of imitation and simulation, rather than empathy per se, because of the missing cognitive dimension: Lipps's target is a catalyst for activating his observer's memories.

Stein's intervention was to propose that empathy can produce new knowledge, if the observer imaginatively reconstructs the target's intentionality. This intentionality is not directly accessible to the observer, but by actively attempting to make sense of the target's experience, the observer falls into the "intentional pull" of the target and is drawn closer to his state of mind.[49] Stein's observer does not, as Lipps suggested, project herself into her target's experiences; rather, Stein's observer imagines the object-ness of the target's experience as a subjectivity that can be re-created and understood,[50] which draws the observer closer to her target. By treating her target as a fellow center of intentionality,[51] the observer attends to her target's intentions, which pull the observer into a deeper understanding of why and how the target acts as he does.

Stein's intentional pull is not appresentational in and of itself, since it refers more to the force of attraction through which an appresentational image reorganizes the observer's bodymind. However, intentional pull's implied motion, process, and progress suggest that empathetic solicitation is a process of getting increasingly close to the target until the target's selfhood and intentionality can compel the observer to action from within the situational reconstructed self. The observer's reconstruction of the target's intentionality produces new knowledge for the observer, which pulls the observer closer to her target. Each step closer to the target within that intentional pull likely expedites the observer's subsequent motions towards her target. In other words, this means that an actor's process of soliciting her empathetic connections has options for what aspects of the target's intentionality she should latch on to first, in the hopes that an initial partial connection will make subsequent partial connections easier and more compelling.

The actor's capacity to generate and respond to specifically targeted intentional pulls makes physical imitation and bodymind simulations into valuable stepping stones en route to her empathetic connections. For example, in preparation for his role in *Taxi Driver* (Martin Scorsese, 1976), Harvey Keitel developed a richly affective physical vocabulary for his character after socializing with real-life street pimps.[52] Keitel imitated the pimps' gestures, postures, and speech patterns as a means of delineating his verisimilar performance choices. These imitations helped to ensnare Keitel in his character's intentional pull, since the vocal and physical constraints prompted Keitel to imagine compelling appresentations from within their boundaries. Keitel transferred this corporeal knowledge to the imaginative dimensions of the role, thereby exploring

Figure 2.1 Harvey Keitel (left) and Robert de Niro (right) in *Taxi Driver* (Martin Scorsese, Paramount, 1976)

the interpersonal and performable affordances of moving and talking like that.

Coplan and Decety's Criteria for Empathy

Amy Coplan and Peter Goldie examine how the widespread contemporary interest in empathy across the humanities, social sciences, and life sciences has transformed the concept of empathy into a compelling, if somewhat unwieldy, term.[53] Rather than attempt to define empathy per se, Coplan offers three uncontroversial foundational criteria for what bodymind experiences can qualify as empathy across disciplines and social contexts. First, empathy exists only when the observer "affectively matches" her target, meaning that the affective states of the observer and her target must be "qualitatively identical."[54] This qualitative similarity must go beyond affective congruence, wherein someone might feel pity for someone else who is sad, and reactive emotions, in which someone may become angry at someone else's mistreatment. Affective congruence and reactive emotions can certainly bolster the affective match, but are not enough on their own to satisfy the empathetic criterion because they do not engage the observer's imagination.[55] Coplan's affective match requires an imaginary cognitive reconstruction of the target's affective state grounded in the observer's perceptual experience of her target.[56]

Second, the observer must imagine herself as the target and process the target's experiences and situation as if she were the target. This "other-oriented perspective-taking"[57] requirement bears a striking similarity to neurophenomenological appresentations such as Stanislavsky's "Magic If," the seminal acting lesson wherein the actor imagines that she is living as her character within that character's narrative circumstances. Of all of Coplan's criteria, therefore, other-oriented perspective-taking is often the most readily accessible component of the empathetic solicitation for realist screen actors.

Third, Coplan's empathizing observer remains aware of the distinction between herself and her target, in that empathy is a process of reconstructing experiences, rather than self-erasure through over-immersion.[58] The observer does not meld with her target, nor does she seek to feel what he feels if she were in his situation. The self–other distinction requires the observer to reconstruct what her target feels as she understands how he feels in his situation, based on her available bodymind resources. This empathetic criterion is a primary site of contrast between major American Method acting practitioners. Whereas Lee Strasberg's Method and its experimental off-shoots often sought to blur and minimize the self–other distinction to quite literally turn the actor into her character, Sanford Meisner and Stella Adler's Methods sought to preserve and navigate the boundaries between the actor and her character as a site of productive difference.[59]

Overall, Coplan's criteria underline the cognitive, intentional aspects of how the empathizing observer re-creates her target's experience. The emphasis on imaginative cognition as a vital aspect of empathy differentiates these primarily philosophical criteria for empathy from unimaginative imitation and unmotivated simulation. Coplan's criteria and Stein's intentional pull qualify empathy's functions and metaphorical spatialization without unpacking the substance of intentionality; specifically, the place of memory and imagination within the appresentations that the actor uses to connect with the situational self of her character.

Although Coplan's criteria for empathy generally align with those of leading empathy researcher Jean Decety, the areas of slight mismatch create interesting spaces to consider the social and industrial cultures in which actors solicit empathetic connections. The rest of this book relies more on Coplan's criteria than those of Decety because of how Coplan's self–other distinction's prompts an analysis of how actors keep their quotidian distance from —and go in and out of—the situational self of the actor-as-character. That said, this chapter proceeds by establishing some continuities between Decety and Coplan's models of empathy so as to further substantiate the actorly empathetic connections in Chapter 3, and then examine how they play out in some of screen acting's cognitive ecologies throughout the remainder of the book.

Decety's interest in empathy's roots in evolutionary biology often stresses empathy's role in prosocial behavior and community formation, on the premise that group membership increases the likelihood of humans helping likeminded others.[60] Beyond upholding one's moral obligation to one's community, Decety defines empathy as "a complex multi-faceted construct that involves perspective-taking, affect sharing, and a motivated concern for other's well-being."[61] The empathetic bond between observer and target is not inherently altruistic, and may even encourage the observer to act outside of her community's moral code of conduct because of her empathetic biases.[62] I take Decety's emphasis on empathy's importance to community formation and the cultural principles of the community in question as an opportunity to examine empathy's role in screen acting's creative cultures and professional communities.

Most of the determinative components of empathy in Decety's definition align with Coplan's criteria. Decety's affective and emotional sharing, for example, seems generally similar to Coplan's affective match, in that the observer has the same affective experience as her target. The main difference between Decety's affective sharing and Coplan's affective match is the social goal of the matching as opposed to the fidelity of what the observer matches about the target. Decety sees the shared emotional experience as a motivation for the observer to care for an ailing target, on the assumption that the observer and target are part of the same community.[63] The ensuing emotional contagion, "the experience of emotional similarity," between observer and target becomes readily associated with accruing interpersonal benefits in future social interactions, especially if the observer witnesses the target to be in pain or distress.[64] Coplan, on the other hand, sees the affective match as going beyond contagion to the observer's qualitative replication of the target's disposition.[65] The intensity of the matched emotion can vary, but the match between the target's emotional state and the observer's reconstructed version of that state must be identical. For both Decety and Coplan though, the common bodymind state between observer and target is only possible through the observer's attention to the target's affective experiences.

Decety's requirement that empathy includes some sense of perspective-taking aligns well with Coplan's other-oriented perspective taking. In both sets of empathetic criteria, the observer must have some interest, investment, and engagement with the target's lived experience. Decety and Cowell describe perspective taking as being quite taxing on the observer's working memory.[66] This is not surprising since the observer's executive cognitive functions must carry the weight of both the observer's situational self and an emerging situational self based on the perceived disposition of the target. When actors are rehearsing or performing a character, the deliberate construction of a new situational actor-as-character, based on prompts from the script about the character's cognitive scaffolding, tends to override the actor's quotidian self. Far from viewing the selfhood override as a problem, actors typically consider the exertive nature of the outward-directed attention to the dramatic moment at hand as essential required to keep the actor "in the moment": a state of ideal and deep attunement within the actor-as-character's selfhood wherein the reorganization of the quotidian actor's bodymind is sufficiently firm as to automatically respond to fictional events in the character's with the moment-to-moment experiences as if they were real. Without an attempt to somehow adopt the target character's perspective, realist acting simply does not happen.

The largest variation between Decety and Coplan is Decety's insistence on the observer showing care and concern for the well-being of her target, whereas Coplan's self–other distinction asserts that the observer never permanently becomes her target or gains access to the target's actual personal lived experience. Rather than opposing these two empathetic criteria to each other, I suggest that they are non-contradictory ways of accounting for different parts of screen acting's empathy-inducing practices. Moreover, I argue that a performing actor's empathetic connections position a limited version of Decety's criteria of care for the target's well-being as a pre-condition for Coplan's self–other distinction.

Acting work is precarious, and an actor who does not care about doing the work of making the requisite connections with her targets will likely find herself not working as an actor. The limited version of empathy's motivation to care for the target's well-being manifests insofar as the industrial and artistic imperatives of acting culture compel the actor to care about making connections with her targets.

In what the next chapter calls the intrasubjective connection, the actor must care enough about her character's goals, deadlines, and worldview to reorganize her bodymind into a new situational self, whether or not the actor agrees with the moral decisions made by or about her character. Some actor training regimens insist that actors fight for what their character wants and needs until the end of every scene, regardless of how petty, cruel, unsympathetic, or greedy the character's motivations may be, or however inevitable the scripted end of the scene may be. This tenacity is based in the realist acting maxim that a character who has nothing left to fight for is at the end of her story, and therefore ceases to be dramatically interesting. At Toronto's Professional Actors Lab, for example, screen acting instructor Bruce Clayton sometimes responds to actors who abandon their characters' goals too early in the scene with a rendition of the Kate Bush song, "Don't Give Up."[67] If an actor cares about their work, she will care about connecting with the situational self of the character and let that care motivate the actor-as-character's pursuit of their goals. At least on the level of character, Decety's criterion of care for the target's well-being motivates the actor to care enough about the scripted character as a new situational self to pursue her goals with and as her, while still keeping the actor-as-character situational self who is distinct from the actor's quotidian self.

The actor's intersubjective connection requires that performing actors open themselves to the creative output of their scene partners, often by establishing some sense of care for and trust in each other. Sebastian Gerold, a professional screen actor and instructor of Sanford Meisner and Ivanna Chubbuck's acting styles, encourages actors to "become addicted" to the mutually supportive "safety net" that they can feel for each other when they work together.[68] For Gerold, this reciprocated feeling of care is best established when the performing actors are genuinely listening to each other and responding in the moment. Put another way, by offering one's scene partner the trust that she will remain immersed in the scene, and that she will help to keep the scene partner immersed in the scene as well, actors establish a sense of mutual care for each other so that they can bring the best work possible out of themselves and each other. To be fair, this culture of reciprocated care is more of an ideal than a given situation; Chapter 6 considers how actors on set can seek emergency empathetic bandages to compensate for mismatches in the casting in which the actors simply have no creative "chemistry" together. For now, Decety's criteria of care goes hand-in-hand with Coplan's self–other distinction: the foundational trust and care between working actors recognizes them as fundamentally distinct selves from each other who need each other's professional help to realize their scenes together.

Last, the actor's performative solicitation of the anticipated audience's empathy stems for the actor's fundamental care that their work will be comprehensible to whoever will see it in the finished film or episode. One of the key differences between theatrical and screen acting is the presence of the intended audience during the actor's performance. Whereas theatrical actors feel connected their performance spaces *and* the attending audience,[69] and can even gage the audience's attunement to the performance, screen actors receive no such immediate feedback from anticipated audience because the film is not yet finished nor in theaters when the actor is performing. The actor must therefore extend a great deal of trust to her on-set collaborators, from the director and other actors to the technicians other below-the-line production personnel,[70] that they will help her complete the performance in the most artistically compelling manner possible. This trust often means that actors must work around the logistical hurdles of film and television production which rarely prioritize the actor's convenience, readiness, patience, or creative flow. On a more fundamental level though, the actor wants their performance to be comprehensible—if not enjoyable—for her audience, and therefore must make the most of the on-set affordances as a matter of care-laden professional due diligence when inviting the audience into the actor-as-character's lived world.[71]

The kinds of actorly care described here are admittedly a stretch from the evolutionary and biological foundations of empathy, even if Decety readily acknowledges advanced forms of empathy in which people can empathize with humans outside their communities and with non-humans.[72] The in-group empathetic care bias that I feel for my son's pre-naptime tantrums are categorically different from the empathy I feel for my first-year undergraduates' stress about their midterm deadlines, even if I feel attuned to their collective anxieties, frustrations, and general exhaustion. In a similar vein, the heightened levels of imaginary abstraction in acting depend on a significant amount of out-group attention which strains and restricts the likelihood and intensity of any ensuing sense of empathy. There is no guarantee that every actor will actually make vibrant empathetic connections in every role they play across their career; sometimes the care criterion is not enough to overcome a character with flimsy cognitive scaffolding, the demands of a picky casting director, the working habits of an impossible co-star, or adverse conditions on set. There is also nothing inherently altruistic or morally righteous about an actor's solicitation of empathetic connections. The activities previously described as examples of the actor's criteria of care are easily intertwined with the actor's sense of professional survival, and therefore have at least as much to do with the actor caring about her own career and well-being as with caring about anyone else.

Rather than seeing this stretch as weak argumentation about acting and empathy, this book stresses the actor's solicitation of empathy, rather than its assured presence. Even if there are many creative and industrial factors which can restrict, inhibit, or prevent vibrant experiences of actorly empathy, the nature of acting work still prompts the actor to go in search of those connections. Whether or not the final performance compels audiences to empathize with the actor-as-character, the actor still presents the actor-as-character as legible text with a cognitive scaffolding for the audience to construct for themselves. The actor still pushes the actor-as-character's intentionality towards the audience as best she can, hoping that they will become ensnared in the intentional pull.

The Project Ahead: Screen Actors as Solicitors of Empathy

This book attempts to pull together the many theoretical threads outlined in this chapter, from neurophenomenological notions of selfhood to principles of realist acting and models of empathy, to produce a conceptual model of screen acting that speaks from the actor outwards. In the chapters to come, this book argues that the creative process of screen acting aims to solicit empathetic connections across a range of targets, such as the actor's situational character, her fellow actors-as-characters, and the anticipated audience. Actors are key hubs of embodied cognition within the network of distributed cognition that produces screen performances; the bodymind reorganization they undertake to reify the actor-as-character as a situational self is deeply reliant on the connections they attempt to establish with other selves. This approach to studying acting prioritizes the bodymind movement of actors' imaginations, training, and creative habits, thereby presenting actors as authoritative experts on how their work is done. Any such analysis of a screen actor's situated expertise must necessarily account for its situatedness; the later chapters of this book in particular contextualize the screen actor's empathetic solicitations within the industrial hurdles and practicalities—in other words, the cognitive ecologies—of film and television production.

Notes

1. Thompson, *Mind In Life: Biology, Phenomenology, and the Sciences of the Mind*, p. 37.
2. Varela, "Organism, cognitive science and the emergence of selfless selves," p. 175.
3. Ibid. pp. 186–7.
4. Ibid. p. 187.
5. Thompson, *Mind In Life: Biology, Phenomenology, and the Sciences of the Mind*, pp. 49–61.
6. Varela, "Organism, cognitive science and the emergence of selfless selves," p. 192.
7. Kemp, *Embodied Acting: What Neuroscience Tells Us about Performance*, pp. 104–5.

8. Ibid. p. 123.
9. Frederique de Vignemont, "Body schema and body image—pros and cons," p. 672.
10. Antonio Cayonne (actor), in discussion with the author, August 2016.
11. See Chapter 5 for a more extensive discussion of actors combining imaginary and remembered selves during character development.
12. Blair, *The Actor, Image, and Action: Acting and Cognitive Neuroscience*, p. 59. See also Antonio Damasio's *The Feeling of what Happens: Body and Emotion in the Making of Consciousness* (1999), p. 23.
13. Blair, *The Actor, Image, and Action*, p. 60.
14. Jackman, "Training, insight and intuition in creative flow," p. 116; Csikzentmihalyi, *Creativity: Flow and the Psychology and Discovery of Invention*, p. 110.
15. Vervaeke, Ferraro, and Herrera-Bennett, "Flow as spontaneous thought: insight and implicit learning," p. 309.
16. Ibid. pp. 311–12.
17. Ibid. 311.
18. Varela, "Organism, cognitive science and the emergence of selfless selves," p. 179; Thompson, *Mind In Life: Biology, Phenomenology, and the Sciences of the Mind*, pp. 260–1, 383.
19. Thompson, *Mind In Life: Biology, Phenomenology, and the Sciences of the Mind*, p. 391.
20. Ibid. p. 386.
21. Thompson, *Mind In Life: Biology, Phenomenology, and the Sciences of the Mind*, p. 391; Corradini and Antonietti, "Mirror neurons and their function in cognitively understood empathy," p. 1153; Smith, "Empathy, expansionism, and the extended mind," pp. 104–5.
22. Meisner and Longwell, *On Acting*, p. 15.
23. Thompson, *Mind In Life: Biology, Phenomenology, and the Sciences of the Mind*, p. 383.
24. Thompson, *Mind In Life: Biology, Phenomenology, and the Sciences of the Mind*, p. 388; Drummond, "Imagination and appresentation, sympathy and empathy in Smith and Husserl," p. 129.
25. Johnston, "Stanislavskian acting as phenomenology in practice," p. 74.
26. Zahavi, "Self and other: from pure ego to co-constituted we," p. 153.
27. Gallese and Cuccio, "The paradigmatic body—embodied simulation, intersubjectivity, the bodily self, and language," p. 5.
28. Ibid. p. 8.
29. Orban, "The mirror system in human and nonhuman primates"; Mikulan et al., "Homuncular mirrors: misunderstanding causality in embodied cognition"; Alford, "Mirror neurons, psychoanalysis, and the age of empathy"; Arévalo et al., "What can we make of theories of embodiment and the role of the human mirror neuron system?"

30. Lamm and Majdandžić, "The role of shared neural activations, mirror neurons, and morality in empathy—a critical comment."
31. Gallese and Cuccio, "The paradigmatic body—embodied simulation, intersubjectivity, the bodily self, and language," p. 9.
32. Ibid. pp. 16–17.
33. Gallese, "Visions of the body: embodied simulation and aesthetic experience," p. 5.
34. Ibid. p. 9.
35. Gallese and Guerra, *The Empathetic Screen*, pp. 4–5, 50–1, 201–2.
36. Gallese, "Visions of the body: embodied simulation and aesthetic experience," p. 14.
37. Ibid. p. 14.
38. Feagin, "Empathizing as simulating," p. 149.
39. Ibid. pp. 158–61.
40. Bal and Veltkamp, "How does fiction reading influence empathy? An experimental investigation on the role of emotional transportation."
41. Mirodan, "Acting and emotion," p. 110.
42. Gallese, "Visions of the body: embodied simulation and aesthetic experience," p. 14; Wojciehowski and Gallese, "How stories make us feel: toward an embodied narratology."
43. The term "sides" often refers to the script/screenplay excerpts used as audition material. During film production, "sides" may also refer to the portion of the script that is to be shot that day.
44. The details of this mirroring and translation from page to the actor's body will be taken up in greater detail in Chapter 3.
45. Gallese and Cuccio, "The Paradigmatic Body—Embodied Simulation, Intersubjectivity, the Bodily Self, and Language," p. 16.
46. MNS researchers such as Gallese and Iacoboni have both invoked Lipps to support their research on emotional and behavioral mirroring, but as the previous section of this chapter has argued, the lack of a one-to-one connection between MNS and empathy means that theories of imitation should not automatically expand to become models of empathy. Imitation does involve corporeal and emotional recognitions, which could be a step towards an empathetic relationship. Imitation, however, does not of itself require the observer to take on her target's emotional or mental disposition. The observer's intentional focus while imitating is on gestural detail rather than necessarily on investigating and re-creating the target's intentions behind the gesture itself. Without the cognitive attention to intentionality, imitation is at best a stepping stone on the way to an empathetic connection between target and observer; imitation is, in a way, empathy without the imagination.
47. Zahavi, "Empathy and other-directed intentionality," p. 130.
48. Ibid. p. 131.
49. Ibid. pp. 134–6.

50. Ibid. p. 136.
51. Zahavi, "Self and other: from pure ego to co-constituted we," p. 153.
52. Levinson, "The auteur renaissance, 1968–1980," p. 100.
53. Coplan and Goldie, "Introduction."
54. Coplan, "Understanding empathy: its features and effects," pp. 5–6.
55. Ibid. pp. 8–9.
56. Ibid. p. 6.
57. Coplan's other-oriented perspective taking criterion has considerable theoretical precedent in the simulation models in contemporary theory of mind (ToM) research, especially what Buckner and Carroll (2007) call "self-projection", wherein the subject appresents herself into a target perspective which resembles but is not synonymous with her present self. This is especially interesting in relation to realist acting practices because Coplan's second criterion avoids Goldman's "quarantine failure" (2006) in that the actor is free to blend her own quotidian experiences of the world with those implied in the scripted character's cognitive scaffolding.
58. Coplan, "Understanding empathy: its features and effects," p. 15.
59. The differing ways in various Method and non-Method acting styles satisfy Coplan's criteria will be taken up extensively in Chapter 3.
60. Decety, "The neural pathways, development and functions of empathy," pp. 3–4.
61. Yoder and Decety, "The neuroscience of morality and social decision-making," p. 284.
62. Decety et al., "Empathy as a driver of prosocial behaviour: highly conserved neurobehavioural mechanisms across species," p. 2.
63. Decety and Cowell, "Friends or foes: is empathy necessary for moral behavior?"
64. Ibid.
65. Coplan, "Understanding empathy: its features and effects," pp. 6–7.
66. Decety and Cowell, "Friends or foes: is empathy necessary for moral behavior?"
67. See Chapter 5 for a more detailed analysis of the Professional Actors Lab.
68. Sebastian Gerold in a Chubbuck masterclass at Amsterdam's Mulholland Academy, November 2015.
69. Lutterbie, *Toward a General Theory of Acting: Cognitive Science and Performance*, pp. 211–31.
70. Caldwell, *Production Culture: Industrial Reflexivity and Critical Practice in Film and Television*.
71. Some of the tactics by which actors "make the most" of their on-set resources are the focus of Chapter 6.
72. Decety and Cowell, "Friends or foes: is empathy necessary for moral behavior?," p. 533.

CHAPTER 3

The Actor's Three Empathetic Connections

This chapter unpacks the three empathetic connections that western screen actors solicit as part of creating realist acting's verisimilar illusion. These connections position the actor as the "observer"—the one who solicits the empathetic relationship—and the sel(ves) with whom she aspires to connect as her "target."[1] The major exception to this pattern is the *performative* connection, wherein the actor presents herself as a target for an anticipated observer in the audience by intentionally pushing herself towards that spectator's attention.

In unpacking these three connections, this chapter attempts to qualify how various twentieth-century American acting traditions prioritize specific empathetic connections over others as key to their Method's conception of compelling *acting*, often supported by training exercises for developing appresentations towards that prioritized connection. These training exercises are best understood as the conditioning of tactics for soliciting the empathetic bonds, rather than prescriptions for ensuring them: neither actors nor acting come with assembly instructions. The emphasis here is on the actor's attempt to form an empathetic bond with her target, hence the recurring use of the word "solicitation." Simply put, not all acting is compelling; the connections are essential but there is no guarantee that they will each be adequately realized by every actor in every performance.

Realist screen acting is the solicitation of three complementary and simultaneous empathetic relationships: an intrasubjective relationship between the actor and her character; an intersubjective relationship between performing actors and among actors as characters; and, a performative empathy between the performing actor and her audience. These empathetic relationships collectively enworld the quotidian actor as the situational actor-as-character within the fiction. The actor's transformation from quotidian self to situational self is a strategic reorganization of her quotidian bodymind schema into a situational configuration that is not inherently recognizable as the actor's quotidian self. And yet, the bodymind movements within this self-reorganization are what solicit the actor's necessary empathetic connections with her situational self, her fellow actors and surroundings, and her anticipated audience as a self-reinforcing, iterative, dynamic system. In placing the solicitation of empathy at the center of a model of realist acting, this study examines how each empathetic relationship solicits and sustains its appresentations and its target's intentional pull, with the ultimate goal of producing verisimilar performances. What, however, are the empathetic connections that iteratively produce and are produced by these bodymind movements? What kinds of tactile, imaginary, and emotional activities shape these movements, and how do various prolific traditions of western realist screen acting operationalize them?

This chapter analyzes how each of the actor's intrasubjective, intersubjective, and performative solicitations fulfill Coplan's criteria for empathetic relationships: the affective match, other-oriented perspective-taking, and self–other distinction. This chapter exemplifies the intrasubjective and intersubjective connections with a brief historical case studies that demonstrate how prolific American Method acting practitioners such as Lee Strasberg and Sanford Meisner prioritized this particular empathetic connection as the foundation of an actor's craft. This necessarily accounts for the solicitation of appresentations in each connection's observer/target relationship, often in relation to what the actor does with the screenplay.

The performative solicitation is far less codified by these Method practitioners because, as this chapter suggests, the performative solicitation is largely contingent on how the actors navigate the intrasubjective and intersubjective connections in front of the camera. In a perfect world for Method actors trained in these styles, the performative solicitation falls into place as the audience—the performative target—becomes ensnared in the actor-as-character's intentional pull. Therefore, this chapter sketches how the solicitation of a performative connection develops appresentations while realizing Coplan's criteria. Chapter 5 provides a detailed examination of some performative tactics used by the actors interviewed during this study.

In the meantime, I have chosen to use ideas and techniques from American Method acting practices, particularly from Strasberg and Meisner, as my primary illustrative case studies for several reasons. These styles of Method acting have many acclaimed and commonplace examples in western realist film acting, from Robert de Niro's radical experimentation with Strasberg's techniques to Diane Keaton's Meisnerian training. The intense stylistic differences between Strasberg, Meisner, and other Stanislavski-based methods in terms of an actor's priorities, strategies, and training exercises are well-documented, which helps them to serve as time-honored examples of the diversity of film acting styles. Moreover, some of the actors who were interviewed as part of this research credit some aspect of their approach to acting to these key practitioners: Joe Dinicol, for example, regularly draws in his extensive training in Meisner's techniques for his work in film and television; Natalie Lisinska, on the other hand, explains that many of her most influential acting instructors were heavily influenced by Uta Hagen's approach to acting.

It would be completely misleading, however, to imply that all actors are Method actors. Many established, successful, and respected film and television actors have never explicitly studied Strasberg, Meisner, Adler, or any of their contemporaries, and may even consider themselves better off for it. Nevertheless, these methods represent three distinct and often-mutually opposed codifications of Stanislavsky's principles of realist acting, many of which find some sort of parallel, resonance, or correlative in other non-Method styles. Acting is an inherently diverse and amorphous practice, and accounting for every style and system ever used in front of a motion picture camera is beyond the scope of this book. Even Method arch-rivals like Strasberg and Adler could agree that actors should gravitate towards the specific techniques that happen to work best for them individually, further underscoring that there is no one "correct" or "best" way to do acting work.[2] It is therefore beyond the scope of this—or any—book to account for all realist acting styles across all time. My interest here is in how these Method practitioners and their contemporaries navigate core Stanislavskyian principles of realist acting for use in theater and film. I therefore offer empathetic readings of these three systems to illustrate the common applicability of my theoretical approach to some of Stanislavksy's most prolific twentieth-century interpreters on the premise that an empathetic analysis of these classic examples provides a template for future studies of other acting styles another day.

Intrasubjective Empathy

In the intrasubjective solicitation, the actor connects with her character by reorganizing her quotidian bodymind to align with the situational self of the scripted character. This translation from script to body requires the actor to develop useful appresentations to ensnare herself in the scripted character's intentional pull. These appresentations often blend cues from the script as to the character's cognitive scaffolding with the results of the actor's creative experimentation with compelling reference points in her quotidian bodymind schema that somehow resonate with her interpretation of the situational character. This section illustrates the some of the diversity of strategies for intrasubjective connections by contrasting the intrasubjective solicitation tactics between the American Method acting styles of Lee Strasberg and Stella Adler.

The intrasubjective connection's prompt to the actor to turn outwards towards the script and inwards towards her imagination and memory for creative fodder makes sense in terms of its place in filmmaking as an industrial process: a great deal of intrasubjective appresentation development occurs when the actor is working alone. She may make further creative intrasubjective discoveries about her character's goals and desires while rehearsing with other actors or while collaborating with directors, costume designers, and other production personnel. She may also uncover valuable details about her character's experiences by experimenting with performative choices like blocking directions, consciously varied vocal intensities, and so forth. Ultimately though, much of the work that an actor does to prepare her inner monologue,[3] including her character's backstory and finding pertinent physical and mental appresentations in her quotidian self to somehow embody within her character, happens privately and early in the actor's creative process. This workflow has as much to do with practicality and pragmatism as with artistic priority: most film actors have access to their script before meeting the other actors and having a chance to rehearse. The actor is presented with a script laden with the cognitive scaffolding of the situational self with whom she must align, and subsequently build the appresentations that pull the actor from imitating the character to empathetically experiencing the world as her character.

To that end, intrasubjective appresentation creation typically blends cues from the script with physical and emotional exercises that improve the actor's access to her bodymind resources, thereby giving the actor more to work with while aligning herself within a character's intentional pull. Stella Adler, for example, encouraged her students to study the arts and history, and to practice the habits of observing and imagining things in great critical detail, to generate experiential fodder for future re-interpretations. Strasberg, on the other hand, developed relaxation and introspection exercises to help connect the actor to memories that trigger affective responses that can be recalled in performance to put the actor in the right bodymind state for the scene at hand; as Anna Strasberg describes, to introduce "the actor's sensory life back to her."[4]

In many traditions of script analysis, the actor targets the scripted character by identifying the beliefs and desires as evidence of the scripted character's emotions. By reconstructing a realist character's cognitive scaffolding, the reader—in this case, an actor—can first simulate and imitate the character's imaginative and emotional experiences en route to ensnaring herself within the scripted character's intentional pull, literally pulling the character off the page and into the situational bodymind of the actor-as-character.[5]

The empathetic process of translating the character from page to body in Stella Adler's Method, for example, begins with simulation as a path to the emotional truths behind and within the words. Adler insists that, in addition to conducting diligent dramaturgical research to gain informed access to the world of the drama,[6] the actor must be profoundly aware of the script's words in order to transcend the script and unleash all of the affective power and possible selves imbedded within them.[7] At the same time, the actor should develop her own paraphrases of each line to hone in on the character's intentionality before memorizing her lines to avoid becoming so fixated on the words that she loses the emotional connection to the dramatic moment.[8] The actor's ability to first understand the play's ideas[9] and to then use these ideas to excite her fruitful creative imagination[10] is a cornerstone of Adler's Method.

This same tactic of mining the script for emotional through-lines and then making the script subservient to the affective power of the enacted moment also manifests in some non-Method styles of film acting. For Canadian screen acting instructor Bruce Clayton, the script is a "roadmap" to the character's journey throughout the scene but, as with Adler, any "preciousness" about the words must be discarded if it impedes the acting work behind the words. The actor may start with the scripted words, but must move away from the script by translating the cognitive scaffolding within the words into her body, and let that cognitive scaffolding reorganize the quotidian self into the situational character, for those words to take on meaning in performance. Similarly, British screen acting instructor Bill Britten acknowledges the affective potential of a script's "intricate" words and "detailed" descriptions; it is the actor—and not the writer—who scripts the emotional inner monologue of the performed character by connecting with the emotional content embedded within and between the lines.[11] The cultural politics behind how an actor ought to "respect" the script's words differs greatly across nationalist and artistic traditions. Beyond simply memorizing her lines, the actor's translation of the character into her own body gradually places more value on how the actor-as-character enacts the narrative than on strictly adhering to a script that the audience will likely never see.

Formal script analysis is not the only way for the actor to reconstruct a character's cognitive scaffolding from the script's page. In some acting traditions, the desire to move from simulation to empathy prompts the actor to use external and internal objects to begin the serious entry into the character's intentional pull. Actors often couple script work with experiments with props and costume pieces that are appropriate to the character to gain a firsthand sensorial experience of how the character might move.[12] Laurence Olivier was famous for finding character inspirations in costume pieces from crowns to fake noises: the "one or two externals" that sparked his imagination as to who the character could be to him.[13] More recently, Viggo Mortensen wore a sword on his belt for months before and during the shoot of the *Lord of the Rings* films to help him find a convincing physical vocabulary[14] for the films' fantastical heroism, enworlding his situational self with the corporeal knowledge of someone accustomed to carrying a large sharp object on his hip at all times. This type of experimentation presumes a productive connection between physical action and creative imagination. This creative investigation of potential body schemas can prompt a corporeal knowledge that will help the actor to imagine her script from within the character's intentional pull. For Olivier, Mortensen, and many other screen actors, the intentionalized actions motivated by the object help to specify the script's cues towards the character's beliefs and desires because it prompts the actor's top-down imaginative processes to collaborate with the bottom-up sensorimotor experience of the object.

Additionally, some actors will supplement their immersion in a character's intentional pull with firsthand research and skill acquisition. In an example given earlier in this book, Harvey Keitel's experiences while studying and interacting with New York pimps proved to be a potent source of character information for his role in Scorsese's *Taxi Driver*. Beyond addressing production concerns, such as when Robert de Niro learned to box to play prizefighter Jake LaMotta in *Raging Bull* (Martin Scorsese, 1980), acquiring skills can be a productive point of entry to the character's intentional pull because they provide a firsthand experience of a meaningful aspect of the target character's experience and intentionality. Skill acquisitions can impact performative empathy as well as intrasubjective because they can easily transform the actor's image and body schema: not only can an actor look, move, or sound different from learning a new skill, but the corporeal knowledge of that skill can be imaginatively applied throughout the performance.

Coplan's Criteria and Intrasubjective Connections

Many schools of Method acting insist that the actor must "become" her character during performance or else the result will be unconvincing, insincere or manipulated.[15] In terms of Coplan's criteria, the intuitive priority of this situational becoming treats the intrasubjective other-oriented perspective taking as direct conduit to the intrasubjective affective match. The actor constructs the situational character's cognitive scaffolding to take on the character's perspective by identifying a compelling Magic If. By taking on the perspective of a situational character in terms of that character's lived circumstances, the quotidian actor starts to enworld herself as the situational character. Since the character is a situational reconfiguration of the quotidian actors' own bodymind, however, she will inherently accomplish a rudimentary affective match with the situational character by virtue of reconstructing that cognitive scaffolding and taking on the situational perspective. Eventually, the other-oriented perspective taking and the affective match reinforce each other as the actor continues to refine her intrasubjective connection with her character through rehearsal and creative experimentation.

This focus on "becoming" the situational character suggests that intrasubjective Method acting techniques risks obfuscating the self–other distinction required for empathetic relationships. The marginalization of the self–other distinction is at its most visible in the radically intrasubjective Method acting experiments by Strasberg-based practitioners in the 1970s, who began altering their quotidian bodies to better match the intended body for a character[16]; this will be taken up in greater detail later in this chapter. That said, the American Method acting movements are not the only Stanislavsky-based theories of screen acting available to contemporary actors, however influential the Method has become in screen performance practices. Moreover, and despite the lack of explicit training for establishing a productive self–other distinction, it is important to remember that the self–other distinction is always still accessible to the actor or else she logically could never "stop" acting once the filming process is complete.

In other words, an essential facet of intrasubjectively connecting to the situational character is the ability to disconnect afterwards. This disconnection principle has wide consensus among key acting practitioners and critics. Rick Kemp cites prolific director and acting instructor Michael Chekhov's insistence on keeping actor and character distinct as a key principle of stimulating the actor's creative imagination.[17] Sharon Carnicke's historical analysis of Stanislavsky's theories of acting positions the Magic If as a valuable safeguard against the actor losing control of these invoked and applied emotions and then genuinely reliving them as her character.[18] Even Strasberg's notes from Boleslavsky's classes stress that "hallucination" is not acting, but to be able to recall and manipulate emotional experiences is a powerful boon to one's performances.[19] Instead, the appresentational Magic If preserves and negotiates the bodymind distance between the quotidian actor and the reorganized actor-as-character.

Only in the most radical of intrasubjective practices does the actor refuse—or become unable—to break out of character. The underlying bodymind interconnectivity through which Daniel Day-Lewis, for example, finds emotional and imaginary creative fodder through physical experimentation and then transfers it to the situational actor-as-character disrupts any clear distinction between his quotidian and situational selves. I suggest that an excessively weakened intrasubjective self–other distinction forced Day-Lewis to leave Richard Eyre's 1989 production of *Hamlet* at London's National Theatre. The role of Hamlet is famously demanding on its actor's emotional and mental resources, and Day-Lewis is known for his intensely immersive approach to acting. During the Ghost scene during one performance, an exhausted Day-Lewis-as-Hamlet broke down mid-performance and left the stage, convinced that he had just seen the actual ghost of Day-Lewis's quotidian father.[20] Day-Lewis was traumatized by the experience and could not return to acting for many years.

Day-Lewis's film acting career is similarly peppered with stories of his unwillingness to come out of character between takes. He insisted on remaining paralyzed on the set of *My Left Foot* (Jim Sheridan, 1989), much to the annoyance of the film crew who had to physically move him on, off, and around set each day,[21] and insisted that he personally lived under the torturous prison-like conditions depicted in *Name of the Father* (Jim Sheridan, 1993).[22] Day-Lewis greeted visitors to the set of *Gangs of New York* (Martin Scorsese, 2002) as his sociopathic character, "Bill the Butcher", refused pneumonia medication on set that did not exist in Bill's nineteenth-century New York,[23] and severely injured his nose during rehearsal by headbutting a stand-in mannequin for co-star Leonardo DiCaprio.[24] For Day-Lewis, acting is more of a "childlike" imaginary immersion in the life of another person than formal artistry, even if his difficulty in ending that immersion often comes at a painful personal cost:

> "I'm told that people find it strange that I do the work the way I do it, but then I think, 'Well, yes, but the work is inherently strange. [. . .] [Even] stranger from my point of view to have the capacity to jump in and out which some people undeniably have. I'm kind of in awe of those people. They'll probably live longer and happier lives.'"[25]

Although, as Kemp explains, these harsh physical preparation conditions have stimulated Day-Lewis' imagination[26] into producing many deeply memorable performances, the suspension of the intrasubjective self–other distinction in the hopes that the intrasubjective affective match and other-oriented perspective taking will overcompensate come at a considerable cost to Day-Lewis's personal health and well-being. In other words, the preservation of the self–other distinction is essential for intrasubjective realist acting because it preserves the quotidian actor's psychological well-being while keeping the actor-as-character enworlded within the drama.

Intrasubjective Case Study: Lee Strasberg and the Affective Memory

Strasberg's version of the Method explicitly prioritizes the actor's intrasubjective connection as her primary task, on the presumption that the intentional pull of a strong intrasubjective connection will inevitably organize and fuel the actor's connections with her fellow performers and the anticipated audience. In Strasbergian acting, the actor searches within herself for powerful emotional memories to invoke in performance. By putting the actor in a dramatically suitable emotional state, Strasberg's actor will appear to genuinely feel *as* her character, and thereby enworld the actor-as-character within the drama.

Strasberg's Method for intrasubjectively reliant acting stems from his interpretation of Stanislavsky's early experiments in emotional recall. In the early 1920s, Strasberg and Adler were among the first American theater practitioners to study Stanislavsky's System at the New York workshops led by Moscow Art Theater expats Richard Boleslavsky and Maria Ouspenskya.[27] This early version of Stanislavsky's System pioneered the affective memory technique, wherein the actor treats her own emotional memories as a "mine from which all psychological truth must be dug."[28] The hope of this affective memory work is that the actor becomes able to recall sincere feelings on command.

Strasberg was fascinated by both the prospect and the process of invoking genuine emotions on stage, so much so as to be described by his former colleague Harold Clurman as a "fanatic on the subject of true emotion."[29] The unremittingly truthful expression of the actor's emotions became the primary goal of Strasberg's Method, and affective memory work became one of the primary teaching exercises for that skill. Anna Strasberg, a student of the Actors Studio who later married Lee Strasberg, exemplifies the utter conviction in affective memory as the best training for realist actors:

> Emotional memory is the key to unlocking the secret to creativity. When anybody creates, he is unconsciously using memories of senses and emotions. All people have emotional memories, but not everyone can re-create them. The emotional memory exercise provides a technique for doing so.[30]

Both Strasberg and—at least in his early career—Stanislavsky treated the psychological conditioning required by affective memory work as Pavlovian rather than Freudian.[31] Rhonda Blair explains that Stanislavsky's goal was not to probe the actor's inner psyche but to develop methodical techniques—similar to Pavlov's contemporaneous research on producing consistent reactions to external stimuli—for activating the actor's full capacity for artistic expression.[32] Emotional recall was not about psychological recuperation, but rather about conditioning a learnable and desirable skill that would protect the actor from giving an insincere performance: "the Method teaches actors to re-create—not to copy, not to make believe, but to connect with what you know and use it as a character."[33] The empathetic underpinnings of this Pavlovian connection "with what you know" through affective memory work carry important consequences for the performing actor's body schema.

Strasberg's affective memory exercises treat the quotidian actor and the situational character-on-the-page as centers of intentionality to be pulled together. This pulling-together occurs in Strasberg by invoking an intermediary remembered situational self who can satisfy the conditions of the appresentational Magic If. In affective memory exercises, the instructor guides the student through the reliving of a buried memory by making the student describe aloud its associated sensory experiences and subsequent emotions. Although Strasberg insisted that his students focus on the somatic experience of the recalled emotion rather than the story behind the memory,[34] some narrative prompting was required to make sure that the actor was recalling something sufficiently moving as to be dramatically meaningful. First, the exercise awakens a body schema associated with the recalled memory within the actor. This intermediary remembered self, grounded in the recalled body schema and dramatically relevant to the character's narrative condition, helps the actor to feel her way into the character's lived world. If the intermediary body schema is a compelling fit within the Magic If, the actor transposes her recalled self into the situational self of the character. This creates the verisimilar illusion that the actor has become the character by wholeheartedly embracing the intermediary appresentations as being real.

Strasberg's techniques aim to establish a firm intrasubjective connection that satisfies Coplan's criteria for empathy. Through the affective memory exercise, the quotidian actor improves her access to her emotionally charged memories to better affectively match her situational characters. The other-oriented perspective-taking goes hand in hand with the affective match, in that the choice of emotions to recall is determined by the cognitive scaffolding that she has reconstructed from the script.

The affective memory, as a professional practice, is predicated on the notion that the actor never fully overcomes the self–other distinction: the recalled emotional material informs the experiences of the situational character, but only in affective proximity to the actor's quotidian memory. In other words, if the recalled emotion was not intensely and specifically personalized to the quotidian actor, that emotion would not be chosen to be adapted to the needs of the situational—and inherently non-quotidian—self. This heightened emotional access trained by the affective memory exercise allows the actor to transform the scripted character's cognitive architecture into a resonant bodymind appresentation that blends the intrasubjective affective match with its accompanying other-oriented perspective-taking. The Strasbergian actor thereby creates a verisimilar performance since she appears to feel exactly what her character feels.

The emotions recalled during an affective memory exercise become part of the actor's performance repertoire and, for Strasberg, her resourcefulness in conjuring these deep memories becomes a test of her skill.[35] The inevitable analogy of Strasberg as an amateur psychotherapist became a popular weapon among Strasberg's critics, a group that included many former colleagues and students. Actors Studio co-founder Robert Lewis eventually condemned affective memory as "pathology, not art," arguing that Strasberg was not equipped to deal with the traumas that might surface during the exercise, and that these traumatic memories push the actor too far from the drama and too far into herself.[36] Morris Carnovsky declared affective memory to be useless as a rehearsal method, and Phoebe Brand accused Strasberg of "crippling" actors by encouraging a "moody, personal, self-indulgent acting style."[37]

Stella Adler was so incensed with Strasberg's insistence on affective memory that, in 1934, she left New York to visit the elderly Stanislavsky in Paris. During their meetings, Adler learned that Stanislavsky had abandoned the affective memory exercises in favor of techniques that encouraged the actor to physically and mentally imagine her way into the actor-as-character's situational selfhood. Stanislavsky's new Method of Physical Actions insisted that characters emerged though physical experimentation and an imaginary immersion in the character's fictional world,[38] rather than relying as heavily on recalled emotions as the version of his System that Strasberg and Adler had once learned from Boleslavsky and Ouspenskya. Blair indicates that, by the mid-1930s, Stanislavsky no longer viewed memory as a photograph, but as an event which is reimagined along similar lines to how it was first processed without needing to be an identical re-creation of that event.[39] If the actor's imagination was inevitably going to inform her emotional reference points for the actor-as-character's cognitive scaffolding, the goal was to now stimulate the imagination with physical experimentation, rather than treat the inventiveness of the actor as an artistic liability:

> We no longer need to be concerned about reliving a past event as truthfully as possible, but can tap into memory as a tool to be used to make the present more alive, as part of the powers of imagination to make the actor's range of expression as wide and deep as possible.[40]

Stanislavsky's Method of Physical Actions therefore is much more consistent in practice to the modern neuroscientific understandings of imagination, emotion, and empathetic responses to fiction[41] than Strasberg's exclusively introspective process of awakening emotional memories. Upon returning to New York, Adler severed her connections with Strasberg and the Actor's Studio and formed her own school of acting based on Stanislavsky's later work. Not surprisingly, Adler's Method would eventually conceive of emotion as "only a frame of reference for the action itself" since emotions were best expressed through the actor-as-character's actions.[42,43] What was it, though, that so many expert practitioners eventually found so destructive about affective memory?

When transposing the actor's allegedly internal emotions to those of the character, the interconnected bodymind must adjust physically to accommodate the emotional choices. Since the ensuing body schema is organized around the needs of the actor-as-character, however, the quotidian body that houses the Strasbergian character may struggle to match the character's story and circumstances. Put another way, the remembering body may not match or be able to adequately accommodate the remembered body in a way that suits the verisimilar needs of the actor-as-character. Strasberg's conviction in the truth of memory and the artifice and deceit of imagination, coupled with his penchant for intimidating and bullying his actors who performed with "artificial" emotions,[44] dissuaded many actors from freely imagining bodymind circumstances to close the discontinuities between the actor and her character.

The irony, as Kemp argues, is that Strasberg's emotional recall exercises are as much about spontaneously reimagining the emotion as remembering it, since memories need to be re-created within the bodymind rather than rolled like videotape.[45] Strasberg's commitment to memory as the actor's exclusive path to performing real emotions and simultaneous distrust of imagination is also refuted by modern neuroscientific understandings of cognition and emotion. Kemp argues, via Joseph LeDoux and Antonio Damasio, that the emotion which the actor recalls is not necessarily identical to the one she remembers, and—beyond the boundaries of Strasberg's mediative techniques—that physical actions associated with emotional states and specific personal memories are reliable triggers for emotional experiences.[46] However, Strasberg's vehement insistence on using introspective memory over imagination often forced the actor to make uncomfortable mental adjustments in the hope that her body will keep pace. If the actor's body schema cannot resolve the ensuing tension, the Strasbergian actor may need to either develop new memories through research and experimentation, or to change her body to fit the character.

Many Strasbergian actors in the late 1970s and early 1980s experimented with physical transformations for overcoming the implicit self–other distinction through altering their quotidian bodies to better match the imagined body of the situational character. Dustin Hoffman's inebriated and sleepless preparation for some scenes in *Marathon Man* (John Schlesinger, 1976) famously drew the ire of co-star Laurence Olivier, who asked Hoffman why he was physically harming himself rather than "try acting" instead.[47] Robert De Niro filed his teeth down for his role in *Taxi Driver* (Martin Scorsese, 1976) to better imitate the symptomatic teeth-grinding of his PTSD-afflicted Vietnam veteran character. A few years later, De Niro's extensive physical conditioning and weight fluctuations during production on *Raging Bull* (Martin Scorsese, 1980) grew out of extensive personal research on LaMotta's life and boxing career. The intense emotional labor and potentially dangerous physical transformations of radically intrasubjective Method actors coincided with a larger American cultural impulse towards emotional honesty and self-awareness. Julie Levinson connects the critical acclaim for this intensely immersive new style of Method acting with the popularity of contemporary pop psychology, which often stressed the importance of "uncovering" and "rediscovering" one's true essential self.[48] Once the emotional intensities and risk of physical self-harm became normalized as a commendable commitment to the craft of acting,[49] the radically intrasubjective practices of 1970s Strasbergian actors became inseparable from conversations of screen actors bodies. From the representational gender politics of Charlize Theron's weight gain for *Monster* (Patty Jenkins, 2003), to Michael Fassbinder's self-emaciation for *Hunger* (Steve McQueen, 2008), to *The Atlantic*'s proclamation that Jared Leto tormenting his fellow actors on set as the Joker in *Suicide Squad* (David Ayer, 2016) had finally destroyed Method acting as a whole,[50,51] the version of the screen actor that arrives within the character inevitably raises the question of where performances stop and—radically intrasubjective—acting begins.

Across all of these techniques, however, is the impulse towards catachresis, which Vivian Sobchak borrows from Merleau-Ponty to qualify a spectator's affective responses to a film:

> Reciprocating the figural literal representations of bodies and worldly things in the cinema, the spectator's lived body in the film experience engages in a form of sensual catachresis. That is, it fills in the gap in its sensual grasp of the figural world on-screen by turning back on itself to reciprocally (albeit not sufficiently) "flesh it out" into literal physicalized sense.[52]

For actors, intrasubjective catachresis is a process of completing the actor-as-character with pieces of the actor's quotidian self, letting the appresentational Magic Ifs pull the actor's recalled intentionalities into the performance score of the actor-as-character. These quotidian patches in the situational meshwork can provide a wealth of creative fodder by fostering deeply resonant appresentations, but also increase the risk of blurring the empathetic self–other distinction.

Acting styles differ widely on the importance of extensive emotional catachresis to the actor, in terms of what kinds of memories—if any—should be transferred to the actor-as-character, and how the recalled material should be used. For Strasberg, the intrasubjective intimacies of emotional catachresis provide the detailed authenticity of an ideal verisimilar performance. In a direct challenge to Strasberg, Adler saw an over-reliance on catachresis as a mistaken reduction of the character to fit the smaller "size" of the actor, famously cautioning that "Hamlet was not 'a guy like you'."[53] Catachresis can, however, productively inform a performance if the actor uses the transferred material to spark her imagination to rework the recollections to fit the character. By reimagining memories to suit the character, Adler's actor pulls the actor-as-character's intentionality into her body by magnifying, extrapolating, or otherwise reworking her quotidian experiences to fit the actor-as-character's world.

Sanford Meisner was far more skeptical of catachresis because he feared that it removed actors from the world of the drama by making them more involved with themselves than with the dramatic moment. Instead, Meisner instructed his actors to emotionally particularize key moments in the drama to provoke an intended personal reaction. Otherwise, Meisner's Method places far more emphasis on the spontaneity that arises organically from the dynamic system between the actors than on the personal meaningfulness of how and what the actor inserts of her quotidian self into the scene. Although the actor should emotionally prepare herself to enter a scene in the dramatically appropriate emotional state, there is no reason that this state should revive an experience outside the actor-as-character.[54] Even then, any catachresis must be used to prompt sincere reactions from Meisner's actor-as-character, rather than let it become an emotional excavation that traps the actor inside herself.

In any case, catachresis is a potent and potential force in generating intrasubjective appresentations, thereby closing the perceptual gap by literally inserting versions of the actor's quotidian experiences into the actor-as-character. Little of this intrasubjective work, however, is apparent outside of the dramatic world: although the actor's immersion in the dramatic world begins with the script, the enworlded actor-as-character is rarely alone in that narrative world.

Intersubjective Empathy

The iterative and often unpredictable relationship between performing actors is crucially important to realist acting's verisimilar illusion. In many schools of acting, the circular causality of the actors' responses to each other is a testing ground for the malleability and relevance of her intrasubjective appresentations in light of the spontaneous intersubjective connections that manifest while collaborating with her scene partner. The intersubjective solicitation occurs within two related yet distinct sets of observers and targets. The primary intersubjective connection positions the quotidian actor as the observer, who connects to her scene partners as the co-creators of the dramatic action. The secondary intersubjective connection positions the actor-as-character as the observer, and her scene partner's actor-as-character as her often-uncooperative target within the dramatic world. Through the actor-as-character, the quotidian actor is also often attuned to her scene partner's actor-as-character in order to understand why he does what he does. Although both the actor and the actor-as-character observe the people around them as different selves, the cognitive and corporeal structural similarities between the actor and actor-as-character allow them to engage with their respective worlds in the same manner: reading and responding to the intentional cues of others, while simultaneously presenting herself as a center of intentionality with whom those others can connect.

The primary intersubjective affective match between quotidian actors is based on the mutual trust and the professional focus that the actors bring to the scene is a necessary precondition for their creative co-enworlding. If the dramatic world between the actors is to become verisimilar, each actor must contribute to its construction by remaining "in the moment," sustaining her intrasubjective appresentations amidst the dynamic system of the creative interaction with the scene partner. This shared "in the moment"-ness implies a matching creative investment in the scene at hand: the creative enworlding can only be sustained when both actors are actively participating within it. If one actor changes the verisimilar terms of that enworlding, through oblique responses, for example, or by responding outside the realist cognitive scaffolding with non-realist performance cues, the dynamic system of the diegetic world cannot maintain its verisimilar illusion. The actors' shared state of trusting preparation enables a co-creative state in which their intentional pull keeps them performing in the same play.

The secondary affective match among actors-as-characters is difficult to ascertain because, simply put, situational characters do not always agree with each other. It is reasonable to assume though that, following Feagin's claims on the cognitive structural similarities between situational characters and quotidian readers, the situational characters will attempt to make sense of each other and the world around them. Whether the characters—or the actors-as-characters—succeed in affectively matching each other or not, the trust and matching effort established in the primary intersubjective connection allows the actors to remain in the same situational world, so that the circular causality of the actors-as-characters relationship can make space to pull them closer together.

If the actors-as-characters do happen to empathize with each other, the secondary affective match is the result of the actors' inner monologues aligning across the subtext. Intersubjective appresentational Magic Ifs guide the actor's trajectory in relating to the other actors-as-characters, even if the relationships among actors-as-characters may vary significantly throughout the drama. In the film adaptation of *Who's Afraid of Virginia Woolf?* (Mike Nichols, 1966), for example, the relationship between Richard Burton's George and Elizabeth Taylor's Martha constantly fluctuates across combinations of love, boredom, exasperation, malice, playfulness, hatred, and vulnerability. Even amidst the characters' interpersonal cruelties, Burton and Taylor sustain George and Martha's marital commitment to each other, whether the connotations of that commitment are entrapment, acceptance, tolerance, or begrudging obligation. In this film, the complex intersubjective relationship between Burton-as-George and Taylor-as-Martha is only possible when Burton and Taylor create the appropriate appresentations within Burton-as-George and Taylor-as-Martha to guide how their bodymind intentionalities will react to each other as a dynamic system.

The primary actor-to-actor other-oriented perspective-taking goes hand-in-hand with Decety's criteria of care. These empathetic criteria are best met during rehearsals, where actors experiment with creative choices by running a scene and then discussing their experiences afterwards amongst themselves and with the director. Rehearsals enable a process of creative trial and error, in the hopes of finding a version of the scene that lets each actor accomplish whatever her character requires during the sequence in question. This part of the creative process helps actors to establish the mutual trust which will help to keep them enworlded together as the actors-as-characters. Although far more common in the theater, some film directors will hold script read-through rehearsals and "tablework sessions," where the leading actors will often share their ideas about their characters and reveal preliminary work on their performance scores. Many actors will also tell stories about how the relationships among actors-as-characters influenced the personal relationship between the quotidian actors who perform them, much to the professional gratitude of celebrity gossip journalists. Rehearsals can therefore reinforce the trust-based affective match while giving each actor some idea of what to expect from her colleagues during performance.

This is, however, an idealistic take on the working dynamics between hypothetical actors, which does not necessarily account for the time constraints, labor conditions, or the personal friendships and rivalries that shape the way actors and directors work together. Otherwise, a performing actor will only wonder about the other actor's perspective if something in the scene is going wrong, or if a health or safety issue develops from the way the scene is being performed. As long as the actors sustain their trust-based affective match, there are few bodymind resources left available for imaginatively projecting oneself into the quotidian shoes of one's scene partner.

The secondary other-oriented perspective-taking among actors-as-characters is more accessible than its primary counterpart because, in the circular causality of their relationship, the actor is constantly taking stock of her fellow actor-as-character's reactions. The film actor shifts a great deal of attention to the scene partner who, as Canadian film acting instructor Bruce Clayton suggests, is a mirror who reflects the result of the actor's performance back to her through his iterative reactions.[55] In the absence of a spectatorial audience, the actor gages the effectiveness of her performance score by the reactions that she provokes in her scene-partner-as-character.

Even if the actors are aware of each other's perspective through a scene's iterative actions and reactions, the nature of their creative work means that the only perspective that they each fully take on is that of their own respective actor-as-character. The actor's secondary intersubjective other-oriented perspective-taking is necessarily synergetic with her intrasubjective other-oriented perspective-taking with her own character. The quotidian actor can learn just as much about her actor-as-character through individual efforts, like skill acquisitions and immersive behaviors, as she can from collaborating with scene partners to see how their interaction can pull the actor closer to empathizing as an actor-as-character. The target is still one's own actor-as-character, but some of the appresentations that pull the actor towards the actor-as-character can manifest in the scene partner. As the actors experiment with performance choices to pull themselves from imitating their actors-as-characters towards empathetically re-aligning as the actor-as-character, they may discover new performance choices based on the dynamic system of their interaction.

During the rehearsal process for *Who's Afraid of Virginia Woolf?*, for example, Taylor and Burton likely experimented with how to align their performance scores to not only reveal pertinent character information but to establish a mutually productive understanding of how each round of emotional attacks on each other should resolve. The near-constant animosity between Taylor-as-Martha and Burton-as-George requires a meticulous collaboration to determine which attacks are brushed off and ignored, which escalate the fight, which are unnecessarily cruel and which are emotionally justifiable, and how these decisions enable future reactions as their relationship develops throughout the long film. Taylor draws a deep understanding of Martha's beliefs and desires from Albee's screenplay, but needs Burton-as-George to catalyze much of her performance score.[56] Taylor's intersubjective preparations therefore likely included scoring decisions such as "If Burton-as-George says X, I cannot let him see how much it hurts me so I must laugh it off. Burton-as-George can only upset me visibly with X if he also mentions Y," and so on. Part of the dynamic system of the actors' iterative exchange therefore requires the intrasubjective other-oriented perspective-taking to mesh—however imperfectly—with the secondary intersubjective other-oriented perspective-taking.

The self–other distinction in the actor's primary and secondary intersubjective empathetic relationships are fairly straightforward. For all of the intentional cues drawn from and offered to her scene partner, the actor is sufficiently busy balancing her intrasubjective relationship with her character within the circular causality of her interactions with her scene partner to ever worry about becoming the other actor or his actor-as-character. The actors remain distinct collaborators in their co-creative enworlding. Some intersubjective appresentations, drawn from close attention to one's scene partner, can reinforce the self–other distinction by creating opinions about the other actor-as-character. In the scene from *Romeo and*

Juliet where Juliet laments to the Friar that Romeo has been banished, for example, the actor-as-Juliet must continually decide whether she trusts the Friar to help her or whether she fears that he will now reveal her secret marriage. Either way, the intersubjective appresentational Magic If in this scene reinforces for the actor-as-Juliet that she must collaborate with the Friar as a distinct target: an autonomous center of intentionality who may no longer be sympathetic to her cause.

Many realist styles of acting suggest that the actor somehow prepare for her intersubjective relationships by creating an appresentation about how her actor-as-character relates to each other actor-as-character, knowing that their relationship will often fluctuate throughout the narrative. This often involves projecting an imaginative substitution on the scene partner: in the previously mentioned scene between Juliet and the Friar, the actor-as-Juliet must imagine how Juliet would speak to a benign patriarchal friend in a time of urgent emotional need. These kinds of projections often raise parallel intrasubjective questions—"How does Juliet relate to authority?" and "Is Romeo's banishment worse for Juliet than Tybalt's death?," for example—and the answers can be mutually informing across both intrasubjective and intersubjective layers. These performance score choices are crucial to enworlding the actor-as-Juliet within the enacted narrative, since her action must seem internal and external at the same time.

Neo-Strasbergian[57] film acting instructor Ivana Chubbuck proposes a particularly radical intersubjective self-other distinction by suggesting that the actor should imaginatively substitute other actors-as-characters with emotionally resonant figures from her quotidian life.[58] In the prior example of Juliet and the Friar, Chubbuck would insist that the actor playing Juliet not only speak to the actor-as-Friar as if he were the quotidian actor's best friend who has helped her during past crises, but that the actor-as-Juliet should relive all of the emotional traumas that the quotidian actor has shared with that friend to make the emotional stakes of the scene more compelling. Chubbuck's substitutions graft an appresentational Magic If on to the scene partner, in that the actor treats her scene partner as if he is a response-provoking and emotionally resonant self from the actor's quotidian life. This kind of appresentation is therefore an intersubjective catachresis, since the actor is completing her empathetic perception of her scene partner with pieces of her quotidian self so that her actor-as-character will react to the scene partner in a way that provokes emotionally charged iterative reactions.

Like Strasberg, Chubbuck's interest in psychotherapeutic techniques for releasing suppressed emotions translates directly into her work with actors.[59] Chubbuck's substitutions are a complicated technique to manage effectively, since the actor will be encouraged to substitute other actors-as-characters with emotionally resonant quotidian figures, like deceased parents, abusive ex-lovers, and alienated friends.[60] Although these substitutions can generate powerful empathetic connections for the actor by giving the performed moment an immediate point of emotional entry to the scene,[61] they can also exacerbate the intrasubjective over-immersions against which Meisner vehemently cautions. Instead, Meisner's Method challenges the presumed priority of intrasubjective connections to realist acting by allocating most of the actor's creative attention to responding to and being affected by her fellow actors.

Intersubjective Case Study: Sanford Meisner and the Repetition Game

Meisner's intersubjectively reliant Method was a deliberate break with Lee Strasberg and the Actors Studio. Exasperated with Strasberg and his introspective emotional recall exercises, Meisner sought to create verisimilar performances that de-emphasized internal emotional associations in favor of outward action, famously declaring that "The foundation of acting is the reality of doing."[62] In Meisner, action leads to spontaneous creative ideas, telling the story by showing what the character thinks and feels.

Meisner's actors embrace this spontaneity through improvisation exercises that fix the actor's utmost attention on the behavior of her scene partner, thereby encouraging the actors to think and do together. The actors' earnest reactions create the verisimilar effect because their ensuing dynamic system enworlds the actors together within their scene on the actors' own terms. More specifically, Meisner's Method trains the quotidian actor's sensitivity to primary intersubjective prompts so that similar prompts in the secondary intersubjective connection can generate spontaneous and sincere reactions, whatever the scene at hand might be. In this case, Meisnerian appresentations are the results of the actors responding to each other's performance cues, which provide clues to the scene partner's—and their own—character's cognitive scaffolding. Meisnerian actors conceive of their performance in terms of how the situational character reacts to the people and events around her, rather than rely on an inward-facing Strasbergian rolodex of emotional memories. Meisner therefore relies on spontaneous intersubjective reactions to inform intrasubjective choices, inverting the Strasbergian pattern of using intrasubjective sincerity to determine how the actor-as-character relates to her scene partners. Although Meisner recognized the importance of script work and its intrasubjective cues, and that performative clarity and sincerity are necessary goals for any actor, the intrasubjective and performative connections are largely configured as by-products of a potent intersubjective connection.

Like Strasberg, Meisner developed training exercises that prime actors to solicit the prioritized empathetic connection. Meisner's Repetition Game and its core principle of "the pinch and the ouch" are his pedagogical response to Strasberg's affective memory because of how Meisner's exercises prioritize the intersubjective connection as the foundation for realist acting. Meisner's foundational training exercise, the Repetition Game, is the basis for his Method's co-creative enworlding through soliciting a potent intersubjective connection. In the Repetition Game, two actors have a thoroughly unnatural conversation about their observations of each other. The actor is not allowed to pose questions to her scene partner, or to talk about herself, except in response to her scene partner's observations. Focus and a brisk pace are essential, although the actor is only allowed to speak when she feels compelled to do so by her scene partner. Meisner calls this circular causality "the pinch and the ouch," the iterative loop of spontaneous cause-and-effect perturbations to each actor's state of disequilibrium which motivate the next exchange. The "pinch and the ouch" puts a premium on not only provoking responses from one's scene partner but also investing enough attention on the scene partner to pick up on all the embodied connotations of each "pinch."

In the Repetition Game, unless an actor perceives a change in her scene partner and feels immediately compelled to name the perceived behavior, the actor must repeat what she has just heard her scene partner say. The actors must respond to each other immediately, focusing their attention on the interaction while preventing them from "going into their heads" and being clever with words. The situational selves of Meisner's actors-as-characters are constantly perturbed by each other's spontaneous and intentionalized actions, and by naming the perturbations that they observe in each other, they define each other's characters by acknowledging how they do what they do. The unfiltered impulses triggered in one actor by the other, and the subsequent impetus to speak, are pedagogical tools for recognizing subtext and intent—in other words, clues towards cognitive scaffolding—expressed through verbal or corporeal language. The Repetition Game shoves the actor into the intentional pull of her scene partner through the deliberate attentiveness to the other actor's experience, not only in recognizing and reconstructing the other's experience, but in articulating and "working with" it as a collaborative project.

As the variations on the Repetition Game become more advanced—adding relationships between the characters, attention-diverting physical activities, opinions about each other, or entering the scene in the context of something imaginary that has just happened—the actors come closer and closer to the dramatic circumstances of playing a scripted scene on the understanding that they must still play off each other rather than become too absorbed in something external. The point of the Repetition Game is to make the actor more adept at detecting and responding to these subtextual cues so that when a script is added, the verisimilar enworlding through attentive listening will carry over. As such, the Meisnerian actor develops appresentations from not only her heightened observations of the scene partner's performance as cues to the other actor-as-character's cognitive scaffolding, but from her own experience of responding to them. In this way, Meisnerian appresentations are a sincere "ouch" and a motivated return "pinch" to the scene partner.

In scripted scenework, the actors are not only connecting with each other as collaborators, but also with the scene partner's character *as* her own character. This implies that the intersubjective bond between the quotidian actors is a foundation for the verisimilar enworlding of the situational characters; by constantly attending to each other's subtextual responses, the performed characters appear to be interacting as people trying to understand—and maybe even empathize with—each other. Part of Meisner's intervention was effectively to train actors to read each other with the same focus and intensity as their scripts, thereby co-creating a narrative world through the iterative loop of their interactions. The intersubjective empathy solicited by Meisner's Method is predicated on the actor treating her scene partners as active texts, collaborators in the co-creative act of storytelling. Although Meisner emphasizes action over thought per se—one of his most famous maxims was "an ounce of behavior is worth a pound of words"[63]—the overarching framework for this action is a deeply invested attention to one's scene partners.

When done correctly, Meisner's Repetition Game is an iterative loop of action and reaction that supports an empathetic connection between the actors that satisfies Coplan's criteria. The invested and attentive curiosity constitutes an overarching affective match between the actors, even if the performed responses may differ. The other-oriented perspective taking and self–other distinction in Meisner go hand in hand: the unremitting focus on the other actor's experiential state demands that the actors can see the world and themselves from each other's perspective, all the while maintaining their observer-target distinction since the exercise does not allow an actor to talk about herself as more than a repetition en route to a new impulse. These named impulses from the purely improvisatory version of the Repetition Game become the subtext of the scripted scene since what the actors-as-characters are ultimately responding to are the perceived affordances of his bodymind schema and the intentionality ascribed to the scene partner's reactions. This puts a premium on the active work that the actors must do to really listen to each other and to work with what they give each other to make the characters seem truthful, which supports the appearance of the characters living in the same situational world. Meisner's actors therefore enworld themselves within the drama by co-creating their dynamic system's boundaries: the world of the actors-as-characters is verisimilar because the actors-as-characters respond to each other as fellow inhabitants of the dramatic world while simultaneously co-creating the dramatic world they inhabit.

Meisner's Method achieves its intersubjective other-oriented perspective-taking by integrating the imaginary circumstances of the drama within the actors' iterative relationship. In Meisner, character is the by-product of how one actor iteratively relates to another, rather than a set of foregone conclusions from the beginning. The Secondary intersubjective relationship between the characters is therefore only possible with the primary relationship between the actors firmly in place to support the exchange. The close attention to each other's reactions *as the character* bonds the actors by creating the characters—and experiencing one's own character's imaginary circumstances—together. The intrasubjective other-oriented perspective-taking in Meisner occurs through the emotional preparations that an actor will undertake to enter a scene in the desired bodymind state. Even then, Meisner only allows these preparations if the actor is willing to "leave them at the door" once the scene begins. The important acting work must happen during the scene, and not before, and if the emotional state that the actor prepares is to remain in play, it must start to derive from the actor-as-character's exchange with her scene partner's actor-as-character.

If Meisner's Method has an intrasubjective affective match, it is through appresentations that adapt some quotidian beliefs and desires to fit a dramatic moment. Meisner partially interpreted Stanislavsky's Magic If as preparatory tool that can, if necessary, "particularize" or specify the actor's observations of her target to fit the requirements of the scripted drama so that the observations will be relatable for—and therefore useable by—the observing actor. The emotional stakes of the reaction must be real to the observing actor so that her response will foster a compelling dramatic world, so if the textual perturbation is not meaningful in and of itself to the observer, she must privately substitute something else that will be appropriately resonant for her. In Meisner's example,[64] an actor in his class is playing a woman who is accused by her homophobic boyfriend of being a closeted lesbian. The scene codes the accusation as "a deadly secret,"[65] but Meisner accuses the actor's response to the accusation of being too emotionally weak because the quotidian actor has no negative associations with lesbianism. Meisner suggests that the actor privately substitute "lesbian" with something that would produce the appropriately shocked response, such as "heroin addict" or "child murderer" to particularize the moment to something that will provoke a more emotionally potent and specific response. This use of the Magic If as a particularization has some foundations in the actor's intrasubjective relationship with her character. The actor is aligning the actor-as-character's beliefs with her quotidian own, and then forcing these beliefs to intrude upon the actor-as-character's intersubjective relationship with her fellow actor. The whole point of the particularization, however, is to serve the relationship between the actors by magnifying the emotional terms of their interaction beyond the contents of the words they must say. By particularizing "lesbian" to mean "child murderer," Meisner's actor from the above example paradoxically plans a verbal substitution to provoke a spontaneous reaction.

For Meisner, a script's words are not as important as the "emotional essence"[66] behind them; if an imaginary word change clarifies the moment's emotional essence, so be it. This kind of substitution is significantly different from the radically personal substitutions encouraged by Chubbuck because the point is still to prepare a response in anticipation of future responses, rather than to invoke a bodymind state from outside the drama that will visibly unsettle the actor-as-character. Meisner's substitutions may be personalized, but they are not quotidian-personal to the same magnitude as in Chubbuck. This enables Meisner's actor to remain connected to her scene partner's actor-as-character as he is playing it, while preventing the actor from going into her own head.

The co-creative enworlding of Meisner's technique maintains the self–other distinction on the primary and secondary intersubjective levels. The actor never loses touch with herself, even when caught in the intentional pull of the other actor. On the primary level, the collaborative cognition valorized in Meisner requires that the other actor is someone to connect with, and not someone to become. On the secondary level, Meisner de-emphasizes the notion of character as a fixed entity. Character is instead the by-product of how the actor reacts to the drama as the character; how she, to quote Meisner, lives truthfully under imaginary circumstances.

The performative aspects of this emotional preparation become extremely important for film actors, who likely have to undertake the same emotional preparations many times in close succession over multiple takes during a film shoot. The tight schedules and budgets of many film shoots allow very little time for the actor to emotionally prepare once the shot's technical preparations are complete. If the actor cannot shift her preparations to her scene partner repeatedly over many takes, the performance will seem either emotionally monotonous or disjointed and unmotivated. Entering the emotional state and then leaving the preparation behind on a film set with limited time to shoot each scene takes tremendous performative discipline. To that end, many Meisner actors will start their emotional preparations and the necessary emotional transitions before the camera starts rolling to ensure that her performance occurs "in the moment" once the director calls "action."

The intrasubjective self–other distinction in Meisner is fairly straightforward: the character is simply the result of what the actor-as-character does, so the situational self cannot manifest outside of the performance. The performative self–other distinction is, in a way, the culmination of the actor's intentional push. The actor presents her actor-as-character and her situational enworldment to the spectator. If the verisimilar illusion generated by the rest of the acting work is strong enough, the spectator will see the actor-as-character as a center of enworlded intentionality. The actor-as-character remains distinct from the spectator, while also imploring him to imagine that she and her situational world are real. The performative intentional push of Meisner's Method reward the disbelief-suspending spectator with a compelling realism that invites comparison to the quotidian world while asserting its difference. To this spectator, the actor-as-character is not imitating the fiction but is imaginatively, empathetically engrossed within it. Whatever else the spectator derives from the film performance, in terms of representations of race, class, and gender, are the result of the actor's intentional push and her collaboration with her colleagues and within rest of film form. As Meisner suggested, "Don't be an actor. Be a human being who works off what exists under imaginary circumstances. Don't give a performance. Let the performance give you."[67]

Meisner's system for soliciting intersubjective empathy among actors as a path to verisimilar truth is a cornerstone of later styles of acting. David Mamet and William H. Macy's Practical Aesthetics explicitly embraces Meisner's Repetition Game as its main performance training technique, while also re-configuring the Repetition Game to make a strong connection between its improvisatory impulses and the narrative needs of a given script.[68] Mamet studied acting with Meisner at the Neighborhood Playhouse for a year (1967–8) before Meisner refused to readmit Mamet for a second year of training.[69] Far from becoming disillusioned with Meisner or acting, Mamet devised a performance style that is heavily indebted to the Meisner training that he received with a strong emphasis on script analysis.[70]

Mamet and Macy's intervention into Meisner is to ground intentionality in the script, which is clarified, embodied, and articulated by the performing actor, rather than for actors to primarily draw from each other with the script as a necessary hurdle to be overcome. Enthusiastically deriding Stanislavsky, Strasberg, Adler, and the Method as "a cult,"[71] Mamet insists that all emotional connections, imaginative substitutions, and enworlding intrasubjective backstories are counter-productive to real acting because they make the performance about the actor's quotidian self rather than what the actor can create. As in Meisner, the Practical Aesthetics character is a by-product of how the actor-as-character does what she does. The emphasis remains on actions that present the actor-as-character's body schema as a target for another's observations.

The progressive stages of Mamet's Repetition Exercise move the actors from straight repetition, which is very similar to the earliest levels of Meisner's Repetition Game where the actors repeat each other until one makes the other change, to what Mamet called active repetition, wherein the actors commit to a strategically motivated delivery with significant freedom to vary one's responses. The progression of Mamet's Repetition Exercises from pure reaction to expressive subtext is useful in clarifying an actor's response to a scripted moment, pulling the actor from an imitation of the scripted material to living truthfully within it.

Whether based in Meisner, Mamet, Strasberg, or other acting styles, intersubjective appresentations are powerful forces in enworlding the actor-as-characters within the drama while simultaneously asserting their autonomy within it. This world, however, must be intelligible to its audiences, which means that actors must have ways of presenting their situational enworlding to their spectators.

Performative Empathy

Performative empathy is the actor's medium-specific solicitation of her anticipated audience's attention, gained by intentionally pulling the anticipated spectator towards the actor-as-character. The actor's technical training allows her to manipulate her body schema, and to collaborate with the rest of film's formal construction, in such a way that she solicits an intentionalized connection with an anticipated spectator, who reconstructs the actor-as-character's cognitive scaffolding as if the actor-as-character were a quotidian self. With sufficient experience on set and medium-specific training, the film actor engages in both an intentional pull of the filmic spectator into her imagination, and an intentional "push" of herself towards the anticipated spectator as a center of situational intentionality and thereby ensnare the anticipated spectator in the actor-as-character's intentional pull.

This combination of intentional pushing and pulling operates largely as a by-product of the intrasubjective and intersubjective connections. Strasberg and Meisner's Methods both presume that the proper intrasubjective and intersubjective connections will be enough to solicit and sustain the spectator's attention. Although Adler insists that she does not train actors' physical and vocal capacities, she stresses the importance of effectively expressing detailed ideas through performance so that the audience will imagine the idea as clearly as the actor,[72] thereby merging intentional concerns with elocution and habitual gesturing. Otherwise, the medium-specific solicitation of the anticipated spectator's attention is largely left to technical training that prepares actors to act deliberately for and with the camera, as opposed to, for example, Meisner, Strasberg, and Adler's conceptions of acting as a general art form. The performative solicitation therefore requires the actor to present her intrasubjective and intersubjective connections to the anticipated spectator, on the condition that these connections are articulated, accentuated, and clarified by the actor's strategic use of on-set production affordances, such as the performance space itself and, in particular, the camera within it. Additionally, actors may draw on their own experiences of watching their own performances on-screen, recalling which technical adjustments tend to "work" for them and which are best avoided, when gaging the ideal combination of performance choices for a given role, with the goal of pushing their intentionality towards the spectator. In this light, the performative solicitation of the spectator plays upon the actor's ability to cast themselves within what the audience will accept as a compellingly verisimilar actor-as-character. Amy Cook argues that performed characters are

> [built] through a dynamic interplay between a number of conceptual spaces: the body (age, race, gender, physical attributes); textual information (actions taken or lines said about or by the character); what we already know or anticipate based on historical information; the reputation of the character (and the actor); and what we know about other roles the actor's body has taken on.[73]

Actors therefore learn to make the best use possible of the character-expressing bodymind resources that they have, based on the affordances and constraints of the on-set conditions and their experience of watching their own performances in the hopes that the audience will connect with the actor-as-character in a manner similar to how the actor first encountered that scripted character.

The details of how Coplan's criteria for empathetic relationships are satisfied by the performative solicitation vary widely, depending on the combination of strategies that the actor uses to bolster her intentional push. The aforementioned medium-specific strategies for incorporating on-set affordances into one's performative solicitation will be summarized later in this section, and will be analyzed in depth in Chapter 5. For now, the rest of this section will qualify the actor's performative solicitation through Coplan's empathetic criteria by focusing on the importance of the anticipated spectator's attention for the soliciting actor. In this case, the adjustments made to the actor's performance score often involves developing appresentations of anticipated spectators while fostering a trusting collaboration with the camera.

Despite the creative commensurability of stage and screen techniques in intrasubjective and intersubjective solicitations, the technical requirements for resonant screen and stage acting—regardless of the size of the stage—are quite different in terms of how the audience shapes the performance. Theater actors have much more direct access to their audiences, and often claim to be able to feel the affective energy of the auditorium fluctuate during a performance. The film actor, on the other hand, is aware that she will be watched, and film acting allows actors to be part of their own audiences, but the film actor receives no such direct affect from her future audiences while she acts.

Consequently, film actors have had to develop additional appresentational tactics to compensate for the lack of immediate feedback from their anticipated audiences. In many cases, the problem of the absent audience during a screen actor's performance before the camera can be remedied by reimagining the camera as an audience of one. In the absence of immediate reactions from an audience, the film actor draws on her experiences of watching herself on-screen and adjusts her performance accordingly. The absent-but-anticipated film spectator becomes, in a way, a performative appresentation that informs the performing actor's body schema, iteratively altering the performance experience so that it will intentionally push itself towards the spectator. Not only does the camera give the screen actor a focal point at which to orient her performative address to the spectator, but the actor learns to imagine the camera as a co-collaborator in the performance, even if the camera's role within that collaboration is sometimes to stay out of the actor's way.[74]

For example, in a film acting masterclass by actor Michael Caine for BBC Television, Caine insists that the camera is "the greatest lover" that the actor could ever wish for because it will meticulously capture even the subtlest qualities of a performance, and all the actor has to do is ignore the camera's presence.[75] On the surface, this suggests that the camera is more of a passive observer than an active collaborator. Caine, however, spends the majority of the class advising actors on how to convey the most narrative and character information as possible to the camera, from technical tips on eye-line matches and hitting one's marks consistently to overarching theories about listening and reacting to one's scene partner in ways that will be the most lucid on-screen. Therefore, even if the actor's primary objects of attention while shooting a scene are her fellow actors, the manipulation of the body schema to make this attention legible primarily for the camera demonstrates a complex and delicate balance of ignoring and embracing the camera.

To this end, actors have developed a wide range of training strategies for the performative solicitation, beyond the specifics of individual film shoots. In particular, habits for learning from one's own on-screen performances,[76] and for appresentationally immersing oneself deep within a film set, aid the actor's performative solicitation by reinforcing her intentional pushing of her situational self towards the spectator.[77]

Many screen actors have on-set habits aimed at specifying and pushing their intrasubjective and intersubjective connections towards the spectator, based on the creative affordances of the actual film set. Some actors, for example, develop appresentational on-set objects based on props, set pieces, and costume items found on set. The actor imbues these objects with potent intrasubjective and intersubjective appresentations that help to immerse the actor in the *mise-en-scène*. Adler actively encouraged her actors to make every object on set real to their characters by filtering the objects through the actor's imagination in order to make the actor-as-character come to life in that performance space.[78]

Similarly, acting guru Uta Hagen suggests that actors must imagine the "fourth wall"—the side of the stage left open to the audience or, in the case of screen acting, the vantage point of the camera as an audience of one—to complete the actor-as-character's perception of her situational lived world.[79] Hagen's actor can only connect with her audience if she makes her situational self "alive" within the "magic circle of [her] playing area".[80] In practice, this means that the actor must appresent the contents of that fourth wall, endowing every object on set—including those in the imaginary "fourth side"—with imaginary qualities that [they] do not possess to make the entire performance space real to the actor-as-character. The importance of appresentationally-endowed objects to screen acting is that the actor has the opportunity to embed her intrasubjective appresentations within the film set, which gives her more creative fodder to intentionally push towards the spectator.

If, for example, an actor had to play a mad scientist who is discovered in her cluttered laboratory by her aspiring protégée, the actor playing the mad scientist could imbue the on-set laboratory's mounds of half-read books, scattered papers, and overflowing lab equipment with appresentations that make the room belong to the situational actor-as-character. The props of the messy laboratory would not necessarily represent the character's lackadaisical attitude towards housekeeping: instead, the endowed appresentations could be that the musty books are deliberately left open at useful reference pages; the mounds of papers could be meticulously arranged by genius-level understanding that only she can appreciate; a piece of personal memorabilia positioned amidst the laboratory equipment as a cherished memorial to an ill-fated former assistant. These appresentations ground her intrasubjective and intersubjective appresentations in physical objects on set, which reinforces her performative solicitation by making her character appear not only enworlded but also at home in her current surroundings. The spectator who is caught in the intentional pull of these cues feels a more compelling connection with the actor-as-character because of the performance's heightened verisimilitude: the spectator reconstructs the actor-as-character's cognitive scaffolding more easily because, like the spectator, the actor-as-character has a psychologically plausible relationship with her environment.

As a further means of preparing for the inevitably missing audience, film actors often train in part by performing in front of a camera and then studying the results. Beyond knowing the performance maxim that screen acting generally occurs on a smaller physical scale than most stage acting, the actor must gain a firsthand sense of how her bodymind schema communicates on-screen, lest her creative work become lost to small-scale vagueness. Many screen actors eventually watch the films and television episodes in which they appear and vicariously study their own performing image, comparing their immediate recollection of their body schema experience while performing to how it manifests on-screen. As the actor learns how to best articulate her character for the screen—vicariously improving her capacity to solicit a connection with her anticipated audience—the actor simultaneously learns to appresent her own medium-specific performance techniques from the perspective of an anticipated spectator.

Even the most sincerely habitual and creatively intentionalized facial expressions, postures, vocal intonations, and physical gestures can create performances that misrepresent the actor's skill, intentions, or affective state: simply put, some things simply look and sound wrong on camera.

The process of performative trial-and-error refines the actor's command over her bodymind instrument, partly by forcing the quotidian actor to connect to her on-screen situational self to study the efficacy of that on-screen self in intentionally pushing her intrasubjective and intersubjective connections towards the spectator. First and foremost, the quotidian actor-as-spectator must learn to view her on-screen situational self as a distinct self, predicating all analysis on the suspension of disbelief required to establish a self–other distinction between quotidian and situational selves. By being critical of her situational on-screen self, the actor-as-spectator is inherently assessing how and what the actor-as-character is communicating via the camera. The actor-as-spectator thereby undertakes a complex process of other-oriented perspective-taking by studying her own skills as a screen actor by cross-referencing what she feels about her situational self on-screen with her personal recollection of her performance score. In assessing the emotional efficacy of her performance, the actor-as-spectator pays attention to what affective matches are prompted by the actor-as-character's solicitations to the spectator. Moments of potent affective match will likely suggest to the actor that the strategies she employed during that shoot were sufficiently compelling. This self-knowledge impacts how she intentionally pushes herself towards the spectator, commanding her bodymind instrument to present itself as a strategic rearrangement that is not immediately recognizable to the spectator as her quotidian self.

It would be foolish to over-extend the claim that the actor has no audience on set whatsoever. Key production staff, such as the director, collaborate with the actor throughout the filmmaking process, collectively transforming the actor's work on set into the finishing filmic performance. The collaborative nature of filmmaking becomes a major enabler of screen acting work, in that the actor is able to focus intensely on her creative work since the film crew has a vested interest in supporting her performance. With sound technicians to make sure that the dialogue is clearly heard, a director of photography (DOP) to make sure that the actor is framed and shot properly, etc., screen actors are free to focus on their intersubjective and intrasubjective connections while collaborating with the crew to solicit the performative connection.[81] As skilled professionals who think along with the actor's performance while it is filmed, these production personnel begin to populate the cognitive ecology of the film set as the landscape which is preconfigured to, among other things, complete the on-set acting work with a finished performance.

Neither the director nor the production team constitute an audience, however, in the same sense of the anticipated audience whose intentionality she solicits through the camera. The film's production staff is primarily interested in realizing their own part of the filming process, from carrying the boom mike to the many tasks of the assistant director team. Although it can be gratifying for an actor in a comedic role to occasionally hear the crew laughing at his performance after a particularly compelling take, the screen actor should not anticipate, expect, or require this kind of direct feedback. Moreover, since many jokes become less funny each time they are told in short sequence, the sheer number of subsequent takes required to film comedy often prevents anyone other than the actors and directorial team from paying much extended attention to the performed comedy.

The on-set creative collaboration between the director and the actors can range anywhere from a very hands-on to a very hands-off process. Many of the actors interviewed for this study reported that remarkably few film directors are explicitly interested in the actors' work. Overwhelmingly, the director's focus on set is often on technical composition of a given shot. This practice forces the actor to compete for directorial input with traditional auteurist investments in cinematography and *mise-en-scène*, while indirectly relegating the actor to being only one *mise-en-scène* concern among many. More often than not, and assuming that the actor's performance is not flagrantly contradicting the director's overall vision, screen actors are left to their own devices in terms of the creative fodder for their work on set. The actor is expected to be ready when needed, to work within the shot's formal composition, and will be directed to change her performance if such a change is deemed necessary; otherwise, screen actors must learn to self-perpetuate their creative work without excessive reliance on a director. The actor's on-set tactics for staying focused and "in the moment" amidst the long and unevenly paced shooting schedule is a test of her technical skill and the strength of her empathetic connections. Some actorly techniques for working around these kinds of production challenges are analyzed in detail in the three ensuing case study chapters.

Conclusion: "Camera rolling . . . and, action!"

The industrial affordances of film production literally and figuratively frame the screen actor's empathetic solicitations. If her intrasubjective and intersubjective appresentations are sufficiently compelling, the actor will be able to continually re-enworld herself as the situational actor-as-character within the narrative world, and thereby overcome creative challenges imposed by film production's industrial nature. The audience for whom the screen actor acts is a performative appresentation, endowed in the camera as an audience of one, which galvanizes the intrasubjective and intersubjective connections into the actor's solicitation to the audience.

It is important to remember that, although these three empathetic relationships have been presented here as mutually distinct phenomena, they are not nearly so compartmentalized in practice. This chapter has attempted to show that the three empathetic solicitations of realist screen acting have significant precedent within enduring ideas about realist screen acting from major twentieth-century practitioners. Some practitioners certainly privilege a particular empathetic solicitation as the ideal starting place for compelling acting work, such as Strasberg's intrasubjective probing though affective memory work, or Meisner's intersubjective spontaneity through the Repetition Game. That said, it is far too reductive to assume, for example, that a Strasbergian actor has no interest in her fellow actors-as-characters, or that a Meisner-based actor makes no solicitation to her anticipated audience. In practice, when the camera is rolling and the director calls "action," the actor must coordinate her intentional efforts to engaging all three connections simultaneously, often with some presumption that establishing one connection will initially clarify and support the others. The actor's preparations for, and on-set collaborations with, his scene partners and the rest of the production team are the focus of this book's remaining chapters.

Notes

1. Zahavi, "Empathy and other-directed intentionality"; Coplan, "Understanding empathy: its features and effects," p. 5.
2. Carnicke, *Stanislavsky in Focus: An Acting Master for the Twenty-First Century*, p. 66.
3. Britten, *From Stage to Screen: A Theatre Actor's Guide to Working on Camera*, p. 29.
4. Strasberg, "Lee Strasberg technique," p. 18.
5. Feagin, "Empathizing as simulating."
6. Adler, *The Art of Acting*, p. 85; Oppenheim, "Stella Adler technique," p. 37.
7. Adler, *The Art of Acting*, p. 26.
8. Carnicke, *Stanislavsky in Focus: An Acting Master for the Twenty-First Century*, p. 201.
9. Adler, *The Art of Acting*, p. 60.
10. Britten, *From Stage to Screen: A Theatre Actor's Guide to Working on Camera*, pp. 5, 29.

11. Bandelj, "How Method actors create character roles," pp. 391–2.
12. Levinson, "The auteur renaissance, 1968–1980," p. 97.
13. Young, "The other side of Viggo Mortensen," p. 46.
14. Carnicke, *Stanislavsky in Focus: An Acting Master for the Twenty-First Century*, p. 42.
15. Strasberg, "Lee Strasberg technique," p. 23; Hirsch, *A Method to Their Madness: The History of the Actors Studio*, p. 134; Adler, *The Art of Acting*, p. 35; Meisner and Longwell, *On Acting*, pp. 37, 128.
16. Levinson, "The auteur renaissance, 1968–1980," pp. 99, 115.
17. Kemp, *Embodied Acting: What Neuroscience Tells Us about Performance*, p. 122.
18. Carnicke, *Stanislavsky in Focus: An Acting Master for the Twenty-First Century*, p. 159.
19. Strasberg, *A Dream of Passion: The Development of the Method*, p. 69.
20. Thompson, *Why Acting Matters*, pp. 45–7.
21. O'Toole, "Step by step toward creating 'My Left Foot'."
22. Kemp, *Embodied Acting: What Neuroscience Tells Us about Performance*, p. 151.
23. Ibid. p. 152.
24. Lyall, "The Daniel Day-Lewis Method: a kind of vanishing act."
25. Ibid.
26. Kemp, *Embodied Acting: What Neuroscience Tells Us about Performance*, pp. 152–4.
27. Carnicke, *Stanislavsky in Focus: An Acting Master for the Twenty-First Century*, p. 42; Bandelj, "How Method actors create character roles," p. 399.
28. Clurman, *The Fervent Years: The Group Theatre And The Thirties*, pp. 44–5.
29. Ibid. pp. 20–1.
30. Blair, *The Actor, Image, and Action: Acting and Cognitive Neuroscience*, p. 31; Hirsch, *A Method to Their Madness: The History of the Actors Studio*, p. 141.
31. Strasberg, "Lee Strasberg technique," p. 18.
32. Blair, *The Actor, Image, and Action: Acting and Cognitive Neuroscience*, p. 29.
33. Hirsch, *A Method to Their Madness: The History of the Actors Studio*, p. 140; Strasberg, "Lee Strasberg technique," p. 21.
34. Frome, *The Actors Studio: A History*, p. 105.
35. Ibid. p. 107.
36. Hirsch, *A Method to Their Madness: The History of the Actors Studio*, pp. 76–7.
37. Ibid. p. 126.
38. Carnicke, *Stanislavsky in Focus: An Acting Master for the Twenty-First Century*, p. 66; Kemp, *Embodied Acting: What Neuroscience Tells Us about Performance*, p. 146.
39. Blair, *The Actor, Image, and Action: Acting and Cognitive Neuroscience*, p. 73.
40. Ibid. pp. 74–5.
41. Kemp, *Embodied Acting: What Neuroscience Tells Us about Performance*, p. 150.
42. Carnicke, *Stanislavsky in Focus: An Acting Master for the Twenty-First Century*, p. 193.

43. This insistence on imaginatively motivated actions as being more important to acting than the personal authenticity of the actor's performed emotion is also quite similar to the core ideas of Sanford Meisner's Method, which will be discussed later in this chapter.
44. Levinson, "The auteur renaissance, 1968–1980," pp. 96–7.
45. Kemp, *Embodied Acting: What Neuroscience Tells Us about Performance*, p. 161.
46. Ibid. pp. 161–7.
47. Levinson, "The auteur renaissance, 1968–1980," pp. 113–14.
48. Ibid. p. 101.
49. Coplan, "Understanding empathy: its features and effects," p. 6.
50. Bastién, "Hollywood has ruined Method acting."
51. See Chapter 7 for a closer analysis of *The Atlantic*'s critique of Leto's preparatory work.
52. Sobchak, "What my fingers knew," p. 82.
53. Meisner and Longwell, *On Acting*, p. 98.
54. Chubbuck, *The Power of the Actor*, p. 53.
55. Bruce Clayton, masterclass at Pro Actors Lab, Toronto, Canada, September 2006.
56. The same is of course hypothetically true for Burton's relationship with George and Taylor-as-Martha.
57. Carnicke, *Stanislavsky in Focus: An Acting Master for the Twenty-First Century*, p. 149.
58. Chubbuck, *The Power of the Actor*, p. viii.
59. Ibid. p. 53.
60. Ibid.
61. Meisner and Longwell, *On Acting*, p. 4.
62. Ibid. p. 27.
63. Ibid. pp. 137–9.
64. Ibid.
65. Ibid. p. 151.
66. Hart, "Meisner technique: teaching the work of Sanford Meisner," pp. 76–7.
67. Meisner and Longwell, *On Acting*, p. 128.
68. Bella, "Practical aesthetics: an overview," p. 225.
69. Collard, "Living truthfully: David Mamet's practical aesthetics," p. 333.
70. Mamet, *True and False: Heresy and Common Sense for the Actor*, p. 6.
71. Bella, "Practical aesthetics: an overview," pp. 242–4.
72. Adler, *The Art of Acting*, pp. 60, 79.
73. Cook, *Building Character: The Art and Science of Casting*, p. 38.
74. Some basic strategies for the actor's relationships and collaborations with the camera will be taken up in extensive detail in Chapter 6.
75. Croft, "Acting on film with Michael Caine."
76. See Chapter 6 section on Metaphors of Trust for the Camera.
77. See Chapter 6 sections on Lisinska's Tears and Dinicol's Jazz.

78. An attributed derivative of Adler's object-oriented approach to acting appears in Chapter 6, wherein Canadian actor Natalie Lisinska describes how the presence of emotionally charged personal objects on set gave her access to the high emotional intensity required for a scene on *Orphan Black*.
79. Hagen, *A Challenge for the Actor*, p. 154; Rosenfeld, "Uta Hagen's technique," p. 139.
80. Rosenfeld, "Uta Hagen's technique," p. 144.
81. Jamie Spilchuk (actor), in discussion with the author, August 2016; Joe Dinicol (actor), in discussion with the author, June 2016.

CHAPTER 4

Acting Culture and Audition Preparation

Practice, Constraint, and Affordance

The core principles of major acting practitioners such as Meisner, Strasberg, and Adler have proven formative and inspiring to generations of western realist screen actors. It is essential to any study of acting as a practice, however, to frame these principles as idealistic suggestions to guide an actor's work, as opposed to requisite assembly instructions for compelling performances. For all of their internal disagreements, Meisner, Strasberg, and Adler all viewed their Methods as practices for actors to work with: to embody, to experiment with, and to enact, and not to be pondered as abstract philosophies.[1] As such, the insistence on practical application emphasizes how actors adapt these teachings as required to their own tastes and to the needs of a given role. Since each Method's core techniques prompt different approaches to soliciting empathetic connections and moving across selves, the ways in which actors blend and adapt canonical techniques requires an understanding of acting practices alongside the creative principles behind those practices. The empathetic solicitations framework provides a useful analytic vocabulary for both the theoretical components of Method techniques and their practice-driven applications.

The next three chapters will trace how some idealistic principles of realist screen acting manifest in the messiness of screen acting practice, where they are invoked when deemed useful without any pretense of correctness or attributable fidelity. The industrial pragmatism of a film set is a fundamentally different creative environment than the insular seclusion of an actor's training studio, and so it should be of no surprise that actors adjust their technique to accommodate the needs of the film production at hand. My contention across the next three chapters is that the industrial culture that frames screen acting's empathetic work is an ongoing balancing act between collaboration and the actor's individual agency to control as much of her work as possible. Creative training and industrial logistics will be treated as enculturing forces that the actor's malleable bodymind meshwork will navigate in order to solicit empathetic connections when creating a screen-specific verisimilar performance.

In order to ground this theoretical analysis in screen acting as it is practiced, Chapters 4 through 6 will draw heavily on my interviews with fifteen professional and frequently working Anglophone Canadian screen actors during the summer and fall of 2016. These actors are Toronto- or Vancouver-based women and men between the ages of twenty-five and sixty-five whose primary source of income is their screen acting work.[2] The interviews were semi-structured one-hour conversations in which the actors were prompted to reflect on their own creative training, practices, and experiences. Although the professional experiences of fifteen of the thousands of Canadian screen actors cannot count as an exhaustive ethnography of their artistic craftsmanship, the diverse range of professional experiences and accomplishments represented within this study offers an informed sketch of how actors form meaningful empathetic connections as a necessary condition of their work.

To further contextualize how screen acting practices intersect with and operate within the cognitive ecologies of their industrial circumstances, these chapters read my model of empathetic solicitations alongside the psychological and technological notion of constraints and affordances. Psychologist J. J. Gibson initially posited that human perception should be understood as the iterative relationship between the observer and the target, rather than the then-dominant cause-and-effect view that the observer's perceptual apparatus constructs a fixed target. Specifically, Gibson argued that human perception does not simply identify objects in the world but evaluates the variables—the *affordances*—for how the observer and the target could interact with each other.

James Greeno helpfully explains Gibson's affordances with the example of an obstructed doorway,[3] upon which I embellish here: Alice wishes to walk from Room A to the adjacent Room B, but the doorway between Room A and Room B is of an irregular shape, the floorboards under the doorway look flimsy, and a cumbersome potted plant blocks part of the already limited space in front of the doorway. With her goal in mind, Alice does not simply perceive a strange door, flimsy flooring, and a potted plant. Rather, Alice perceives her options for passing through the doorway amidst the obstacles: how she might contort her body to fit through the strangely shaped doorway without putting too much pressure on the precarious floor; whether she ought to remove the potted plant, climb over top of it, or ignore it completely while squeezing through the door; whether the combined obstacles are simply impassable and Alice is better off searching for an alternative way into Room B; and so on. The affordances of how Alice could navigate this complicated passageway are fundamentally wound up in her perception of how this location could be navigated, obviously exceeding the mere identification of a doorway, some floorboards, and a plant.

Hand in hand with Gibson's notion of affordance is that of constraint, a fixed condition of a perceived object that eliminates various affordances. Following another example from Greeno, the steering wheel on my car is constrained to its ability to change the direction of the wheels.[4] I cannot turn my steering wheel to accelerate the car's speed or to turn off the headlights. The affordances of the steering wheel manifest in the size and texture of the steering wheel, the amount of force that I must exert with my hands and arms to turn it, and so forth; the constraint of the steering wheel is that it can only alter the direction in which the car drives. It is important to note that I do not perceive the constraints of the steering wheel as an inherent impediment to my driving: if I turn the steering wheel and the car's direction does not change but instead the vehicle speeds up and the lights go out, my entire perception of the car's operation is fundamentally altered.

When read into film and television acting practices, constraints and affordances provide a useful vocabulary for describing how an actor works with whatever resources, opportunities, requirements, and restrictions she faces throughout the creative process. The actor's empathetic work does not happen in a vacuum; it is inextricably wound up in the specificities of the script, the collaborations with the rest of the cast and crew, the industrial logistics of that stage in film production, and the serendipitous creative discoveries that emerge therein. Put another way, the actor's empathetic solicitations of the actor-as-character, her scene partners, and her anticipated audience form dynamic systems of bodymind reorganization as she navigates the various cognitive ecologies of the acting industry, from the audition space to the full film set.

From the audition through to filming the scene on set, many screen actors' processes for developing their empathetic connections comes down to working with what they have in front of them, and making best guesses towards the rest based upon the perceived affordances and constraints. Lucy Fife Donaldson and James Walker, for example, compellingly analyze how James Gandolfini's acting work on *The Sopranos* was often shaped by his use of the set's affordances, specifically those of his character's car. In a key scene in which his car's malfunctioning CD player triggers a violent anxiety attack while driving, Gandolfini's use of the driver's seat's affordances largely determines the performance and significance of Gandolfini-as-Tony's breakdown:

> [Gandolfini-as-Tony's] ease is quickly compromised, however, when the CD track skips. At first, Gandolfini responds by prodding at the player's buttons and briskly tapping the dashboard, as though Tony was attempting to coax the technology back to recovery. But it is not only an effort to coax. Gandolfini's deft performance of these "heavy-handed" gestures encapsulates Tony's appetite for control and his belief that he can exert control over the elements within his life, especially those elements found within the close, comfortable interior environment of his car. [. . .] Gandolfini's performance balances this strength and vulnerability, illustrating the extent to which an intimate, safe space can become claustrophobic and dangerous for his character.[5,6]

Although auditioning actors rarely have access to set pieces like Gandolfini's car, let alone a complete film set[7] to help catalyze their work, the constraints and affordances of audition acting itself have tremendous sway over the actor's ability to convince casting directors, producers, and directors to hire her, instead of her talented rivals. Amy Cook describes the greater cognitive phenomenon of casting as an instance of cognitive blending which reduces "the astonishing complexity of the world around us by casting particular faces in particular roles"[8]; for actors, this means a competitive struggle with other actors over who will have an acting career and who will not, and where the conditions of success are not necessarily clear from the beginning.

"It's nice work if you can get it . . .": Auditions and Precarity

The fundamental constraint about acting auditions is that, no matter how many actors are invited to audition, only one actor will be cast. The supply of actors always vastly exceeds the demand for their work. A 2010 industrial report on the practicalities of being an actor in Canada paints a grim portrait of an actor's working life on- and off-set. As in many European and the American film industries, the vast majority of professional Canadian actors will not be paid for working as actors within a given calendar year,[9] despite the historically steady flow of locally and internationally produced film, television, and theater in major cities across the country. Moreover, a 2007–8 ACTRA[10] Toronto poll showed that 40 percent of its unionized membership did not work as actors during those years, and the average acting-based income for ACTRA members during that time span was less than half of the national average for all labor nationwide.[11] Even a regularly working actor like Natalie Lisinska refuses to separate the precarity of steady employment from her sense of professional accomplishment:

> As far as Malcolm Gladwell is concerned, I think I've logged my 10,000 hours of being a screen actor at this point, so I feel very comfortable. It feels like home. That being said, I'm 34 years old and I've had a baby, and this industry is not kind to women.[12]

Although the ACTRA-approved pay scale for film and television work mandates a better-than-livable wage for working actors to compensate for the infrequent nature of the work, the percentage of screen actors who make the majority of their annual income from their acting work—let alone those who live off their acting work exclusively—is small, to say the least. But for the absolute pinnacle of Hollywood's A-list celebrity actors, very few actors have the luxury of being able to freely choose their roles, let alone be offered a role without any audition at all. All of this is compounded by the demographic and personal banalities of typecasting,[13] the fickleness of artistic taste, and the unpredictability of how many and which productions will be locally cast.

The inevitable financial anxieties and professional frustrations between acting jobs can be potent distractions.[14] Many actors must hold non-creative jobs to support themselves between acting jobs, often in the service and hospitality industries, even though these industries are not always as accommodating of the film industry's manic schedule as an actor might like. There is no guarantee that an aspiring actor's restaurant employers, for example, will take kindly to last-minute shift cancelations because of an audition. The lingering financial threat of losing one's day job—even an uninspiring and otherwise undesirable one—just to attend an audition with no guarantee of being hired for the role simply adds to the actor's sense of anxious urgency over booking consistent acting work. Therefore, the economic pressures surrounding the scarcity and precarity of acting work add an unforgiving sense of desperation to how screen actors approach their creative empathetic work. Unpleasant though it may be for many actors, the constant professional instability affords the actor a complicated blend of assertions of individual control with an openness to trust-based professional collaborations.

The actor must therefore assume control over her own contributions to the creative process[15]: from supplementary physical conditioning to help the actor imagine from within a body she more closely associates with the character; to relevant research and skill acquisition for roles that require specialized tasks such as horseback riding, tap-dancing, fencing, etc.[16];

and, above all else, as much individual script preparation as possible.[17] Many Toronto-based casting directors expect actors to arrive at their auditions in clothing that plausibly resembles the character's future costume. Not only do costumes help to inform the situational actor-as-character's body schema,[18] but audition costumes are seen as evidence of the actor's professionalism; according to Toronto casting director Brain Levy, "If you were interviewing for a job at a legal firm, you would wear a suit, right? If you're auditioning to play a lawyer on tv and you wear shorts and a t-shirt to the audition, no one will take you seriously there either."[19] The casting director's opinion on whether or not a given actor suits a role comes down to a judgment call about whether the actor's unavoidable significations of age, gender, ethnicity, etc., and her perceived talent and professionalism align with the historical and cultural expectations surrounding the type of character being cast.[20] Since the final casting decision is largely out of the actor's hands, all that auditioning actors can do is prepare as thoroughly as possible, give their strongest performance of the scene when the casting director calls "action!", and then hope for the best.

Ultimately though, screen actors must be prepared to delegate and entrust the formal construction of their performances to a film editor, cinematographer, and director. Although the actor is an active collaborator with her fellow actors and the production crew, the final assemblage of her performance is ultimately beyond her control. Many actors would agree that their acting work on set provides the raw material of their performances, which will eventually be shaped and assembled by the actor's co-collaborators. What the actor can control during this deference of final responsibility is to join the collaboration as vehemently as possible, in that the actor does everything in her willing ability to produce as compelling a performance as possible. The necessity of this collaboration coincides with the time-pressed urgency of film production schedules: the freelance nature of most acting work means that even steadily working actors can go months between gigs, which places tremendous pressure on the actor to build and maintain strong social and professional relationships with key production staff in the hopes of being hired again.

Noticeably absent from the actors' collective responses to interview questions about "connections", "craftsmanship", and industrial context of an actor's work in the collaborative project of storytelling, was any anxiety over the cultural significations of their performances. For most actors, concerns over the representational politics of those performance choices are secondary to the affordances of their skills as professional performers: connecting to their character and the story at hand, articulating that connection lucidly to the camera through solid artistic craftsmanship, collaborating with the cast and production crew to tell the story, and building a portfolio of strong performances that will hopefully lead to future acting work opportunities. As actor Sheila McCarthy summarizes, "If you can live with [what you perform], or if you really need the work and you take the gig, you have to do [whatever is in the script]. Otherwise, don't take the gig. That's all it is."[21] Although the audition's function is to show what the actor could hypothetically do with the role if hired, the actor who proposes dialogue or story revisions during the audition is all but guaranteed to be turned down for the role, if not also blacklisted by the casting team.

Instead, the closest most interviewees came to expressing concern over the socio-political ramifications of their performances was the importance of using compelling performance choices to enrich narrative moments in the hopes of impressing directors and producers who may wish to hire them again. Actor Matthew MacFadzean summarizes this link between the fickle economics of the acting industry and the importance of strong performance choices neatly in his description of auditioning for the role of a defense attorney on a police procedural television drama:

> If you're hired for one of the smaller roles [but you make interesting performance choices], they'll hire you back. I start with is what is required. And then, "Where can I pull the threads a bit? Where can I make it a little more me?" Let's say I'm playing a defense attorney and my client is a child molester. How do I let my opinion into this scene to make it more interesting? If I'm talking to my client who is a child molester and he says something that is offensive, and I hold on [that moment] for just a little while, even though I'm supposed to be sympathetic to this guy, [the subtext makes my character more interesting].[22]

MacFadzean's priority in his general approach to this hypothetical defense attorney role is not, as a hypothetical critical analysis of its representational politics might argue, to interrogate the discourses of white cishet patriarchal authority and its intolerance of sexual non-normativity. Instead, MacFadzean's bodymind commitment to the appresentational Magic If of the attorney–pedophile scene is, on some level, always aware of his performance's industrial circumstances and consequences. MacFadzean is certainly aware that uncomfortable political discourses can be present in the scene but must enact those discourses through performed actions and reactions within the scene, rather than meditating only on the scene's greater symbolic or thematic resonances. In this hypothetical defense attorney scene, MacFadzean can feel whatever he wants about his client's pedophilia, but those symbolic socio-political resonances are only valuable to him as an actor insofar as they motivate a compelling performance choice, such as the moment of unease and repulsion at his client that MacFadzean implies with "holding on to that moment." In this way, MacFadzean would show primary intersubjective empathetic care for his scene partner by making performance choices that are uncomfortable for his scene partner's character but could inspire interesting iterative creative reactions with the other actor. In other words, the creative affordances of inflecting a line of dialogue with the affordance of a nuanced reaction is a better representation of the actor's abilities than a self-reflexive censoring of a socio-political abstraction. If MacFadzean can personally justify his symbolic complicity in his performance as a pedophile's attorney, he should take the job and, as actor Kevin McGarry concludes, "leave the rest to the critics."[23]

"Hurry Up and Wait"

Beyond the stressful imperative to get the job, audition performances are framed by the industrial and logistical constraints and affordances of auditions themselves. The audition format in particular provides a clear—and clearly restricted—range of affordances and opportunities for the actor. The overall cognitive ecology of the audition tests the navigation of the actor's engagement with the affordances of the sides amidst the industrial constraints of the audition format, on the presumption that this audition performance indicates what the actor would do with her role if chosen by the casting director, producer, and director. Paradoxically, and as this chapter argues, the acting work required for auditions does not always correspond to the kinds of acting work that the role will require on set; compared to script preparation once hired or her work on the actual film set, the actor's navigation of the audition's cognitive ecology is an empathetic grasping at straws, without necessarily knowing where the straws are.

One of the overarching industrial constraints on realist screen acting practices is the constant shortage of exploratory time. Compared to many live theatrical productions, the breakneck pace of screen production schedules allows considerably less time for creative experimentation, from the audition process through to post-production. Whereas theater actors often have multiple weeks of rehearsal time to experiment with character choices and to eventually draw strength from their close familiarity with their characters and colleagues, many screen actors receive their audition sides[24] within forty-eight hours of the audition, have little to no meaningful rehearsal time on set prior to shooting, and may be greeted at the casting director's office with a revised version of the audition sides. At auditions, actors often wait around in the lobby of the casting director's office for prolonged periods of time surrounded by other actors who, judging by their demographics and wardrobe, are clearly auditioning for the same role. While flagrant eavesdropping on a rival actor's audition is rare and frowned upon, the auditioning actor must learn to deal with the struggle of remaining focused and emotionally prepared[25] when it is often unclear how long she must wait among her equally anxious competitors to give the performance she has prepared. Once called in by the casting director, the audition is carried out with decisive urgency: as MacFadzean summarizes, "You have to be amazing *now*. There's no time for fucking around because there's a lot of money involved."

Even if the actor passes the audition, she will likely run into similar creative complications on set. Many screen actors struggle to sustain their empathetic connections amidst the frequent and often unpredictably long breaks between technically complicated takes, across long days of shooting multiple scenes, and within emotionally intense scenes that require particularly long shoots to fully capture. Actor/producer Lauren MacKinlay explains that screen actors must learn to emotionally navigate the "hurry up and wait" of film shoots: maintaining a state of constant bodymind readiness for emotionally intense material without exhausting oneself during the down time.[26] The screen actor is just one part of a busy, expensive production process, wherein the monetary and temporal constraints are often more easily alleviated by inconveniencing the actor's preparation than needing to rebuild the set, refocus all the lighting, recompose the musical score, etc. Actor Natalie Lisinska observes that navigating the "hurry up and wait" of film production is a necessary but difficult task:

> It's tricky because when you're in your trailer, you want to prepare [emotionally] but you don't want to accidentally give your entire performance to the make-up mirror. It's [a difficult balancing act] of thinking about it and mulling it over, and then [distracting yourself], and trying to leave [the pending scene] alone. And then the 3rd AD[27] will come knock on your door and say, "this is your 10 minute warning."[28]

Not surprisingly, on set and at auditions, many screen actors report that they must rely on medium-specific techniques to connect and reconnect quickly and efficiently with the scene at hand.[29] In fact, any veteran screen actors see time constraint issues as a major enabler of their creative work since fast-paced production schedules place a premium on disciplined acting technique and the ability to develop compelling empathetic bonds with speed and efficiency. Established and up-and-coming screen actors tend to agree that the manic pace of film production, from the audition onwards, energizes their creative work in at least two closely related ways.

First, the general goal of audition preparation goes far beyond simply memorizing the words: reconstructing the character's cognitive scaffolding[30] requires the actor to identify and understand the character's goals and desires within the sides, as well as pertinent moments of emotional and physical transition. Many actors, like Julian DeZotti, refer to this in-depth process of intentionally pulling the character from the page into his body as "homework": just as the student who only skims his textbook will likely fail the exam, the actor who merely skims over her sides is doomed to produce a sub-par audition or performance on set:

> Essentially you have to bring your imagination to make it real, but the only way you can do that is if you know your lines [perfectly], and all the ins and outs of what the scene is about. You have to do your homework first.[31]

For some performances, the preparations for and intimate knowledge of DeZotti's "ins and outs" of the scripted scene extend beyond learning one's lines by rote while forming intrasubjective connections between the actor and her character. The often-brief amount of time that the actor can spend with her sides before the audition necessitates an efficient script analysis process to ensnare the actor in the scripted character's intentional pull. The efficiency of the script analysis presents the scripted character to the actor as a relatively stable situational self that can be adapted as required on set. The prepared flexibility to creatively reorganize the actor-as-character's bodymind schema therefore makes the actor far more likely to collaborate well with her fellow actors and the production team, which vicariously increases her chances of being hired for more acting work in the future.

Second, the manic, unpredictable pace of film production prevents the actor from "overthinking"[32] her creative choices, and encourages her to sincerely trust her own storytelling, performance-driven instincts. These creative instincts are in part an artistic judgment call: the actor introduces a personally potent and narratively relevant re-imagination into her bodymind meshwork and then incorporates this re-imagination into her character's actions. When pressed for time in his own practice, Spilchuk finds that "committing" to spontaneous narrational choices that are personally evocative and meaningful will foster a compelling performative solicitation that will ensnare the audience within his character's intentional pull: "go with your first instinct, because normally the first one is the right one anyway. [. . .] You just do it, whether it's an audition or the actual [gig]."[33] In another sense, the habitual conditioning of the actor's bodymind that enables her to connect and immerse herself in the appresentational Magic

If of the scene must also enable her to clearly articulate the bodymind state that comes with the re-imagining. In this way, part of an actor's technique is a balancing act between spontaneity and restraint in the command of her bodymind instrument.

Similarly, Lisinska emphasizes that the actor must trust her technical training, narrative impulses, and her script-based homework to immerse herself as-the-character "in the moment" and thereby react as her character:

> The moment when you actually achieve an authentic emotional connection is the moment where your lines leave you *because* you're connected and you're *there*, and so they've got to be in you to the point where it's instinctual and reflexive, so that means that when it comes out of you, you're just a conduit.[34]

In order to get to the state of connected, instinctual "in the moment"-ness that Lisinska describes, actors train habits of bodymind immersion to align their intentionality with that of their characters. Actor Chris Baker connects bodymind alignment to technique by insisting that these immersive habits must also give the actor command of her bodymind instrument, so that she can adapt her performance plans quickly enough to accommodate the industrial realities of film production:

> If I'm getting my lines the day before, I have to bang that stuff out with a few exercises. I need to get the lines, and to be able to go out and do that scene [because] I'm not going to have time for [a long exercise process on set].[35]

The recurring themes here of speed, efficiency, alignment, and adaptability manifest across the entirety of acting culture, including the unapologetically fickle nature of the casting process.

Audition Logistics and Empathy

At their most optimistic, many screen actors regard auditions as an opportunity to practice their craft in front of a camera. Not far beneath that optimism, however, is a keen understanding that only one auditioning actor will get the job, and that a strong audition is never a guarantee that one will be hired. As Jamie Spilchuk quips, "First of all, as an actor, you need to get really good at auditioning. Second of all, there are three kinds of actors: film and tv; theater; and auditions. They're completely different things."[36] Tongue-in-cheek cynicism aside, auditions require distinct performance practices from the rest of screen acting, and the underlying empathetic work for auditions must vary accordingly.

The industrial and creative circumstances of auditions shape the empathetic connections that the actor presents to casting directors, producers, and directors when she is under consideration for a role. An actor's timeline and workflow for a screen audition are essentially the same for film and television productions: first, the actor receives her sides from her agent, usually within forty-eight hours of the audition, although less than twenty-four hours is quite common. She then prepares intensely with the sides, performs her audition for the casting director, and anxiously waits for her agent to call with some good news.[37] Although the actor's screen audition practices must necessarily overlap with her screen acting practices, the sparse formal conditions of the audition shoot and the urgency of the audition process streamline her creative process by prioritizing her ability to make primarily intrasubjective and performative connections.

The sparse shooting conditions of screen auditions eliminate formal distractions in order to assess the actor's expressive potential from the raw material of her performance. Screen auditions are likely filmed as a two- to five-minute long take[38] in a medium- to medium-close shot under simple bright lighting against an unobtrusive background. Actors are encouraged to dress in a similar manner to what their character might wear, since the clothing that an actor wears to an audition is likely the only costume that the audition will include. The actor will often perform one or two takes of the sides, and the casting director may provide some direction between takes.

The audition's formal "neutrality" purportedly affords a distraction-less showcase of the actor's work, since there is essentially nothing else in the footage to look at other than the actor's performance. Popular industrial wisdom suggests that this neutrality emphasizes the actor's capacity for imagination.[39] Although casting directors will provide a "reader" to fill in other character's lines for conversation-heavy audition sides, this reader is rarely an actor auditioning for the other role. More often than not, the reader is the casting director's assistant, another actor hired to read the lines in a neutral voice off-camera, or perhaps the casting director himself. A meaningful intersubjective connection between the actor and the reader is largely impossible, so the actor must perform the scene without relying on her scene partner for any significant creative collaboration. At best, the overlookability of the reader affords the actor to play the scene with an imagined ideal scene partner. More often though, the actor overcompensates for her non-creative scene partner by focusing her efforts on work that she can control: her intrasubjective character preparation, and her performative articulation of that work before the camera. In this sense, Spilchuk's earlier quip about how actors who audition well are categorically different from actors who excel at screen and stage work affirms the importance of intersubjective connections and on-set collaborations.

Auditions are therefore an inherently limited style of screen performance that makes great demands of the actor's capacity for intrasubjective and performative solicitations while marginalizing acting's necessary intersubjective connection. The industrial and empathetic challenge for actors in this cognitive ecology is that audition performances require two-thirds of acting's skill set to be sufficiently compelling in and of themselves, without betraying the absence of the last third of the acting's empathetic solicitations. To convince the directors, producers, and casting directors who will evaluate the audition that the actor's audition performance is a faithful demonstration of her total skill set, the actor develops habits for temporarily bolstering her intrasubjective and performative solicitations to overcompensate for the unavailable intersubjective connection.

Empathetic Connections for Audition Performances

The intrasubjective and performative connections for auditions go hand in hand. The intrasubjective work for an audition begins with script analysis, and the urgent focus with which the actor begins searches the sides for clues about her character's cognitive scaffolding, in the hopes of ensnaring herself in the character's intentional pull. As MacFadzean's attorney–client example shows, this search for cognitive scaffolding can afford the actor valuable opportunities to showcase her creative potential, even if the actor is constrained by sides' dialogue and narrative arc. The performative connection is a combination of articulating the character to the camera while buttressing the actor's intrasubjective focus against the anti-verisimilar distractions of the audition shoot. Whereas the intrasubjective solicitation will be based on limited access to the character's cognitive scaffolding through extensive bodymind extrapolation of the sides, the performative solicitation must pretend that the intersubjective solicitation is perfectly intact without needing attention, or is completely unnecessary.[40]

The "panicked focus"[41] of audition preparation, exacerbated by the brief time between receiving the sides and the audition itself, prompts many actors to quickly identify the sides' narrative trajectory, including her character's goals and tactics towards those goals. Many actors frame their analysis as a series of questions of interview-like questions, ranging from biographical basics such as "how old is my character?" and "what does she do for a living?" to scene-specific details, such as "what does my character want in this scene?", "what does my character want fundamentally, and what actions does this character pursue?" and "how does she react to changes in the situation?"[42] Although the specific wording and priorities of these questions varies across acting traditions and from actor to actor, the overarching goal of connecting the quotidian actor to the situational character of the sides remains the same.

The emphasis on speedy analysis, however, forces the auditioning actor to limit her creative explorations at the audition stage to character details to which the actor has relatively immediate bodymind access. This problem is easily exacerbated by the often-sparse nature of the sides themselves, which are likely only one or two scenes from the whole screenplay and may not come with much of an overarching synopsis of its whole narrative. Cayonne explains that excessively detailed audition preparations can interfere with the basic connections that the audition aspires to showcase:

> In the audition room, my goal is to be present: to be grounded, to be honest, to connect with my character, and—chief among all those things—is understanding what is happening in the scene so that you're *doing* something. [. . .] I love having all of that detailed stuff, and it is relevant in theatre when I have a two-month rehearsal process. For film and television auditions, I have 24 hours to show up, be a [verisimilar] human being, say my lines, effect change in that human being, and walk out of the room. So, a lot of the [details] I get rid of are things that don't allow me to really connect with somebody or with the text.[43]

This expedited process of character creation therefore places a great emphasis on the imaginative resources that translate the character's identified goals and tactics into a person to whom the actor can relate.

Cayonne's insistence that he must be "*doing* something" to effect a change in someone else while he is reorganized as the situational character stresses that whatever details and personal nuances that Cayonne brings to the audition character must be immediately and clearly actionable within the sides themselves. These performable actions, whether a physical gesture or a social transition within the drama, are an excellent opportunity for the auditioning actor to present her situational body schema to the evaluative viewer as a compelling center of intentionality within the narrative. Moreover, in the absence of verisimilar acting's necessary intersubjective solicitation, the audition performance effectively breaks realism's fourth wall by presenting the actor to the evaluative viewers as a creative center of intentionality who demonstrates how she would perform *if* she were hired. In this sense, the cognitive ecology of the audition setting and format is primarily arranged to find a performer, rather than create a performance, positioning the actor to show a restricted version of their acting skills as fodder for the casting process. The acting work which occurs within that cognitive ecology must endure a Sisyphean struggle of trying to create the entire performance itself, even if the final performance given by the actor who is eventually hired will co-create that performance with the aid of the director, costume designer, cinematographer, and other personnel,[44] all the while knowing that giving even the second-best audition will not ultimately be good enough.

Spilchuk expands upon Cayonne's point about "doing something" by arguing that the auditioning actor must be able parse her character's life goals from her immediate goals within the sides. Although the greater narrative context of an audition's sides is valuable, that greater context is only valuable in so far as it impacts a relevant action in the sides:

> You can only play one scene at a time. If my character's goal in the whole script is to avenge my father's death, but in the audition sides I have to order a pizza for my mom, I can't always play "revenge" at the pizzeria. I just need to get the pizza.[45]

The verisimilar effect of the audition performance depends on the actor becoming sufficiently caught in the character's intentional pull that she enacts only the scene at hand, while bearing the screenplay's greater narrative in mind without becoming overburdened by it. The auditioning actor reorganizes her bodymind schema into a situational self that, in turn, re-self-organizes in relation to its changing environment and socio-narrative circumstances.

In other words, part of the challenge for the auditioning actor is to immerse herself within the appresentational Magic If of the sides while balancing being "in *the* moment" as her situational self with being "in *that* moment" within the greater narrative. To preserve this situational bodymind location, many actors attempt to find the continuity "in your own body" as a progression of narrative beats across the arc of the scene.[46] This corporeal continuity depends heavily on connecting textual prompts from the sides towards the character's cognitive scaffolding with habits of imagining and recalling bodymind experiences as the character.[47] The clearest way to express these continuity-preserving connections is through performable actions afforded by the narrative, inviting the producers and casting director into the auditioning actor's intrasubjective connection with the character. In other words, auditions stress the performative other-oriented perspective-taking by linking it to the intrasubjective affective match and intrasubjective other-oriented perspective-taking. The actor's invitation is to the producer to see the situational character the same way that the quotidian actor sees the situational character, especially since the producer cannot reconcile the performed center of intentionality with his own ideas about the character.

AUDITIONS, EMPATHY, AND CREATIVE GUESSWORK

Many actors describe their audition preparations as an oscillation between analyzing the sides and experimenting with the sides' enactment. In fact, actors refer to the moment where they can perform a scene "off-book"[48] as an important benchmark in their preparations.[49] Although the process of going off-book likely involves some cold memorization, the memorized lines will only feel meaningful to the actor when she attaches the words to an action-driven intentional throughline. Put another way, the auditioning actor focuses on the affordances of the character's actionable goals within the sides as a means of demonstrating her intrasubjective connections to the character's goals and tactics.

Unlike the preparatory work when the actor already has the role, the auditioning actor must undertake her script-based homework without access to the entire screenplay. This complicates the audition process because the absent screenplay likely contains valuable details and context that the actor could use to better understand her character's imaginary circumstances. There are various reasons why an actor auditioning for a role might not have access to an entire screenplay before an audition. The producers, for example, may wish to protect the intellectual property of their unmade film. In other circumstances, the role in question is generic enough to not require dramatic context beyond the scene in which she appears: an actor auditioning for a one-scene role in an action film as the paramedic who resuscitates the hero, and whose dialogue is confined to medical procedural jargon, does not likely require an extensive backstory for her character. Beyond knowing the basic medical condition of the hero during this scene, the actor auditioning for the paramedic role is more likely to be hired for her ability to convincingly administer first aid than her connection to the character's larger hopes and dreams. It is also not common that the screenplay for television serials may be under active revision or be incomplete at the time of the audition.

In each of these situations, actors often need to extrapolate character and narrative information from the limited sides, and complete any information missing from the sides with material from her bodymind imagination. This narrative catachresis—in this case, completing the gaps in the sides' narrative with verisimilitude-inducing character choices—is a precarious but necessary step in the audition process. Some narrative guesswork is inevitable, and the fickle film industry is quick to overlook the auditioning actor who guesses "wrong" when presented with insufficient narrative information.

This guesswork, however, is also an opportunity for the actor to demonstrate her ability to perform actionable and compelling character choices amidst the sparse sides. These situations showcase the actor's ability to solicit potent performative connections from producers and casting directors, who may recognize the actor's skill and "watchability." At the same time, if the intrasubjective connections are strong enough to immerse the auditioning actor in the character's intentional pull, her immersion as the character can present producers and casting directors with unexpected dramatic opportunities latent within the sides that also fit within their vision of the final film. The narrative guesswork can therefore become a strength of the audition, even if the actor has committed to creative immersions that are somehow beyond the scope of the screenplay.

One interviewee remarked that, in some situations, casting directors and producers do not yet know exactly what kind of actor they are looking for prior to holding the auditions, preferring to become inspired by what they see an actor perform for some narrative choices.[50] Fortunately for the actor, some casting directors will also identify an actor's skillful but inadvertent misunderstanding of the scene and provide helpful commentary before offering a second pass at the scene. In any case, the actor's ability to compellingly complete the narrative gaps in the sides is a question of intrasubjective empathetic connections and also of the actor's interpretive habits. A compelling, performative-empathy-soliciting audition therefore depends not only on the personal identifications and resonances between the actor and the character's intentionalities, but also a performance-driven judgment about what actions supported by those identifications and resonances are playable given the short preparation time.

This kind of audition preparation satisfies each of Coplan's criteria for intrasubjective and performative empathetic connections. On the intrasubjective level, the interview-like questions that a quotidian actor poses to the character in the sides lays the bodymind foundations for the intrasubjective other-oriented perspective-taking, on the premise that the actor ascribes motivated actions to the prompts in the sides. The actor affectively matches her character by attending to the situational character's goals, tactics, and desires, and by enacting these within the emotional throughline of the scene. Finally, as Cayonne suggests by connecting his immersion in the situational character and narrative world with the leaving of the audition room, the actor remains aware that the situational self for the audition is ultimately situational. The situational self of Cayonne's audition must be different from his quotidian self, otherwise his situational-to-quotidian transformation upon leaving the room would not be meaningful.

The performative solicitation to the casting director and producer invites them into the auditioning actor's perspective on the character and her situational world, thereby prompting an affective match with the intended tone of the scene. The most strained empathetic criterion to establish here is the performative self–other distinction solicited by the audition, since at best the auditioning actor aspires to distinguish herself from the other actors against whom she competes for the role. The audition's performative self–other distinction banks heavily on the actor's intrasubjective self–other distinction in the hopes that the casting directors and producers will recognize the artist behind the actor-as-character as a likeminded, desirable, and viable co-collaborator. Although this is a far cry from the full verisimilar illusion created by empathetic realist acting, it does address and satisfy the audition's *raison d'être*: to identify the actor who seems most likely to mesh within the overall vision for the film. The performative solicitation of auditions is as much an enabler of creative work as a solicitor of responses from the producer and casting director. The performative connection intervenes to transform the missing or unobtrusive scene partner into another imaginary character to the actor. The actor performs the scene *as if* there is another actor present and responding, but short-circuits the empathetic connections by focusing on the performative connection. The auditioning actor thereby asserts control over her performance by collaborating with herself to block out the anti-verisimilar performance of the reader while directing her performative attention towards the producer and casting directors.

One of the great empathetic complications faced by the auditioning actor is that her performance cannot rely on any meaningful intersubjective connections to make the performance seem more realistic. The reader is mainly there to unobtrusively feed the auditioning actor her lines, and will therefore provide little by way of creative fodder. Not surprisingly, some actors who have studied Meisner have had at least one "disastrous" audition early in their careers in which they relied too heavily on the unreciprocated feedback from a reader, and consequently gave an unconvincing and unmotivated audition. Since much of Meisner's intersubjectively reliant technique presumes that one's scene partner is an equally engaged participant in the storytelling effort, the reader's unobtrusive recital of dialogue will only fluster and confuse the auditioning actor who is soliciting an action-inspiring connection from her reader.

To avoid this anti-verisimilar hurdle, the auditioning actor prioritizes her intrasubjective and performative connections to overcompensate for the largely impossible intersubjective connection by tuning out her anti-verisimilar surroundings and focusing on expressing her intrasubjective bond through actions. Since audition performances do not look for an in-depth interpersonal collaboration but instead a self-propelled expression of character, the performative connection taps into the intersubjective imagination of what all the other elements of filmmaking would be if they were happening, and manufactures them as appresentations to buttress the actor against the distracting formal sparsity of the audition shoot. In the absence of a compelling scene partner, the actor is not only connecting intrasubjectively to her own character but performatively projecting an intrasubjective conception of what the scene partner and *mise-en-scène* could be.

Intersubjective Opportunities During the Call-back

The performative empathetic shortcuts encouraged by the audition process question the efficacy of the process as a whole: why would any producer hire an actor who he cannot be sure will meaningfully collaborate with her fellow actors? For all of the popular critical attention given to the "chemistry" between performing actors, it seems odd that a producer would undervalue the actor to-be-hired's ability to collaborate with other screen actors.

In some situations, such as a television series where a few principal roles have already been cast, an actor may go for a "call-back" audition, a second round of auditions where she will perform a different set of sides with another actor to see what happens between them on camera. MacFadzean, for example, describes his call-back for a recurring role on the television series *Orphan Black* (2013–17) as a test of his potential collaboration with already hired leading actor Tatiana Maslany. This call-back gave him a welcome opportunity to experiment with bold acting choices with another actor as part of showing what he would do with the role, if hired. No longer preoccupied with "just selling a look," as with many auditions, Maslany's openness to creative collaboration and the artistic strength of the audition material made MacFadzean feel like he could "actually do some acting":

> When you're working with an actor who is paid more than you, and they want to act, then it's going to be fun. They're gonna pitch balls at you and you're gonna be [free to experiment. Maslany] is fun to act with. She's open to things to find what works. The directors were [interested in acting], the producers were [interested in acting]: they said "let's see the dynamic here". It really depends on the actor you're working

with, and the director, if you're allowed to do that kind of stuff, but those are the best experiences for me on film sets.[51]

Like the first day on a film set, this kind of call-back tests the speed and efficacy of the auditioning actor's ability to make a meaningful intersubjective connection with his scene partners, especially when the two actors have never met each other before but are thrust together by the industrial framework of the production schedule. The callback is therefore the actor's first real demonstration of acting work during the audition performance process.

In many call-back and audition situations, however, the auditioning actor's intersubjective potential is mostly gaged by guesswork and inference by the casting directors and producer, based on the actor's audition and any prior knowledge of the actor's work. Not surprisingly, this guesswork during casting inherently favors actors who work frequently and therefore have a larger pool of demonstrated work, on the industrial assumption that an actor who seems to perform well with her fellow actors in one film will do so again.[52] The circular logic encouraged by this sort of casting adds a further level of professional stress for aspiring screen actors: the inability of the standard audition procedure to account for intersubjective proficiency prompts many producers and casting directors to cast known talent over unknown talent, fostering a union-joining structure that effectively conspires against new members from gaining enough credits to join.

This begs the question of how any actor ever passes the audition process and books an acting job. The short answer is that very few actors ever do, and even those that do have no guarantee of ever doing so ever again. Spilchuk's earlier quip about auditions requiring a different kind of actor than film, television, and theater therefore leads to two distinct and related conclusions.

First, the industrial logistics of auditions all but eliminate acting's intersubjective solicitation, thus presenting auditions as a functionary yet reductive performance style based on most of the acting practices that it allegedly tests. Second, what screen auditions seem to assess more than acting per se is how the actor articulates her guesswork about her character's cognitive scaffolding and—more specifically—the casting team's understanding and expectations of that character's realization. This second scenario is fraught with potentially "unfair" complications: simple creative differences could eliminate a skilled actor from consideration; the actor's guesswork may have afforded performance choices that would never appear as such if the actor could see the entire screenplay, which could make the actor seem unfocused or unprepared; some or all of the casting director, producer, and director not yet knowing exactly what they want. While this last scenario is easily and often equated to an open-mindedness to surprises from the auditioning actors, it does little to level the playing field for auditioning actors, who have far more access to their character's minds than those of a bored casting director or uninspired producer. The fickleness and precarity of the audition process—and the actor's experience thereof— therefore comes down to holding of audition performances to the same standards of holistic acting when, at best, the actor's audition is a demonstration of their worst-acted final performance: the audition shows what the actor would do with zero intersubjective chemistry with her fellow performers.

The politics of scarcity, precarity, and industrial fickleness are enabling constraints that shape the urgency with which actors pursue and acquire their work. Despite the industrial shortcomings of the screen audition's ability to showcase all of an actor's empathetic talents, the empathetic work that it encourages does showcase how the actor navigates a crucial aspect of screen production's industrial culture. Auditions are a distinct type of performance based on some core tenets of acting work, rather than a full-fledged acting practice. Auditions therefore seem to test the actor's ability to perform with a bare minimum of creative co-collaborators, in the instance where the hired actors have no interpersonal chemistry while performing.[53] Acting culture's politics of scarcity therefore effectively mandate that actors make sure that they can sustain their intrasubjective and performative connections without any external assistance. This sense of professional self-preservation is also reflected in the individualistic nature of performance preparation, which at the focus of the next chapter.

Notes

1. Adler, *The Art of Acting*, p. 34; Meisner and Longwell, *On Acting*, p. 4; Strasberg, *The Lee Strasberg Notes*, p. 3.
2. Many of the actors interviewed for this study also frequently work as actors in live theatre, as well as working as screen directors, producers, and acting instructors.
3. Greeno, "Gibson's affordances," pp. 339–40.
4. Ibid. p. 339.
5. Fife Donaldson and Walters, "Inter(acting): television, performance and synthesis," p. 361.
6. See Chapter 6's analysis of Lisinska's Tears and object work on set for more examples of how actors can incorporate on-set conditions as constraints and affordances within their empathetic solicitations.

7. See the description of Cary Grant's interactions with set pieces in Andrew Klevan's, *Film Performance: From Achievement to Appreciation*, pp. 32–46.
8. Cook, *Building Character: The Art and Science of Casting*, p. 64.
9. Newhouse and Messaline, "Some career problems: gloomy reality," pp. 18–19.
10. The Alliance of Canadian Cinema, Television and Radio Artists (ACTRA) is Canada's primary screen acting union, comparable to the Screen Actor's Guild (SAG) in the United States or Equity in the UK.
11. Newhouse and Messaline, "Some career problems: gloomy reality," pp. 17–19.
12. Natalie Lisinska (actor), in discussion with the author, October 2016.
13. Cook, *Building Character: The Art and Science of Casting*, pp. 83–95, 105–8.
14. Chris Baker (actor), in discussion with the author, August 2016; Antonio Cayonne (actor), in discussion with the author, August 2016.
15. Jamie Spilchuk (actor), in discussion with the author, August 2016.
16. Kevin McGarry (actor), in discussion with the author, August 2016.
17. Sheila McCarthy (actor), in discussion with the author, September 2016.
18. McCarroll, "The historical body map: cultural pressures on embodied cognition."
19. Brian Levy audition masterclass in Toronto, May 2007.
20. Cook, *Building Character: The Art and Science of Casting*, pp. 64, 65.
21. Sheila McCarthy (actor), in discussion with the author, September 2016.
22. Matthew MacFadzean (actor), in discussion with the author, August 2016.
23. Kevin McGarry (actor), in discussion with the author, August 2016.
24. In acting terminology, the term "sides" generally refers to the excerpt of the screenplay that will be the focus of the day's acting work. In audition setting, "sides" refers only to the material chosen by the directors and producers for the actors to perform during the casting process. Once film production is underway, "sides" also refers to the entire text—often a single scene—from the screenplay that is to be shot that day. For clarity and brevity's sake, I will continue to use "sides" as the term for "the script excerpt at hand," and the terms "script" and "screenplay" interchangeably to refer to the document that contains the dialogue cues for the entire production.
25. Utterback, "The Olympic actor: improving actor training and performance through sports psychology."
26. Lauren MacKinlay (actor/producer), in discussion with the author, October 2016.
27. Third assistant director.
28. Natalie Lisinska (actor), in discussion with the author, October 2016.
29. These on-set habits will be analyzed in much greater detail in Chapter 6.
30. Feagin, "Empathizing as simulating," pp. 158–61.
31. Julian DeZotti (actor/writer), in discussion with the author, July 2016.
32. Jamie Spilchuk (actor), in discussion with the author, August 2016.
33. Jamie Spilchuk (actor), in discussion with the author, August 2016.
34. Natalie Lisinska (actor), in discussion with the author, October 2016.
35. Chris Baker (actor), in discussion with the author, August 2016.

36. Jamie Spilchuk (actor), in discussion with the author, August 2016.
37. This progression is simply intended as a general outline of the audition process. Variations in the details of this progression are common, and likely impact the actor's preparatory work. For example, some sets of sides are longer or more dramatically complex than others; sometimes the producers and director will attend the audition; some auditions occur in casting directors' offices and some require actors to self-tape their work and mail it to the casting director; and so on. My goal here is to indicate a general workflow rather than a fixed process because of the ramifications of how the workflow of auditions impacts the solicitation of empathetic connections for the audition performance.
38. The length of an audition reel is entirely dependent on the length of the sides and speed at which the actor performs the scene. Auditions for very small or very large roles can easily run shorter or longer than the two- to five-minute average provided here. That said, the industrial nature of auditions encourages shorter, more concentrated scenes so that more actors can be more thoroughly assessed in a shorter amount of time.
39. Jamie Spilchuk (actor), in discussion with the author, August 2016.
40. This choice between presuming an already complete or an unnecessary intersubjective connection parallels two actorly habits for collaborating with the camera: Dinicol's Jazz and Lisinska's Tears, respectively. These habits will be analyzed extensively in Chapter 6.
41. Chris Baker (actor), in discussion with the author, August 2016.
42. Antonio Cayonne (actor), in discussion with the author, August 2016.
43. Antonio Cayonne (actor), in discussion with the author, August 2016.
44. Cook, *Building Character: The Art and Science of Casting*, pp. 79–80.
45. Jamie Spilchuk (actor), in discussion with the author, August 2016.
46. Antonio Cayonne (actor), in discussion with the author, August 2016; Lauren MacKinlay (actor/producer), in discussion with the author, October 2016; Danelene O'Flynn (actor/producer), in discussion with the author, August 2016.
47. See Chapter 5 for more on script analysis.
48. The actor no longer needs to refer or hold on to the sides to complete a scene.
49. Chris Baker (actor), in discussion with the author, August 2016; Danelene O'Flynn (actor/producer), in discussion with the author, August 2016.
50. Actors interviewed for this study were invited to make any responses anonymous if they were concerned about being professionally punished should their commentary ever be made public.
51. Matthew MacFadzean (actor), in discussion with the author, August 2016.
52. This industrial reliance on casting actors who work frequently is indirectly mirrored in the professional union structure. Aspiring Canadian screen actors can only join ACTRA if they earn enough credits towards their membership by appearing in professional, ACTRA-sanctioned films, television programs,

and commercials. However, ACTRA regulations demand that all professional film shoots in Canada must consider current ACTRA members first before hiring non-members and other aspiring talent.
53. Actorly tactics for working around these situations will be covered Chapter 6's "Make It Work" section.

CHAPTER 5

Empathetic Work Prior to Shooting

From Guesswork to Scaffolding

Once an actor passes the audition process and is hired for a screen role, she has a great deal of preparatory homework to do before she arrives on set. This work differs from the audition preparations because she will now have to navigate the performance affordances of narrative options across the entire screenplay. This means that the audition's frantic preparation and narrative guesswork expands to uncovering and stockpiling a long progression of referenceable bodymind associations and appresentations along the situational character's intentional throughline, as part of constructing the character's cognitive scaffolding.

This extensive and overarching preparation is important because many film and television productions are filmed out of narrative sequence, which can mean that an actor may have to perform her most demanding scenes before shooting or even rehearsing the crucial scenes that set up these narrative climaxes. Actor/producer Lauren MacKinlay justifies this type of shooting schedule as a matter of industrial practicality:

> As a producer, you need to decide where your money is going. What are the biggest visuals that can support the message and the theme, and what do we want the audience to walk away with? That's how you structure your shooting schedule. You want the actor to be able to offer things and you obviously want the director to be able to realize their vision, but you also need to say "[. . .] Is this where our money needs to go? Is this shot the most important shot of the film? If not, we're moving on."[1]

It is often more efficient for a whole film production to complicate the actor's work rather than extend a shooting schedule to allow for creative exploration on set. These disruptive shooting schedules place a premium on the actor's advance preparations so that the actor can establish some level of character creativity despite performing their scenes out of narrative order.

The disjointed narrative progression throughout the shooting process can pose a great challenge to actors who have not established a firm intrasubjective connection with their character, both on the scene-by-scene level and across the screenplay as a unified narrative progression. Although most of the pre-shoot homework is focused on the intrasubjective work that the actor can control on her own, she can also anticipate crucial intersubjective and performative work that will be of great help once shooting begins.

Tactics for Screenplay Analysis and Intrasubjective Connections

This chapter analyzes three basic clusters of potential strategies used by actors to ensnare themselves in the scripted character's intentional pull and thereby construct the situational cognitive scaffolding[2] prior to shooting: a bottom-up approach; a top-down approach; and, most commonly, a balanced approach. The goal of these strategic trends is to develop the necessarily intrasubjective appresentations—the Magic Ifs of the character and her narrative world—to enable verisimilar performance, based on the narrative affordances of the screenplay. As such, the distinguishing factors between these trends is closely related to the actor's preferred balance of remembered and imagined creative fodder, and how the actor incorporates this fodder into her script analysis to bring her further into the character's intentional pull.

Each of these script analysis habits presumes that the actor will learn her character's lines, and somehow connect these lines to actions informed by the tactics through which the character pursues her narrative goals. Moreover, each set of habits anticipates that the actor will, at some point, need to start collaborating with her scene partners and production staff; the cognitive ecology of the script preparation process is populated primarily by the actor's quotidian self and whichever situational selves may emerge during her creative experimentation. As such, the trends aspire to establish the character as a meaningful and referable bodymind self; stable enough to recall and invoke quickly, but malleable enough to adapt to her collaborators and, by doing so, establish the necessary intersubjective and performative empathetic bonds. In short, the habits here aspire to give the actor a strong sense of the bodymind meshwork's reorganization as the character, and to be able to locate, access, and enact this reorganization as required on set.

A Note on Terminology

I wish to diffuse any potential confusion about the origins of some of the inevitable jargon that will appear in the next two chapters. Since most of the tactics and examples in this chapter come out of the interviewed actors' practices, I will reference specific roles played by these actors as examples, where possible. During the interviews, each actor described tactics, practices, and habits they use in their creative practices. Overwhelmingly, these tactics, practices, and habits were not first developed by the actor who describes it. Instead, the practices described here are an amorphous and ever-evolving amalgam of practices, often handed down across generations and through diffuse networks of actors, with each actor adapting the practices as she sees fit. In order to focus on how forces in acting culture—like creative training and its industrial economics—shape an actor's practice, this chapter and the next will associate some actorly practices with the interviewed actor who most clearly described them during my interviews. The point of the upcoming terminology such as Cayonne's Minotaur and McGarry's Relatability, is to identify and quickly reference a specific acting habit as it is practiced, rather than to credit an originating practitioner. Therefore, just as the apocryphal story of Duse's Blush[3] credits a skilled actor with a practice for which she was likely not the original practitioner, so too with the screen-specific practices described to me by the actors during these interviews. Presented with the choice, this study of actorly practices benefits more from the creation of productive and referable jargon than from adding further layers of theoretical abstraction to describe a fairly specific practice.

Although the following analysis partitions script analysis tactics into loosely bottom-up, top-down, and balanced practices, it is important to note that most actors view the many points on this spectrum of practices as inherently complementary and will not necessarily rely exclusively on one tactic for every role. This division of actorly habits has no pretense of being exhaustive, nor should the top-down and bottom-up categories be considered mutually exclusive. I stress the importance of these strategies as "habits" because they are patterns—rather than prescriptions—of behaviors for how actors create empathetic connections. What these habits collectively demonstrate is that differences in script analysis tactics tend to reflect the intrasubjective priority that the actor ascribes to Coplan's affective match versus the other-oriented perspective taking.

"Bottom-up Script Analysis": Extrapolating Specific Memories into Emotional Common Denominators

Actors often invoke personally resonant emotional memories and other stimuli to ensnare themselves in the character's intentional pull and translate their scripted characters into their bodies. Based on Feagin's argument that the cognitive scaffolding of a realist character will be similar to that of its quotidian reader, an actor may draw parallels between events in her quotidian life and her character's scripted actions, experiences, and narrative situations. Although the character's situational circumstances inevitably vary from the quotidian actor's detailed memories, realist screenplays can afford the actor's intrasubjective bond by prompting the actor into catachresis, recalling and re-imagining experiences from her quotidian life in terms to inform appresentations about her character. In this sense, bottom-up preparation tactics position similarities between a character's experiences and the quotidian actor's memories as affordances to connect the actor to her character. This effectively targets potential affective matches as access points to the character's cognitive scaffolding. These preparatory tactics are only constrained by the actor's tolerance level for such catachresis and her willingness to test her intrasubjective self–other distinction.

In many screenplays, however, the character will experience something that is somehow beyond the actor's experiences, making the empathetic connection in that moment more difficult to establish and sustain. These irreconcilable experiences can range from the subtle to the far-fetched. Many respondents, for example, describe past roles in which the scale and nature of a scripted character's particular trait simply exceeds the actor's experience of that trait: an actor who occasionally drinks alcohol or takes illicit drugs, for example, may struggle to imaginatively extrapolate their recreational inebriations to the scale required to play an alcoholic or a drug addict. For other films, the greater narrative circumstances may be so heightened or fantastical that the actor could not be expected to have a specifically detailed frame of reference: although an actor might enjoy watching science fiction films, she has no personal experience to reference in performance of fleeing Toronto while alien invaders raze the city.[4]

Many schools of acting have tolerated and even encouraged actors to develop life experiences to close the potential bodymind gaps between the actor and her character. Despite the culture of celebrity that can incentivize radical intrasubjective research and its subsequent transformations,[5] some character research is simply legally and logistically impossible—or even personally dangerous—for an actor to pursue in good conscience. Actor Sheila McCarthy reports that Uta Hagen, with whom McCarthy trained, actively discouraged her acting students from investing too heavily in the type of "My character kills her mother so I must kill my mother to know what that's like"[6] research in favor of immersive imaginary work. Nevertheless, an actor in search of parallels between her scripted character's most inaccessible aspects and recalled events in her own life must still establish some level of catachresis between the quotidian and situational selves, in order to establish the empathy-enabling affective match. Many actors therefore attempt to establish an emotional common ground, however basic, with their characters, through appresentational personal substitutions.

Actor Natalie Lisinska often invokes and reimagines emotionally charged memories to connect her to her characters' affective experiences. For example, Lisinska appears in an episode of *Mary Kills People* (Cameron Pictures and Entertainment One, 2017–19) where she plays a woman whose husband is terminally ill. To make sense of her character's erratic emotional states, Lisinska drew on her contemporaneous experience of concern over a seriously ill family member. This substitution of her quotidian relative for her situational husband enabled her to locate her situational character's tumultuous emotions within her own quotidian experience, which led to a profound empathetic connection with her character. After such an intensely charged script preparation, Lisinska reports that she was able to reliably re-create the necessary emotional states on set:

> On my last day on *Mary Kills People*, I walked onto set and I was already crying. I said, "Hi everybody, the crying girl is here," and they laughed because every other day, I had also shown up already in tears.[7]

Lisinska also uses emotional memories in a more abstract manner than the literal transference on *Mary Kills People* to establish her intrasubjective affective match with her character. In a climactic scene from her Screen Guild of Canada Award-winning performance on *Orphan Black* (BBC America, 2013–17), Lisinska-as-Ainsley aggressively accuses her best friend of sabotaging Ainsley's rapidly failing marriage.

To connect her to the character's feelings of anger, betrayal, and sadness, Lisinska referenced her emotional experiences of confrontations that have ended romantic relationships and personal friendships in her quotidian life. "Channeling" her own feelings during those altercations, and her impression of those expressed by her former friends and lovers, Lisinska reports that her preparation for that scene felt raw, powerful, and deeply sincere:

> Ainsley was a treat to play because she's an Alpha "Mean Girl." I've played that a few times in my career, and I've definitely been that in my life. You will always just be you, so it's just an aspect of yourself. That's why acting is fun! You get to explore the darker deeper recesses of yourself that you know exist. You know that they're there, so [be brave] and go there.[8]

Figure 5.1 Natalie Lisinska (left) and Tatiana Maslany (right) in *Orphan Black* season 1, episode 10, "Endless Forms Most Beautiful" (John Fawcett, BBC America, 2013)

The convenient intersection between the character's situation and the actor's lived experience afforded for a potent affective match, even if the actor must give breath to parts of herself she would sooner avoid.[9]

The task of emotional substitution for intrasubjective affective matching becomes more complex when the actor has a less personal connection than those made by Lisinska for *Orphan Black* or *Mary Kills People*. Kevin McGarry, for example, focuses some of his script analysis practices around making his character "relatable" by identifying the core value, emotion, or desire that motivates the action in moments or roles that require creative fodder beyond the "mental rolodex" of his lived experience. This process of uncovering "relatability" is based on the presumption that emotions are sharable between people, and that some essential affective material is at least partially transferable across experiences and across selves, even if the details of those experiences may vary. In short, by identifying and atomizing specific bodymind states, the actor can draw on the "emotional common denominators" of those bodymind states as a starting point for understanding how, what, and why a character may feel as she does:

> Things are only overwhelming when they are [lost in] the bigger picture. I find it so much easier to not dumb it down but to break it down into smaller things. [. . .] I think the actor's job is to make it all relevant, but you're not gonna be moved unless you can relate to what is happening.[10]

McGarry used this practice of breaking down his character's actions to relatable impulses, and then adding increasing layers of emotional and situational specificity, for a scene on *Heartland* (CBC, 2007–present), where he plays a discharged Canadian army veteran who suffers from post-traumatic stress disorder (PTSD) from his military experiences in Afghanistan.

In a dramatic scene, his character must fire a gun for the first time since his combat missions to protect himself from an attacking wolf. In preparation for this moment, McGarry constructed the situational conflict—the need to defend himself clashing with the fear of killing again—by identifying relatable emotions and gradually specifying them to the scene. Although he felt that the "machismo need to 'act like a man'" was sufficiently relatable enough to justify the self-defense impulse, McGarry wanted a strong and actionable connection to the fear of pulling the trigger and killing the wolf since he has no direct experience of PTSD himself. He drew parallels between killing the wolf and his experiences with a *Heartland* co-star who, in her spare time, raises turkeys to slaughter for food:

> If you're ordered to kill, it's the extraction of innocence. [. . .] Those little turkeys follow her around. She's their mother, and then she's going to pick up a gun and shoot them. There's an action right there: where you raise living things, feeling their innocence, and that they trusted you. Then you've gone from "extraction of innocence" to "betrayal," and now you have a word that everyone can relate to.[11]

McGarry then layers on increasingly levels of emotional specificity to the atomized emotion, value, or desire as a means of constructing his character's cognitive scaffolding prior to filming.

Figure 5.2 Kevin McGarry in *Heartland*, season 7, episode 10, "Riding Shotgun" (Chris Potter, CBC, 2016)

This tactic relies on at least three fundamental assumptions about how it will manifest in performance. First, the performed narrative conflict between his character's soldierly masculinity and his bodymind invocation of compassionate guilt will be sufficiently balanced to generate the intended dramatic tension over whether his character will save himself or not. Secondly, McGarry presumes that this emotional conflict will reorganize his bodymind schema in such a way that it will manifest as PTSD-based emotional turmoil on-screen, especially since McGarry knew about the director's plans to shoot this moment as a gradual zoom-in shot on his tension-ridden eyes. Third, McGarry anticipates his audience with his tactic of seeking relatability, on the presumption that his intrasubjectively connected performance will be legible to the spectator and also push its intentionality towards the spectator. Therefore, in this circumstance, McGarry's abstraction of his personal bodymind experience of betrayal and his substitution of this experience into his character prepares McGarry to empathetically connect to the narrative world while soliciting an empathetic connection from his audience. This substitution also anticipates McGarry's collaboration with the production crew, especially the DOP who eventually chose to film the scene as a tracking close-up on McGarry's eyes to accentuate the character's affective state.

As a final thought, McGarry's relatability anticipates some of the balanced approaches between bottom-up and top-down script analysis habits analyzed later in this chapter, in that McGarry turns to an additional level imaginary experience beyond Lisinska's immediately personal substitutions to reach an affective match with his character. McGarry admits that he has no direct personal experience of anything akin to shooting his co-star's adoring turkeys, let alone his character's convoluted feelings about defending himself against the attacking wolf. To manifest his character's PTSD anxiety about firing a gun, McGarry rearranges his bodymind schema around the idea of killing a beloved animal to access the feelings of betrayal and loss that he feels he can communicate to an audience. I continue to qualify McGarry's relatability as a primarily bottom-up practice because the affective match occurs when McGarry substitutes his own experiences of betrayal and loss into that moment of the character's affective progression.

These bottom-up habits for making a scripted character relatable to the actor, exemplified by Lisinska and McGarry, support the development of an intrasubjective empathetic connection by proposing a candidate for a meaningful affective match. Since the situational character choices stem directly from viscerally resonant moments from the actor's quotidian life, the character's emotional life is contingent on that of the actor. The need for an affective match guides the actor in taking on her character's perspective, in that the actor adjusts her own experiences to suit the circumstances of the character's narrative world as a means of accessing what the character might feel. The catachresis of referencing quotidian experiences as part of connecting to one's character seems, at first glance, to betray the self–other distinction upon which an empathetic connection depends. I suggest, however, that establishing the intrasubjective self–other distinction while relating to a character has more to do with being intentionally pulled closer to that situational character than ever arriving at full synchronization: immersion, but not submersion. Implicit in the creative habit of translating the actor's own experience into her character is that the character and actor are fundamentally different selves. Even in moments like those Lisinska describes, in which her characters share significant autobiographical details with the actor herself, Lisinska's goal is not to use her acting work to therapeutically work through her feelings for ill relatives, lost friends, and former lovers. Her goal is to share an affective state known to her quotidian self with her character's situational self to inform subsequent acting choices.

In summary, bottom-up script analysis habits connect the actor to poignant moments and character circumstances in the screenplay on the assumption that these immersive states will prompt verisimilar subsequent actions and reactions as her character. This kind of script work also grounds the actor in a very relatable and quickly-referenceable bodymind schema that helps the actor to preserve her performative continuity across the many takes and out-of-narrative-sequence shooting inherent to screen media production.

"Top-down Script Analysis": Imagination, Abstraction, Archetype

Lisinska and McGarry's habits of relatable common denominators and personal substitutions form a primarily bottom-up approach to catching oneself in a scripted character's emotional pull. Alternately, the primarily top-down correlative to this practice is to reorganize the actor's body schema through wholly invented material that mirrors thematic, emotional, and conceptual cues from the screenplay.

In these top-down practices, the actor opens her bodymind meshwork to reorganizations prompted by evocative, imaginary, and abstract points of reference that correspond to shifting power dynamics and goals across the story and in each scene. The logic here parallels that of McGarry's relatability, in that the actor can connect to the moment by "naming" it something to which she has an emotionally vivid relationship. The main difference between these top-down practices and McGarry's relatability is that the named moments do not originate in the actor's quotidian experiences, but instead mobilize these experiences as an abstract reference point. The priority here is that the abstractions clarify the scripted character's cognitive scaffolding to make it actionable through performance. Put another way, the actor wears a personally evocative metaphor for her character like an imaginary mantle that reorganizes her body schema without excessive reliance on autobiographical substitutions.[12] This evocative image is inherently one that the actor dons as more of a template for potential reactions than a series of substituted emotional benchmarks to pass through. This approach affords the actor considerable freedom to evoke abstract imagery to inform the construction of a character's cognitive scaffolding. The expansive range of affordances, still constrained by verisimilar proximity to the narrative and character at hand, gives the actor access to a wealth of performance choices with which to experiment until she finds a compelling combination of self-reorganizing reference catalysts.

Case Study: Toronto's Professional Actors Lab

One of Anglophone Canada's foremost screen actor training institutions uses a homemade top-down vocabulary to help its actors explore character choices and tactics. The Professional Actors Lab (Pro Actors Lab) in Toronto, run by founder David Rotenberg and long-time instructor Bruce Clayton,[13] grounds its script analysis practices in identifying and naming the character's transitions across the Jungian family archetypes[14] within the sides. The goal of invoking the Jungian archetypes is to connect the gendered power dynamics of the sides to the actor's pre-existing relationship to an imaginary, familial reference point.

Rotenberg and Clayton use the Jungian archetypes as a shorthand schema for a character's tactics in pursuit of her goal rather than the scene's narrative specificities. For example, a Pro Actors Lab actor might label a given scene's character archetypes as "Older Sister and Little Brother," thereby naming the gendered power dynamics between the characters while flagging combinations of recurring tactics for how each character pursues their narrative goals. Characters interpreted as younger siblings—regardless of the character's age or personal relationship to any other characters—will often try to get what they want through sulking, flirting, protesting, demanding gratification, and so forth. Older sibling characters attain their goals by giving or withholding advice, information, support, love, attention, and so forth. These sibling archetypes can be further inflected with the further archetype of "lover"—again, regardless of the character's narrative-specific relationships with others—wherein the character seeks to equalize the scene's power dynamics to create a deeper and more prosperous relationship among other characters in the scene. Alternatively, a character with a supplementary "parent" archetype is one who will never negotiate their dominant power status over other characters.

In the "Older Sister and Little Brother" example, the scene at hand would likely depict a moment where a male character demands something from the female character, who must decide if and how she will oblige him depending on what she wants from their exchange. This relationship can play out in any number of narrative circumstances: a new employee pitches a new business venture to his manager, who must decide if she can justify reallocating scarce company time and money to his risky project; a philandering boyfriend pleads with his furious ex-girlfriend over the phone to give him another chance; a corrupt detective confronts his partner after she has reported his abuses of public trust to the chief of police. Although the power dynamics may oscillate throughout the scene, at least one character will achieve some level of their goal by the scene's end: the reticent manager eventually agrees to support the side project with some conditions; the jilted ex-girlfriend decides her former lover is too immature to warrant reviving the relationship and hangs up; the virtuous detective stands on her moral high ground while realizing that her "betrayal" of the police cultural code of covering for one's partner will have negative professional repercussions for the rest of her career. The Jungian archetypes can help give the actor a preliminary overarching framework for charting the moment-to-moment specificities of her character's narrative arc in a given scene and even across a whole episode or film.

As a script analysis strategy, Pro Actors Lab encourages its students to use the sides' text—and especially its subtext—as a set of clues towards the character's cognitive scaffold. The Pro Actors Lab actor imagines herself into an intrasubjective empathetic connection by using Jungian shorthand vocabulary to quickly clarify the interpersonal power dynamics in the sides, and to use this as an access point to her character's cognitive scaffolding, transforming these abstractions into actionable cognitive references.

This emphasis on fostering intrasubjective empathy through analyzing the character's tactics and power dynamics anticipates acting on-screen, rather than on stage. Clayton encourages his screen acting students to act "off the words," privileging emotional and tactical clarity over the affective potential of the sides' words themselves. Rather than delve into the evocative imagery of the specific words in the sides, as an actor might for a Shakespearean scene study wherein the poetic vocabulary itself is a dramatic force, Pro Actors Lab treats the dialogue's words like a necessary accessory, in that they provide valuable details on the dramatic stakes of each moment but are not in and of themselves representative of that moment.

This anti-theatricalism not only reflects the importance of training screen actors for close-up shots,[15] but is also a symptom of the importance of theatrical training for Canadian actors. The actors interviewed for this study unanimously described screen acting as occurring on a smaller physical scale than theater acting. The reason that this performative concern manifests so early in the establishment of intrasubjective connections is because Canadian actors are predominantly trained for live theater, with screen acting often treated pedagogically as an afterthought or specialization of one's theatrical talents. Drawing just on examples from the screen actors interviewed for this study, Lisinska works exclusively in film and television but spent the vast majority of her BFA acting studies being "groomed" specifically for a career in repertory classical theater at the Stratford Shakespeare Festival; McCarthy worked as a dancer and singer in musical theater for much of her early career before starting any extensive screen work; Dinicol was a professional child actor at Stratford years before setting foot on his first professional film set; MacFadzean switched to screen acting as a personal rejection of the nomadic lifestyle required by working exclusively in Canadian theater; and Baker, Cayonne, Spilchuk, and many others report that they discovered screen acting late in their formal training as actors.

Utterly central to classical theater training is the affective power of the script's words: the actor's job is to use her words to guide her actions, express her character, reveal the text's poetry, and advance the story. This training places great importance on elocution, sustained breath support for long spoken phrases, and developing sufficient command of the dialogue's affective potential to immerse herself and the audience in the compelling complexities of the poetic language. Clayton, himself a former musical theater actor, often explains to his screen acting students that Canadian acting culture's equation of performance skills with classical theater repertoire does not inherently translate well to the screen. The physical scale at which stage actors move, and the thoroughly enunciated lyrical gymnastics that they can perform with poetic texts, often appear as garish and excessive on-screen. To adapt one's acting technique from the stage to the screen—a creative retraining for which the Pro Actors Lab is renowned in Toronto's arts culture—the actor must relearn to use the same creative muscles differently for each medium. Pro Actors Lab therefore encourages Canadian actors who are new to screen acting to put the narrative agency on the actor's bodymind reactions and tactical transitions, instead of acting "on the words[16] as one would in theater: dialogue should be memorized but not slavishly adhered to; lines should be "thrown away" rather than over-pronounced. By focusing on the communicative potential of the filmed reaction, Pro Actors Lab teaches actors to clarify what they "think" and "feel" on camera, without sacrificing narrative details or emotional complexity.

This is not to say that Rotenberg and Clayton's system ignores narrative and emotional specificities: the whole point of the Pro Actors Lab system is to help the actor to establish realistic bodymind transitions across the beats of the scene. Instead, as an acting system intended for the screen, the Pro Actors System embraces the detailed minutiae of what the camera can capture to make acting about choices and reactions rather than actions and events. The hope of this kind of top-down work is that the narrative will become clear through the subtext of how the actor performs, rather than relying strictly on the bodymind authenticity of a performed emotional state.

Top-down Archetypes as Personal Reference Points

Other archetype-driven styles of acting are far less prescriptive than the Pro Actors Lab in terms of the evocative, imaginary personas are available to the actor. Actor Danelene O'Flynn's extensive international screen training and on-set experience has prompted her to think of her creative process as an experiment in "archetypal alchemy," wherein she freely blends metaphorical personas throughout her bodymind to connect her to her character. The personas that O'Flynn invokes as archetypes can range from "roles" she has played in her quotidian life, such as "the Orphan" and "the Wanderer," to pseudo-mythical abstractions, such as "the Wise Woman" and "the Queen." Each of these archetypes lacks a definable, objective definition: what is important to O'Flynn is how her subjective relationship with these appresentational personas helps her to reorganize her body schema to immerse her within the character's lived experience. Significantly, the archetypes that are more closely related to her quotidian lived experiences remain abstractions of those memories: assemblages of associated bodymind perceptions, rather than direct invocations of the recalled material.

O'Flynn describes her archetypes as being reliable sources of creative inspiration, and distinguishes how her top-down script analysis habits anticipate their eventual application on set. Rather than use archetypal references to identify transitions of social power as in the Pro Actors Lab system, O'Flynn envisions her archetypes as the factions of her character's psychological civil war: the names given to the internal forces that create "the wound," the sheering place between the character's overt objective and the personal shortcomings that must be resolved before the character can rest, either with the successful attainment of—or final failure to realize—her objective. The "wound," itself a corporeal metaphor and conceptual blend that clarifies the character's cognitive scaffolding, motivates the character's actions and can also encompass how one archetype transitions into another throughout the narrative. For a role in a recent short film, O'Flynn connected to her character by tracing how the Wanderer became the Queen as the narrative progressed.[17] The accompanying "wound" could then manifest throughout the narrative as a transition between mobility and stability, a tension between freedom and authority, and a balance of unpredictability with self-assertion, however O'Flynn deemed productive throughout the narrative.

Although far more abstract than those of the Pro Actors Lab system, O'Flynn's archetypes are explicitly hers to work with. If the goal is to connect with a scripted character through top-down imagery, O'Flynn's constellations of jostling archetypes are already meaningful and relatable to her. Her highly malleable and personalized system affords deep intrasubjective connections with her characters, and does so while avoiding the explicitly autobiographical insertions of Lisinska's bottom-up substitutions. This top-down practice also relies heavily on the actor's collaboration with the production crew to transmit the performance to the audience: although O'Flynn relates, like McGarry, to her own intrasubjective imagery, her archetypal work does not seek the affective common denominators with the audience with McGarry's vehemence. For O'Flynn, the proof of the archetypes' value rests with how they reorganize her bodymind to articulate the performed narrative that the archetypes support. This script analysis habit therefore willingly trades some control over the final assembled performance in favor of investing significant trust in the how the production team will work with the raw material that O'Flynn will provide.

As a practice of script analysis and performance preparation, O'Flynn's archetypes afford appresentations from their resonances and overlaps with specific story events, character tactics, or specific dialogue cues. O'Flynn is quick to admit that the search for archetypal resonances in complex scripted character becomes very time consuming, in that she prefers to give each archetypal layer time to settle within her situational self to understand how it works before layering in others. The emphasis on layering various archetypes together to help the actor imagine her way into the character's lived experience suggests that the actor organizes the synergies between the named archetypes to connect to the character's strengths and weaknesses.

These top-down approaches have an established history in iconic cinema performances. For example, in press interviews and various other commentaries, Sir Anthony Hopkins has described multiple imaginary personas he invoked while preparing for his role in *Silence of the Lambs* (Jonathan Demme, 1991). Hopkins, as Hannibal Lecter, allegedly layered together multiple evocative imaginary personas, ranging from a tarantula,[18] to the Angel of Death and an ominous black clock,[19] to a house cat and the character of HAL 9000 (Douglas Rain) from Stanley Kubrick's *2001: A Space Odyssey* (1968).[20] Hopkins top-down approach to script analysis anticipates performance in that some of his imaginary invocations apply primarily to enactable possibilities, such as a prowling housecat's wide-eyed mannerisms and Rain-as-HAL-9000's unnaturally calm voice. Other references, such as the tarantula and the Angel of Death, seem more connected to overarching archetypes of menace and mortality to reorganize Hopkins's greater bodymind schema, therefore accounting for the actor-as-character cognition behind the unflinching cat-like gaze and the tranquil, eloquent diction.

Hopkins-as-Lecter, and top-down script analysis habits in general, seem at first glance to reify Stanley Cavell's metaphor of the screen actor as one who rummages through a proverbial attic in search of interesting bits and pieces.[21] Cavell's analogy, however, overlooks the professional training and common creativity across stage and screen acting practices. This comparison of theatrical baseball players to cinematic attic rummagers[22] fails because, as Blair Brown and the professional actors interviewed for this study agree, the intrasubjective relationship between realist actors and their characters is not contingent on the performance medium. Script analysis always anticipates the actor's performance in one way or another. The top-down script preparation habits, described by O'Flynn, Pro Actors Lab alumni such as McGarry and Cayonne, and even demonstrated by Anthony Hopkins, are just as applicable for theater or screen since the importance of the actor-character bond remains the same across media. Top-down script preparation habits simply encourage the actor to play from her imagination and to imagine whatever is required for the role,[23] thereby letting their creatively chosen abstractions manifest through their performing bodyminds.

The invocation of imagined archetypes during top-down script analysis fulfills Coplan's criteria for the intrasubjective empathetic connection between the actor and her as-yet-unperformed character. The other-oriented perspective taking occurs on multiple levels. First, the actor's imaginary archetypes themselves are a vocabulary for situational selves to which the actor can relate and which—in the actor's judgment—manifest in some capacity within the character. The archetypal material is only useful if it is prompted by textual cues to the character's cognitive scaffolding. Moreover, the attention to the character's narrative tactics in pursuit of her goal prompts the actor to work through every line of dialogue as a choice to be made, shaped in part by the imaginary imagery invoked to clarify these choices.

In these top-down approaches, the affective match between the actor and her character occurs as a by-product of the other-oriented perspective taking: with the strong understanding of why the character behaves as she does derived from intentionality of the scripted situational character, and the evocative imagery of the archetypal work spurring further action, the affective content of the performed moment is already shared by the quotidian actor and the situational character. The reconstruction of the character's cognitive scaffolding therefore depends on a logical and premeditated understanding of what a chosen tactic in a given moment, animated by evocative mental imagery, says about a character's affective state and bodymind schema. The actor is able to maintain the self–other distinction because this kind of script work presumes that the character is something *created* through tactical analysis and the layering of evocative images, as opposed to something that the actor *becomes*. As with the bottom-up script analysis practices, the actor remains keenly aware that she is not the character.

The crucial difference between how these top-down techniques and the bottom-up techniques establish empathetic bonds lies in the top-down approaches' emphasis on character tactics and emotional transitions, as opposed to the bottom-up techniques' emphasis on experiential authenticity. The major empathetic distinction between the top-down and bottom-up approaches is therefore effectively the balance of priority between the intrasubjective affective match and the other-oriented perspective taking, especially in respect to the self–other distinction. The bottom-up approaches presume that a potent affective match, established through a personal substitution or McGarry's relatability or another practice, will ground the actor in enough of the character's moment-to-moment affective experience that the transitions across dramatic moments will inevitably follow. In the earlier examples, actors such as Lisinska and McGarry generate enough affective commonality with their characters, all the while knowing that the character is a distinct and situational self, that the situational self's perspective becomes their own. Inversely, the top-down practices manifest in how an invoked mental persona, from Pro Actors Lab's Jungian family to O'Flynn's "Wise Woman," prompts a continuous immersion in the character's perspective by reorganizing the actor's bodymind schema that navigates a scene's affective transitions, in the hopes that the affective match will happen organically from within that immersive continuity.

In summary, bottom-up and top-down script analyses help actors to develop a creative vocabulary for bodymind imagery with the intention of translating it outwards through expressive performances. The archetypes invoked by the Pro Actors Lab system and O'Flynn's individual practice are, in one sense, clarifying terminology given to a hypothetical bodymind schema for quick reference in performance. In another sense, they are evidence of the actor's appresentational attunement to the scripted narrative in that they expedite the empathetic process with body schemas already present within the actor's performative repertoire: in these practices, the actor imagines, invents, and thereby appresents what she needs to form an intrasubjective connection with the scripted character.

Cayonne's Minotaur: Balancing Memory and Imagination to Find the Character's Body Schema

There is no reason why bottom-up and top-down script analysis processes cannot work simultaneously. It is perhaps then more accurate to refer to the bottom-up and top-down approaches to script analysis as being "predominately" top-down or bottom-up, rather than to suggest that one approach always functions at the exclusion of another. O'Flynn readily acknowledges that many of her top-down archetypes are informed to some degree by her quotidian experiences; McGarry enthusiastically embraces the affective potential of evocative mental imagery to inform his choices about memory substitution. More of a spectrum than a binary, these top-down and bottom-up approaches beneficially inform each other when practiced as complementary techniques. The ways in which actors balance top-down and bottom-up imaginary work during script analysis not only reflects the pragmatic individualism of acting practices, but also exemplifies the virtuosity of the actor's skill in reorganizing her bodymind schema as the situational self of the character. The "balanced" actor's implicit freedom to alter, re-imagine, and even invent memories on behalf of her character means that evocative top-down imagery and bottom-up affective authenticity create whatever appresentational material she deems useful in creating an empathetic relationship with her character. This flexible, hybrid approach to memory and imagination is—not surprisingly—by far the most common one in the screen acting community because of the creative agency it bestows on the actor to prepare what works best for her for a given role.

It is hardly surprising that the cast majority of actors rely on a combination of bottom-up and top-down creative ideas to empathize the character's situational self. First, and as has been established earlier, cognitive neuroscientists and realist acting gurus are largely in agreement that memory is effectively a function of the imagination. Second, modern research on the neural foundations of artistic creativity suggests that artistic creation occurs *because* of the bodymind's ability to spontaneously blend a somewhat different sense of loosely bottom-up ephemera with loosely top-down conscious choices. Roger E. Beaty and Rex E. Jung argue that creative artistic thoughts emerge in the dynamic interactions of two different but non-opposed neural networks within the brain. The default network oversees "internally focused mental activity that occurs in the absence of external stimulation," including but not limited to daydreaming, mentalizing, episodic recollection, and future speculation.[24] The executive control network, on the other hand, oversees "experimental tasks that require externally focused attention and cognitive control, such as working memory, response inhibition, task-set switching, and goal maintenance."[25] For actors like O'Flynn, this task-switching and goal maintenance could easily manifest as the conscious inclusion of a top-down personal archetype into her working memory to see what creative resonances it provokes with the rest of the emerging character's situational self. For Beaty and Jung, creative artistic thought occurs when the default and executive control networks cooperate because the goal-oriented nature of creating a dramatic performance, for example, requires the actor to devise and execute a strategic plan for seeing it to fruition.[26]

It seems reasonable to suggest that Strasberg and Adler's battles over the actor's acceptable use of imagination were fought over the types of internal references that the actor's default network ought to access: Strasberg's actor privileges the default network as a repository of personal emotional memories to be excavated on command; Adler's actor privileges the imagination's capacity to adapt and embellish whatever it recalls into something befitting the character's situational self. In both Strasberg and Adler though, the loosely bottom-up self-referential cognitive activities of memory and speculation need to take charge of the executive control network's capacity to execute some manner of pre-planned dialogue and blocking on which the rest of the actor's cognitive ecology depends. Similarly, the outward-action-oriented executive control network seems quite important to Meisner's Repetition Game, which sought to keep the actor in an iterative loop of responses while also preventing the working memory from being able to withdraw internally to assess one's own affective bodymind state. In this light, Meisner's maxim of "Don't give a performance. Let the performance give you"[27] suggests that the actor should be so actively engaged in her scene that the executive control network only has time to grab only the most important and authentic references from the default network since the immediacy of the actor-as-character's iterative responses are where the actor's performance comes from.

In a sense, the distinction between bottom-up and top-down script analysis strategies from earlier in this chapter corresponds to the balance of recollection to invention within the idea that the actor uses to connect with her character. Both the recollection- and invention-based strategies have meaningful presences within the default network. I suggest, however, that the working memory's oversight and execution of all that imaginary material during performance stresses a different sense of top-down pragmatism which many actors factor into their script analysis.

In a balanced script analysis approach, the cooperation of the default and executive control networks are taken as a balanced given from the start. Reworked memories manifest as relatable material tempered by evocative imaginary imagery, on the condition that the actor eventually finds a way to articulate these default network processes outwards in a manner that is comprehensible to the anticipated audience. This forms a creative catachresis wherein the actor completes the character's cognitive scaffolding with not only pieces of her quotidian experience but also that which she can create. Actor Antonio Cayonne's balanced approach to script analysis, for example, freely blends purely imaginary material with re-imagined memories to connect with his scripted character in a form that he feels ready to execute on set. The often incomplete screenplays available to auditioning actors, and the industrial likelihood that the script will change significantly prior to shooting, require the actor to be both prepared and flexible with her creative choices. As a screen-acting-specific tactic of working with this industrial unpredictability, Cayonne analyzes his scripts with an extensive series of questions about his characters as a means of preparing informed options about who his character could be. The questions range from the biographical (e.g., "Where did my character grow up?") to the scene-specific (e.g., "If my character is partially defined by his profession, does he like his job?") to the purely speculative (e.g., "If my character does illegal drugs, what does he take?"). The answers to these questions, prompted by textual and subtextual clues from the sides to the character's cognitive scaffolding, present Cayonne with informed appresentational fodder for who the character could be in performance, all of which come with an action plan for how his executive control network will enact them. Since the point of these questions is simply to foster a detailed understanding of—and connection to—the character, the answers are just as likely to reveal bottom-up relatable identifications with the character as they are to prompt evocative top-down imagery of what the character might be like,[28] insofar as Cayonne's working memory can communicate them in performance.

Since Cayonne's priority is to connect with his scripted character by accessing both what the character feels and the tactics behind his character's actions equally, he feels no aesthetic or cognitive dissonance in freely blending imaginary and recalled materials in the creation of a dramatically compelling situational self, provided that the invoked imaginary and recalled material is productively grounded in the script. Cayonne colorfully describes the creative process of blending imaginary and recalled material as making "Minotaurs" of his characters: "the head of one beast, and the body of another."[29]

For example, Cayonne was pleased with his work at a film call-back audition for a character who searches for his lost young son amidst the environmental conflicts of a post-apocalyptic dystopia.[30] Cayonne drew upon his own experiences of loss, familial love, and betrayal, and substituted relationships from his quotidian life into the sides, and was thereby able to develop a dramatically compelling relationship with his character's urgent search for the child. Although Cayonne has never lived in a post-apocalyptic dystopia before, he made compelling inferences about the ways in which that setting would impact his character's emotional and interpersonal lives. Prompted by cues in the sides as to how his character interacted with the situational world, Cayonne's evocative, imaginary, top-down images of post-apocalyptic society layered upon his re-imagined familial relationships and direct personal experiences. Guided by prompts from the sides to the character's cognitive scaffolding, Cayonne developed appresentational materials from top-down and bottom-up sources alike: in this instance, the affective match from his quotidian memories of loss in the family aligned with his intrasubjective other-oriented perspective-taking, which drew heavily from Cayonne's purely invented representation of life's hardships under desperately impoverished conditions. Although he felt genuinely emotionally moved by the scene and his immersion in the performance, the self–other distinction kept him grounded in the narrative as it was written, lest he become too absorbed in the dramatic action and start improvising his own narrative as his character. Ultimately, Cayonne's empathetic connection to his scripted character depended upon his ability to make the situational self into a "Minotaur", a strategic bodymind rearrangement that blended his quotidian memories with purely invented imaginations, thereby prompting him to act in the situational world as his character. The balanced approach therefore treats memory and imagination as equally valuable sources of creative fodder to be re-arranged and reorganized, as opposed to relying primarily on specified affective common denominators, or the overlapped place between relevant abstractions.

Lisinska uses a similar strategy to Cayonne's Minotaur-making when preparing for a film shoot by loading objects in her physical environment, from props to wardrobe to furniture, with appresentational meanings. Embellishing upon a technique first presented to her by an Adler-based acting instructor, Lisinska externalizes the cues towards her characters' cognitive scaffolding by figuring out how her character relates to her surroundings. References from Lisinska's quotidian experiences and imaginative capacity are freely and openly blended as she attaches her appresentations to significant objects in her character's presence. This practice is predicated on the presumption that the affective connotations of an everyday object, from a family heirloom to a mundane piece of furniture in one's home, are evidence of how a self relates to her environment. Lisinska insists that these re-imagined objects help her to feel grounded on set by transferring her character's relationship to her environment to on-set objects:

> You have so much around you that you need to explore and interact with, and then you start to graft ideas your interaction. If my character is eating breakfast, for example, it looks like I'm eating it the first time, but I actually know exactly what word I eat the toast on, and I know exactly what breath I'm going to pick up my mug of coffee, and there's an organic emotional connection to the mug, the coffee, the toast, everything. That is film acting!³¹

Lisinska's object-oriented balanced approach supports her intrasubjective bonds by testing them with preparatory enactments: if the appresentations linked to an object are powerful enough to propel narrative actions, they likely also suggest connotations about the character's cognitive scaffolding. By grafting emotionally charged ideas into the objects around her, Lisinska trusts in her ability to access the accompanying affective prompts from those objects so they can emotionally trigger relevant aspects of her performance.³² In the scene Lisinska described where her character has toast and coffee for breakfast, the appresentational relationship that Lisinska ascribes to the coffee mug and the toast are loaded with character information: if the mug, for example, is a precious family heirloom made of fragile porcelain, the prop will prompt Lisinska to ponder her character's relationship with her family, her social choice to use precious tableware for a mundane breakfast, the care or recklessness with which she handles the mug, the socio-economic implications about the quality of coffee served within the mug, etc. This flooding of her working memory with imaginary meanings pinned onto objects in the *mise-en-scène* demonstrates the cooperation of her default and executive control networks by giving her working memory an action plan drawn from affective personal recollections as her character's situational self. Lisinska's script analysis practice therefore anticipates her collaboration with key production personnel, such as the art director, costume designer, and scenic decorators.

Lisinska's interrogation of the objects in the character's world mirrors the interview-like questions that Cayonne uses to flesh out his character's lived world in that they both prompt the actor to search through their creative impressions of a scripted character until they find sufficient resonant and evocative material to translate the scripted character into their bodies. Whether this search prompts a compelling affective match before, after, or along with the taking of the other's perspective is less important than the ultimate goal of establishing an the intrasubjective connection with the scripted character by whatever means best present themselves.

The similarities in their analysis habits are not especially surprising when one considers that Lisinska and Cayonne studied acting together for four years at Ryerson University in Toronto, which hosts one of the most prolific and longstanding BFA Acting programs in the Canadian university system. Their related-but-distinct practices reflect the highly individual nature of analysis and, vicariously, performance habits. That Lisinska and Cayonne have comparable levels of professional experience, nearly identical training, and a strong personal friendship to boot, and still use different preparation habits when presented with new scripts underlines the fact that actors assert control over their work by doing what works for themselves individually, rather than slavishly adhering to a single "correct" system. The balanced approach to script analysis clearly supports actors in using whatever recalled and imagined material that the actor deems useful in establishing a viable and enactable intrasubjective connection with the scripted character.

Like the bottom-up and top-down script analysis practices, the balanced approach supports the development of an intrasubjective connection between the actor and the scripted character by giving the actor access to all of her imaginary and recalled fodder to establish the necessary appresentations. All of these script analysis habits position the actor's assertion of control over her intrasubjective bond as the essential pre-filming homework: there is simply not enough time for all of the exploratory work alleviated by these script analysis habits once filming begins. At the same time, this assertion of control over one's preparation practice always anticipates collaboration on set and the dispersal of trust across key production staff. The wealth of creative material generated in Lisinska and Cayonne's balanced approaches to script analysis is well-suited to creating options that will accommodate the inevitable creative adjustments that the actor will have to make on set. After all, once on set, the actor must also attend to the intersubjective and performative bonds that she has—hopefully—anticipated in her script analysis homework.

Conclusion: Arriving on Set

The common assumption is that the actor must arrive on set with a compelling—if preliminary—intrasubjective connection. The intrasubjective appresentations that enable this connection likely stem from the quotidian actor's combination of recalled memories that are in some way informative to the situational character's experience and wholly imagined bodymind references. Since very few actors rely exclusively on purely remembered or purely invented character references, the Cayonne's Minotaur of the strategic re-assemblage of bodymind resources becomes the situational character's cognitive architecture as embodied by the actor.

At the same time, the actor knows full well that her intrasubjective connection will continue to develop once she starts to form intersubjective connections with her fellow actors, and performative connections through collaborations with the director and the camera. The next chapter analyzes common on-set tactics for making that intrasubjective connection legible alongside and within the intersubjective and performative solicitations.

Notes

1. Lauren MacKinlay (actor/producer), in discussion with the author, October 2016.
2. Feagin, "Empathizing as simulating," pp. 158–61.
3. Italian stage actress Eleonora Duse once famously impressed Stanislavsky by visibly blushing during a performance when her character flirted with the object of her affection. Both Meisner and Strasberg invoked Duse's Blush as evidence of a deep and compelling bodymind immersion within the drama's Magic If. For more on the history of Duse's Blush, see Sharon Carnicke's *Stanislavsky in Focus: An Acting Master for the Twenty-First Century* (2009).
4. Jamie Spilchuk (actor), in discussion with the author, August 2016.
5. Levinson, "The auteur renaissance, 1968–1980," p. 101.
6. Sheila McCarthy (actor), in discussion with the author, September 2016.

7. Natalie Lisinska (actor), in discussion with the author, October 2016.
8. Natalie Lisinska (actor), in discussion with the author, October 2016.
9. See Chapter 6 for more about Lisinska's creative process while shooting this scene.
10. Kevin McGarry (actor), in discussion with the author, August 2016.
11. Kevin McGarry (actor), in discussion with the author, August 2016.
12. For an extensive analysis of how physical—rather than imaginary—costume pieces can also help to reorganize the actor's body schema, see Sarah E. McCarroll's "The historical body map: cultural pressures on embodied cognition," in *Theatre, Performance, and Cognition* (2016), edited by Rhonda Blair and Amy Cook.
13. Clayton also administers and teaches the same techniques at the Western Professional Actors Lab in Vancouver.
14. Feinstein, "Archetypes," p. 232.
15. See Chapter 1 for a more detailed comparison of the physical scales of screen and theatrical acting.
16. Bruce Clayton, masterclass at Professional Actors Lab, Toronto, Canada, October 2008.
17. At the actor's request, this film shall remain anonymous.
18. Pierce, "Portfolio 20: Anthony Hopkins and Jodie Foster: 'The Silence of the Lambs' (1991)," p. 106.
19. Weber, "Cozying up to the psychopath that lurks deep within," H1.
20. Ebert, "The Silence of the Lambs movie review (1991) | Roger Ebert."
21. Cavell, "Reflections on the ontology of film," p. 30.
22. Ibid. pp. 29–30.
23. Sheila McCarthy (actor), in discussion with the author, September 2016.
24. Beaty and Jung, "Interacting brain networks underlying creative cognition and artistic performance," p. 276.
25. Ibid. p. 276.
26. Ibid. pp. 276, 280.
27. Meisner and Longwell, *On Acting*, p. 128.
28. Antonio Cayonne (actor), in discussion with the author, August 2016.
29. Antonio Cayonne (actor), in discussion with the author, August 2016.
30. At the actor's request, the title of this production has been anonymized.
31. Natalie Lisinska (actor), in discussion with the author, October 2016.
32. Mirodan, "Acting and emotion," pp. 106–7.

CHAPTER 6

Empathy on Set

With the preparatory homework completed and the shooting schedule underway, the actor expands her empathy-soliciting efforts beyond the script-based intrasubjective work to accommodate the industrial circumstances of film production. The actor's wholehearted commitment to the collaborative process of film production relies heavily on her habits for soliciting empathetic connections while navigating the film set's industrial culture. These immersive habits help the actor to become "in the moment," not only despite the flurry of industrial constraints but also *because* of their habits' creative affordances.

This chapter explores how the on-set empathy-soliciting habits of professional screen actors navigate film production's industrial culture while simultaneously producing the necessary intrasubjective, intersubjective, and performative empathetic bonds. Although hardly an exhaustive account of all the possible habits that an actor may use on set to transform industrial constraints into empathetic affordances, the habits described here had sufficient consensus among the interviewees as viable practices to warrant their inclusion and analysis. Generally speaking, this chapter examines some ways in which actors navigate the cognitive ecology of a film set's industrial culture, collaborate with the camera, and then mobilize that collaboration to establish and configure their empathetic bonds.

Actors and Production Culture: Inductive, Ecumenical, and Self-effacing Practices on Set

Whereas industrial circumstances like shooting schedules and budgets are important details for a given production's on-set culture, the interpersonal collaborative politics of production culture shape actors' on-set work industry-wide. John Caldwell suggests that the industrial culture of film production manifests in distinct patterns of activities through which the entire filmmaking crew "theorize[s] through practice"[1] as to how film ought to be made. Specifically, what Caldwell identifies as the inductive, ecumenical, and self-effacing patterns of practice resonate well with my interviewees' experiences of how actors collaborate with production staff on set, which inevitably shapes the culture in which the actors perform.

The inductive practices of invoking ideas from well-known pieces of literary theory, historical analogy, aesthetic philosophy, and other intellectual references, emerge within the creative collaboration between the actor, screenwriter, and director. For example, MacFadzean's anecdote from Chapter 4 about playing an "interesting" defense attorney instead of a stock caricature demonstrates this inductive production logic through his skillful play with the genre conventions of police procedural television. In this instance, MacFadzean relies on the latent potential for "interesting" performance choices within the sides, as well as the willingness of a director to incorporate a relatively unanticipated and nuanced dramatic moment, which is perhaps in excess of any original planning, into the greater narrative structure.

For many actors, the very act of introducing a compelling intrasubjective association or conscious performance choice within the Cayonne's Minotaur of the situational character—either an imaginative literary metaphor wrapped around the character, or invoking a potent personal trigger—is an inductive aesthetic praxis about how artistic theory can inform the actor's creative work. As just one example, actor Lindsey Middleton explicitly used some of her very recently learned Strasbergian techniques for an episode of popular webseries *Out With Dad* (Jason Leaver, 2010–17). Middleton felt that the intense emotional content of that episode, in which her teenaged character is disowned by her family for her sexuality, would be better served by different acting techniques than she normally uses for her recurring character on that show:

> I just recently started studying Strasberg, so I did all of that kind of prep for this episode. I read the scene, I used [emotional] triggers like we talked about in class. On set, I was ready. In the first take, we've all got tears streaming down our faces. I just let the emotions hit me. When we cut, [the director] said "okay, we don't need to do that again." He said, "that's not what I thought it would be at all. It's so different from what I expected, but I love it this way. We're moving on!"[2]

Middleton's aesthetic judgment and creative approach to this scene contained none of the overt literary references that she might otherwise draw upon, such as a visual or textual analogy to Capulet's attack on Juliet for refusing Paris's proposal. Instead, Middleton's inductive willingness to

Figure 6.1 Lindsey Middleton in *Out With Dad*, season 3, episode 5, "Outed" (Jason Leaver, JLeaver Presentations, 2013)

make Strasbergian performance theory practical for this particular scene led to a compelling performance.

The ecumenical nature of film production, which Caldwell describes as the willingness to "use any solution (any aesthetic tradition or theoretical perspective) as long as it provides a tool to overcome some obstacle or key that fits the film,"[3] is a mixed blessing for the actor. On one hand, this relationship with the production's logistical strategy generally constrains the actor's inclinations towards an inductive performance choice. During production, it is frequently more time- and cost-efficient for the producer to sacrifice consideration of a bold acting choice in the service of a complex auteurist shot composition so that production can better remain on schedule. The ecumenical impulse thus echoes actor/producer Lauren MacKinlay's description[4] of how the creative and industrial priorities of a film shoot are reflected in the shooting schedule: on a film shoot with tight budget, time, and technical constraints, if key production staff deem it more advantageous to marginalize an actor's work in favor of obtaining useable, affordable, timely, and feasible footage, then so be it.

On the other hand, the ecumenical impulse can also afford additional responsibilities to the actor with directors who are open to placing significant narrational weight on acting work, as was the case with Middleton's use of Strasbergian techniques for *Out With Dad*.[5] The need to work amidst a shoot's logistical constraints prompts many actors to start looking for implicit affordances for compelling performance choices. Not surprisingly, many of the actorly examples in this chapter demonstrate the creativity with which screen actors transform performance constraints into affordances by working with what they already have and determining what can be generated quickly.

To that end, many actors rehearse their scenes in part by compartmentalizing the character's emotional journey into sections that do not need to be performed during each rehearsal if the actor understands the emotional arc of each section. This practice of "marking" the key moments allows her to focus her attention on mid-scene moments without needing to perform the entire lead-up to those moments every single time, while still keeping the narrative and emotional journey of the full scene in mind. Edward Warburton suggests that marking a performance while rehearsing it—or between takes on a film set—is a form of cognitive load reduction that lets the performer conserve her focus and expend her creative energy more efficiently by not exhausting herself with full preparations every time a new take starts.[6] If a scene is shot out of narrative sequence or if the director wishes to shoot additional takes after an emotionally intense moment, for example, this ecumenical strategy helps an actor on set to quickly immerse herself into a given moment without needing to fully perform the prior emotional climax every single time; as Natalie Lisinska indicated in the crying scenes from her role on *Mary Kills People*,[7] performing intense emotions day in and day out can be an exhausting but unavoidable prospect in film and television production.

Lastly, although the notion of an actor's work as self-effacing is complicated by actor MacFadzean's assertion that screen actors must "want to be seen",[8] many on-set actors have a palpable sense of being production craftspeople like the rest of the crew. MacFadzean tempers the urgency of the actor's "want to be seen" by explaining that some acting roles are more about narrative function than character expression: to draw again on his example of the defense attorney character from Chapter 4, an actor may have narrational opportunities to make a stock character more compelling, but sometimes the director "just wants the defense attorney, just a guy in a nice suit"[9] to feed the antagonistic client his lines.

Like editors, lighting technicians, and other typically self-effacing production roles,[10] actors in these kinds of functional roles are particularly valued for their adaptable pragmatism: doing whatever needs to be done to tell the story with no visible pretense to overtly show off or self-promote one's individual contribution. The screen actor's performance is always constrained—productively or otherwise—by the shot scale and camera angle, which has inevitable consequences for how the actor must perform as opposed to how she might otherwise like to perform. By positioning the filmmaking process as "a process of physical problem solving based on the obligatory need to overcome production obstacles",[11] Caldwell and the actors' testimonies position actors as welcome and expert co-collaborators in the production process, while also underscoring the lack of any particularly privileged status in that process.

This effectively likens the actor's work to the creative and industrial "problem-solving" work that John Caldwell associates with both "above the line" production staff, such as directors and producers, and "below the line" production laborers, such as gaffers and on-set carpenters. If film production is "essentially a process of physical problem-solving based on an obligatory need to overcome production obstacles,[12] then the actor's agency in meaningfully contributing towards her final performance stems largely from her ability to collaborate within the constraints and affordances of production culture and its industrial logistics. As actors Joe Dinicol and Natalie Lisinska both bluntly explain, "you just have to make it work."

When looking at film and television shoots as distributed cognition networks wherein filmmaking practitioners with vastly different skill-sets think together to record footage of the narrative being performed, it becomes clear that the cognitive ecology which facilitates performance creation does not inherently prioritize acting work. For example, while the director being a key collaborator for the actor is unsurprising, the nature of that creative collaboration is far from guaranteed. Nearly every actor interviewed for this study described collaborations with directors who were deeply invested in the actor's performance as well as—and more frequently—film shoots where the director was fundamentally more interested in cinematographic and *mise-en-scène* concerns than the actor's work. On such shoots, the actors are little more than the director's unpredictable afterthoughts: as MacFadzean summarizes, "sometimes they just want you to do your thing, say your words, and then get the hell out of the way." In these situations, actors must accept that the director will rarely grant time on set for additional takes to primarily satisfy an actor's creative ideas, and that there may be little patience for a flubbed line during a technically intricate shot. Similarly, a director who is sincerely invested in the actors' work may be under sufficient time restraints to push through production with a shooting schedule that is disadvantageous to the actor's sense of dramatic continuity and that has little room for indulgent supplementary takes. Therefore, screen acting can only produce performances within the industrial affordances of the set's cognitive ecology, from the camera and microphone positioning, to the availability of wardrobe and make-up personnel, to the preselection of the daily shooting script, and so on. The greater system of fictional film and television narrative production cannot complete its verisimilar narratives without actors establishing specific kinds of empathetic links with other selves. Acting work forms a vital network of distributed cognition within the rest of the film set, but the total cognitive ecology of the film set expands far beyond the concerns of the actor. This chapter therefore examines actorly tactics for synchronizing her empathetic solicitations within the film set's cognitive ecology, establishing her network of distributed creative cognition within the constraints, affordances, and collaborative opportunities that present themselves.

The actor's creative collaboration with her fellow actors, her industrial collaboration with the production team, and her ongoing rapport with the director, must always navigate the industrial dynamics of scarcity, urgency, and precarity, which shape the actor's ability to solicit and sustain compelling empathetic connections on set. Just as actorly training encultures the actor's self-organizing bodymind with techniques and habits for verisimilar performance, screen media's industrial culture contextualizes the actor's working conditions to produce screen-specific performances. This industrial re-enculturation carries ramifications for how actors solicit and sustain their empathetic connections.

The Actor and the Camera: Habits, Techniques, and Technology

Actor Jamie Spilchuk rightly indicates that the collaboration between the actor and the camera is an essential prerequisite for screen performances:

> If you took out the actors, you could still film the nice set. You could still add subtitles over the nice set. Without the camera, none of this comes together, so [. . .] it's one of the main collaborators, along with the writer, the director, the crew. The camera is there to work with everyone.[13]

The camera is both an enabling affordance and productive constraint on the screen actor's work, and therefore a powerful node in on-set acting's network of distributed cognition. On one hand, the camera's angle, scale, lens, focus, movement, etc. afford the actor a range of options for adjusting their performance for the intended level of visibility. Inversely, the actor's primary on-set contribution to her performance is constrained by its proximity to the camera and its accompanying sound-recording technology: on a foundational level, the actor's performance can only manifest within the finished film if the actor's performance was recorded.[14]

These formal constraints are hardly specific to screen acting. Theater actors must also factor medium-specific affordances into their performance adjustments, such as venue size, open-air versus enclosed performance venue, stage shape, site specificity, multimedia inclusions, and so on. Lutterbie describes the stage actor's relationship with performance spaces as a series of technical adjustments to make the performance legible within the space, emphasizing that the actors' performances should "fill the container" of the theater.[15] Because of the camera's capacity to move between takes and during performance, however, screen actors must fill their performance space while accepting camera usage as co-creative participatory force in the creation of the performance, above and beyond the theater actor's vocal adjustments for a large auditorium, and similar passive concerns. The camera literally mediates the screen actor's ability to fill her performance space, and therefore fundamentally alters the actor's address to the spectator. Whereas stage actors aspire to fill a static stage, screen actors personalize their performance to accommodate the mobile and malleable camera. As such, MacFadzean explains that the technical adjustments—and their subsequent bodymind reorganizations—that the screen actor makes to tailor the performance towards the camera require a firm understanding of how the co-collaborative camera will capture the actor's work:

> The technical stuff is, "here's the box you're going to live in. Here's the fence that goes around you. That's as much as you can use." It's like having a dog: "Here are the rules of your life. If you follow those rules, you can do whatever you want. Within those rules, you have freedom."[16]

The metaphor of animal training is fitting for actors like MacFadzean who have had to adjust their stage training for regular screen work. Many of the Toronto-based actors included in this study were trained for the stage before starting their screen work.[17] The discipline and skill required to constrain their performances to the "smaller" camera without sacrificing the empathetic immersion, emotional commitment, and narrational intensity requires actors to develop a meaningful relationship with the camera itself.[18] This meaningful relationship transforms the camera into co-collaborator, an active participant that provides an ever-shifting performance space in need of filling.

Even for veteran film actors or those who have trained primarily for the screen, the challenges posed by some technical adjustments require extensive personal focus and trust in the on-set collaboration, using the camera's closeness to get to the performative intimacy that screen acting rewards.[19] Actors have many habits for collaborating with the camera by relating to it as a welcome co-collaborator and as an audience of one. Not surprisingly, the technical underpinnings of the performative empathetic connection are tremendously important at this point in the actor's work: without the explicit self-organization to make one's character and one's relationships as the character compelling to the spectator, screen acting never gets further than an unrecorded experimental rehearsal or a complex and convoluted game of make-believe. Actors solicit the performative connection with the spectator through the camera by manipulating the technical affordances and constraints of on-set working conditions to make their intrasubjective and intersubjective connections lucid and compelling to the spectator. This manipulation begins with learning to trust the camera.

Metaphors of Trust for the Camera

The most overt habit for connecting to the camera is to establish an appresentational metaphor that rewrites the camera's identity as a benign, welcome, and trusted co-collaborator. It is somewhat of an overstatement to suggest that the camera is the target of an intersubjective empathetic bond: the actor's often anthropomorphic metaphor for the camera seems to transform the camera into both a character and co-collaborator with whom to connect. Instead, actors collaborate with the formal affordances and constraints of the camera to intentionally push themselves towards the spectator. The point is not to move the camera as a self, but to push the actor-as-character's intentionality towards the spectator and thereby alleviate creativity-inhibiting awkwardness. Instead, screen actors unanimously agree that some level of comfort with the camera is required before one can produce a compelling on-screen performance, even if the ways in which the actor draws upon and mobilizes that comfort often evolve over the course of her career.

The types of metaphors for the camera discovered in this study reflect the affinity that the actor feels for the camera as well as the agency ascribed to the camera within its collaboration with the actor. A common motif is that the actor re-imagines the camera as a close friend, a lover, a trusted family member, or another person in the actor's life with whom the actor feels very comfortable in being honest and even vulnerable. One actor describes how imagining the camera as his best friend motivates him to make sincere empathetic connections on set because the hypothetically observing best friend would know when he is lying:

> I'm a very private person, and I generally don't open up to a lot of people, so it makes me a troublesome actor sometimes because it can make me shy about sharing. To help

me with that, I imagine that the camera is my best friend in the world. I can share anything, and [the audience] won't know, [the film crew] won't know, but my friend will know. That's been a relationship that I still work on every time I have the chance on set: open up to your best friend, share with your best friend.[20]

The moment in the actor's career in which she first appresents the camera as a trustworthy performance enabler is a life-altering professional revelation. Spilchuk describes the moment when the camera went from being a "terrifying black box" to "my best friend" as an unexpected, gradual, and very welcome transition:

At first, you think, "it's staring right at me!," but one day you think, "Ooh, I want to tell you something!" It really just happened one day, all of a sudden. [. . .] Now, I'm both aware of [the camera] and I don't even notice it.[21]

Although it stands to reason that extensive experiences on set will eventually acclimatize the actor to the camera's presence, the fact that many actors create a benign anthropomorphic metaphor for the camera suggests that the actor seeks a connection with a self that includes but also goes beyond the physical camera. One actor reflects on how his revelatory first moment of being truly comfortable in front of the camera changed his perception of all of his prior screenwork:

I don't think that there's anything that trains you really for the task of completing something intimate while forty crew members are [milling around] and the camera is this weird alien that's there for the first many years that you do it. I look at work that I did when I was younger and it's mostly unwatchable: the camera goes on and I forget how my arms work. On screen, we're supposed to pretend like no one is watching. That's a very difficult hurdle to get over, with the camera being there. You should want to be on camera.[22]

The solicitation of this connection aims beyond the camera as its target because the camera is a surrogate for the audience, in which the actor can easily include herself. At the same time, this anthropomorphized camera becomes a welcome and unthreatening presence who is interested in the actor so that the actor can ignore it. The "best friend" metaphor uses the performative solicitation to support the intrasubjective and intersubjective bonds in that screen acting rewards the intimate smallness of the actor's performance. This intimacy is more readily achieved when the "best friend" camera, as one actor explained, "will know when I am lying and will [support me] when I tell the truth."

For other actors, the metaphorical transition is explicitly bound to an on-set experience that shapes the rest of their careers. In a particularly

142   SCREEN ACTING

poignant example, actor Sheila McCarthy describes the moment while shooting *Stepping Out* (Lewis Gilbert, 1991) that she discovered the trustworthy metaphor for the camera that she continues to embrace in her work. In this film, McCarthy's character's abusive husband Frank (Eugene Robert Glazer) discovers that she has secretly been taking tap-dance lessons, and he threateningly demands that she dance for him. Although McCarthy was already a proficient tap dancer from her contemporaneous musical theater career, the challenge of connecting her intrasubjective love of dance and fear of her husband with the intersubjective need to suffer an emotional breakdown, with the performative need to make her character's anxiety fit within the frame while tap dancing to solicit the intended pathos from the spectator, would be a challenging scene in any circumstances.

The added industrial pressures of being amidst the commotion of a tense Hollywood film set with a demanding director made McCarthy feel creatively blocked and distracted, which iteratively fed her anxieties about shooting the scene in question. Although McCarthy prepared herself in her trailer with music that helped to evoke her appresentational choices, the necessary trust in the camera was ultimately established during an encounter on set with co-star, Liza Minelli:

> Liza came in on her day off, and she stood next to the camera, and every time the cameras rolled, she peeked out from beside the camera and mouthed, "It's okay." [...] The discipline of film acting is being able to unlock [your emotions] every single time [in rapid succession], and so [Minelli] doing that unlocked my emotional life

Figure 6.2 Sheila McCarthy (left) and Eugene Robert Glazer (right) in *Steppin' Out* (Lewis Gilbert, 1991)

for me. It was so generous of her. Then after, when I've had to do big scenes like that, I always imagine Liza beside the camera, and it has continued to work for twenty years: imagining her little face beside the camera, giving me permission to plummet to the depths. I'll never forget that.[23]

McCarthy connects her technical and intrasubjective turmoil with the metaphor for the camera that, as she describes, "unlocks" her ability to perform compellingly in front of the camera. By appresenting the camera as her co-star—quite literally as a respected and friendly co-collaborator—McCarthy demonstrates that the performative solicitation enabled by Minelli-as-camera can support the other two empathetic bonds by freeing McCarthy to trust the camera and, vicariously, herself as a performer.

Many actors' metaphors for the camera reflect the camera's co-collaborative and even ecumenical agency, transforming the camera from "a terrifying 800-pound gorilla into a dog that you can play with."[24] Dinicol insists that actors should treat the camera like a dancing partner, the metaphor of which further likens the camera to a trusted and skilled co-collaborator:

> You have to start making the dance with the camera into something that you can enjoy. You should want to be on camera. You don't want it to get in the way. The only way to ignore [the camera] is for you to make [the dance] a part of [the scene]. As much as I say that there's an intimacy on film—because the camera isn't a person but a thing—you have to invite the camera into the dance.[25]

As actors become increasingly comfortable with working in front of the camera, the metaphors for the camera shift from establishing trust to mobilizing co-collaboration. This dance with technology still presumes trust, but now prioritizes how the camera becomes a versatile, co-collaborative conduit through which the actor can solicit the spectator's empathetic connection.

Relatability Revisited

In a parallel metaphor for collaborating with the camera, actor Kevin McGarry thinks of the camera as a filter for his performances. Every detail of the camera set-up, from the lighting and lens size to the location of the microphones and the staging, indicates how the rest of the production crew intends to shape his performance:

> Your performance is getting filtered through [the whole formal set-up] to fit into the camera. It's the audio recording, it's what the shape of the lens does to your face in different set-ups, everything. There are ways to use the camera to your advantage,

and I'm on a big curve of learning as much as I can. Basically, try to get the best understanding of what's going on because it will only enhance your performance.[26]

By understanding what the rest of the production team intends to filter into and out of his performance, McGarry asserts additional control over his performance by self-organizing his performing bodymind to make his solicitation to the spectator as compelling as possible. McGarry's task on set is therefore to provide the raw performed material for that filtering process. In fact, the capacity to imagine and even appresent the intended final shot allows McGarry to solicit a more compelling connection from his anticipated audience by imagining himself as part of that audience. By appresenting himself within that anticipated audience, McGarry can self-organize his bodymind around producing performances that he himself would find compelling, drawing on his extensive experience with studying his own work on screen and also his deep-seated belief in acting's capacity to inspire:

> I really love the idea that an actor can inspire somebody. I don't know if I always wanted to be an actor, but I definitely always wanted to be all these things that I saw actors doing on tv. Then I thought, "If I'm an actor, I can be a doctor, and an astronaut, and a cowboy, all these things!" It's this ability to elicit something—an emotion or inspiration—in people that makes me love my job.[27]

McGarry's relatability therefore extends beyond the emotional atomization of narrative moments to include the performed articulation of that moment, with the actor using herself—or more specifically, her insights from critiquing her own performances—as a litmus test of reacting to her performance and appresenting potential future self-organizations of her bodymind instrument. Although many actors reassess their need to study each of their screen performances throughout their careers,[28] a solid working understanding of how to coordinate one's performing bodymind with the filtering camera is essential for an actor's contribution to the final edited performance.

This collaboration with the filtering camera expands upon how the actor works during auditions because of the vastly expanded range of formal affordances on set, as compared to the limited resources of the casting director's office. Whereas actors eventually become quite comfortable with the basic formal set-up of a screen audition space,[29] the potential formal flamboyance of a professional film shoot demands that the actor has a deep and versatile capacity to collaborate—if not "dance"—with the camera.

In expanding McGarry's relatability to on-set performances, the actor solicits the spectator's empathetic connection in part by envisioning herself as a potential spectator. This solicitation mirrors the appresentation-building process of how actors reconstruct the scripted character's cognitive scaffolding during script analysis. Both processes reorganize the actor's bodymind as a dynamic system to solicit connections with a personal self that is distinct from the self that makes the solicitation. The quotidian actor draws on textual cues to reorganize herself as the character's situational self with immediate personal feedback on the connection's likely compellingness. The situational self then pushes her intentionality towards the anticipated spectators, one of which may be the quotidian actor herself. This performative connection must wait, however, until post-production is done before receiving that same personal feedback. This mirroring of connections, from the quotidian self to the situational self, and then back from the situational self to the quotidian self, is therefore deeply dependent on the actor's collaboration with the camera, which is itself dependent on the actor's trust in the camera as a welcome, benign, and skillful dancing partner.

All of that said, the actor's metaphors for the camera are only of value to the actor if they support her empathetic solicitations once the camera is rolling. Although the intimacy of screen acting technique certainly influences the intrasubjective connection, the metaphorical relationship with the camera is often productively mobilized to establish and sustain the intersubjective and performative bonds, on the assumption that the pre-shooting intrasubjective work will be made vicariously lucid once the intersubjective and performative bonds are in place.

The Other Actor: Creative Labor and Intersubjective Empathy on Set

Actors whose training prioritizes intersubjective connections must mobilize their camera metaphor in a way that supports intimacy and sincerity among actors, in the hopes that an established intersubjective connection will support the realization of the other connections. The intersubjective connection among screen actors on set is, however, fraught with industrial complications. First and foremost, the frequent lack of rehearsal time on set means that the actor must arrive with sufficient intrasubjective preparation already finished so that she can focus on connecting with her colleagues as much as possible. Many of the interviewed actors describe past film shoots where the closest thing to an off-camera rehearsal was a brief dialogue run at the craft services table or while being styled in the make-up trailer immediately before shooting a scene. These impromptu rehearsals are often rushed and better suited to reassuring the actor that she has memorized her lines than to making new creative discoveries.

As MacFadzean explains, "sometimes you end up on set with another actor who you've barely met who is playing your wife of twenty-five years. 'And, action!'" Nevertheless, McCarthy insists that the most important habit for an actor to embrace when creating a verisimilar illusion on-screen is to "play with the other actor, like in a tennis game."[30] The iterative progression of dramatic material between actors provides, for McCarthy and many other actors, a key starting point around which to anchor the rest of their empathetic relationships.

This tactic of beginning on-set work with connecting to one's scene partner is predicated on several assumptions about on-set working conditions. First, the actor assumes that her pre-shooting intrasubjective connections can be refined and strengthened through the iterative relationship with her scene partner. McCarthy, for example, revels in acting gigs where her intrasubjective work is bolstered and reshaped by her intersubjective bonds with her scene-partners-as-characters:

> The actual moment where acting feels best is when everyone is so in-the-moment that I have no idea what is going to come out of my mouth when I speak. I did the movie *George's Island* with Maury Chaykin, and when acting with him, I don't remember learning any of my lines. When you're working with someone [who really tries to work with you], it's like playing jazz with them because every take is entirely different from the one before, and yet we're saying the same words each time. It's really something great.[31]

Actors like McCarthy who excel at this deeply intersubjective work must also vicariously trust that their scene partner wants to work just as intensely in front of the camera with them, spurred by the professional urgency of having little to no rehearsal time prior to shooting. In finding those moments of near-improvisation with the scene in which the characters body image and body schema come together in a compelling situational self,[32] actors align the efforts of their executive control and default networks to produce the intended emotional state.[33] The end result does not need to be fully predictable for the dynamic system between the actors to be a productive force in narrative production.[34] Finally, these actors must trust that the co-collaborative camera and its accompanying production staff will adequately record the iterative exchange between the actors.

Dinicol's Jazz: Habits of Fostering Spontaneity through Structured Improvisation

The on-set habits for quickly establishing compelling intersubjective relationships often presume that the actors must be able to collaborate with each other as professionals before they can productively enworld each other's characters. The pragmatic and ecumenical nature[35] of this intersubjective solicitation is well-realized by actors who are extensively trained in Meisner's Method.

Joe Dinicol, an actor whose practice is heavily influenced by Meisner's Method, views his pre-shooting homework as a necessary foundation for fostering spontaneous and seemingly genuine reactions to his scene partner while filming. Although Dinicol rigorously studies the sides for his scenes for empathetic cues, to gain insight into his character's cognitive scaffolding, and to memorize his dialogue, he makes no firm decisions about how he will perform any given moment. Instead, he defers as many creative choices as possible until he is on set with his scene partner, on the presumption that his actions are only relevantly verisimilar when they are reactions to the scene partner. In fact, Dinicol makes a point of studying the other characters lines as much as his own to give him as much of an understanding as possible to the social context of the narrative moment without predetermining how the narrative will play out:

> A big part [of my script prep] will be about the other person's lines: "they say this and that, and then I feel this" and then you attach your line to that thing, as opposed to going though your stuff, most of it is needing to hear what's coming at me. That's what's going to build the logic of all the things that I say. [Everything] changes when you're sitting up against another human who's done their own work and maybe doesn't say [his lines] the way you thought he would.[36]

Dinicol therefore positions the sides as a binding but non-prescriptive template for a performance, wherein the vital details of its execution will be determined when they are enacted by himself and his fellow performers. Dinicol's preparation therefore depends on developing volatile appresentations, wherein the incomplete cognitive scaffolding of the character intentionally pulls the actor towards a self that is internally cohesive as a situational self while leaving opportunities for significant variations in the details about that self. Moreover, in deferring the decision about those details to the affordances of the on-set collaboration, Dinicol's description of his work prompts a comparison between Meisner's acting technique and how jazz musicians improvise together within the framework of a song's melody and chord chart.

Just as jazz musicians use the rhythmic, emotive, melodic, harmonic, and spontaneous affordances of the jazz chart to coordinate and communicate their largely improvised performance choices to each other,[37] screen actors that embrace Meisner's Method aspire to enworld each other within the drama by establishing an iterative loop of action and reaction.

Implicit within this style of iterative connection is that the performers are in sufficient control of their bodymind instrument to be able to trust that their spontaneous reactions will sustain the flow of the aesthetic text. This is important because the intense and desired intersubjective connection often requires the performer to devalue self-control in favor of attentive collaboration. Frederick Seddon argues that collaborating jazz musicians must "decenter" themselves in order to creatively attune to themselves to the rest of the ensemble, resulting in "an atmosphere of trust [and] creative risk-taking."[38] Similarly, Dinicol insists that Meisnerian screen acting forces the actor to "leave yourself alone" to better connect with one's scene partner:

> "Putting your attention on someone else" is a great tool when you get to a new set and you don't know anyone. You decide, "Okay, well, I can just pay attention to the person in front of me, and they'll give me all this information and all this stuff that I can use." The idea is that you leave yourself alone: the better I know the lines, the more I can stand across from someone—like in the Meisner exercise—and just see what happens.[39]

This decentered approach to collaborative performance, predicated on exceptional preparation, command of one's instrument, and capacity to improvise within the volatile opportunities afforded by the scripted text, constructs the actor's empathetic solicitations in complex but dramatically compelling ways.

For example, Dinicol's Jazz defers the intrasubjective affective match to the intentional pull of the intersubjective other-oriented perspective taking. In other words, this approach to screen acting insists that the actor's experience of her character's feelings is so contingent on the interaction with another actor-as-character that the exchange between the actors-as-characters can be anticipated from prompts in the sides but not fully scripted, per se. This deferral echoes Toronto-based screen acting instructor Bruce Clayton's advice that performing screen actors use their partner's faces as mirrors for the emotional efficacy of their own performance.[40] In this mirror metaphor, the performing actor can vicariously watch her own performance in how it produces reactions in her scene partner. The verisimilar illusion constructed here is predicated on the perception that the emotional exchange between the actors is indeed playing out in real time.

The connection between jazz performance and Meisnerian screen acting is both the creative attunement to one's fellow performers and also the trust among the performers in the reciprocated, iterative "permissions" to react as they will: as long as the reactions are iterative, spontaneous, and aesthetically consistent, the presumption is that the performance will be compelling. These permissions, as Dinicol describes them, can be an implicit working condition as well as an explicit declaration of the intention to experiment creatively with the intersubjective empathetic connection.

For example, Dinicol explains the process of shooting *Passchendaele* (Paul Gross, 2008) as a particularly rewarding instance of decentering and trust among actors. In an emotionally charged scene filmed quite early in the production process, Dinicol's character instigates a drunken fistfight. The subtext of this scene is that his character's mental state is destabilizing rapidly. Dinicol's scene partner, actor Gil Bellows, made a point of helping Dinicol to overcome the immediate challenges instigated by the shooting schedule: namely, that Dinicol would have to perform an emotionally intense scene with personal safety consequences without first establishing a personal and professional rapport with his new colleagues. Bellows not only personally introduced himself prior to shooting but also gave Dinicol explicit professional permission to approach the fistfight sequence with whatever level of ferocity Dinicol wished.

With the explicit permission to "really come after [Bellows]" in place, both actors were able to "jam" with each other throughout the entire shoot because of the ongoing tacit and explicit agreements to support each other:

> I just let go of control, and a big part of that was being given permission, which is a big struggle—especially in film acting—especially because of the circumstances under which we do it. [There are] strangers every time you start a job; it's not a theatre company of people that we know. You're learning new people, how they work, what their boundaries are, and so permission to go for it becomes enormous. Any time you can either read that in someone's eyes, or you get to work with someone who you've worked with before, or someone like [Bellows] takes you aside and says "no holds barred. Just go. Just fucking go," it's so creatively liberating.[41]

Figure 6.3 Joe Dinicol (left) and Gil Bellows (right) in *Passchendaele* (Paul Gross, 2008)

Dinicol and Bellows were therefore able to overcome common industrial challenges to screen acting practices—the lack of rehearsal time, the economic pressure to produce compelling acting work on a major film shoot, the quotidian social dynamics of performing a physically and emotionally intense scene with a relative stranger—by agreeing to decenter their attention and establish an iterative collaboration grounded in the criterion of intersubjective care.

Significantly, Dinicol clarifies that the decentering of his attention is neither a casual disregard for his own performance nor an unflinching focus on his scene partner. The in-the-moment-ness of Dinicol's Jazz requires the actor to be an active reactor to his scene partner, confident that their mastery of their instruments and the spontaneity enabled by their firmly established intrasubjective understandings, will create compelling performances. In a way, the paradox of "being so well prepared that you can forget everything" fosters a vibrant intersubjective solicitation from both performers, who must quickly adapt to each other's spontaneity. And yet, Dinicol is reluctant to describe this collaboration as more than being open to the scene partner's iterative reactions:

> The word "focus" implies that I'm trying to do something other than accomplish an objective: "I want to hit this moment where I get sad for a second and they see it and then they feel a thing for my sadness." You start planning out the whole scene, and that's what you want to stay away from. [. . .] [For example,] Trying to pick where you win in the fight is a clear thing to steer clear from. The fun of film is finding where you win it in that particular take. If you're with a good actor who is really fighting back, they know that they need to lose the fight at some point, but they won't give up without a fight. You don't have to plan anything. You can go in and say "Let's [jam with each other] and see what happens because we might find something beautiful and then it will be captured on film."[42]

As an on-set collaboration, Dinicol's Jazz is as much the active solicitation of an intersubjective connection as the immersion of oneself in the scene partner's intentional pull. Moreover, Dinicol's knowledge that only the best take of the fistfight scene would appear in the final film gave him further creative freedom to "just go for it," confident that director and co-star Paul Gross would likely give his actors another take, if necessary. As such, the Dinicol's Jazz approach to collaborative screen acting accommodates the industrial culture and logistics of film production by assuming that additional takes are inevitable, especially when key production staff, such as directors and DOPs, add performance refining collaborations of their own. Dinicol's Jazz asserts agency within these inevitable extra takes by making the actors take responsibility for the verisimilar worlds they co-create in front of the camera. The hope is that this co-created world is sufficiently compelling to inspire performance-refining additional takes while not making the actors seem "liable" for any perceived slowing down of production.

Empathetically, the intersubjective connections between Dinicol and Bellows, and those between Dinicol and Bellows-as-character, stem from the actors' professional habits for fostering spontaneity. First, Dinicol and Bellows ensure that their on-set relationship affords the necessary intersubjective appresentations by agreeing that they will follow each other's creative lead. By committing to enworlding each other through iterative performance choices based on spontaneously reciprocated reactions, the intersubjective appresentations rely heavily on the decentered attention's ability to support each other's other-oriented perspective-taking, upon which the intrasubjective affective match is contingent. The intersubjective affective match in Dinicol's Jazz is about "leaving yourself alone" and attending to the scene partners, so the affective match here is primarily a synchronization of the affective conditions of the co-created situational world. This affective match is therefore located in both the primary intersubjective connection between the quotidian actors and the secondary intersubjective connection between the actor and the scene-partner as character: Bellows's explicit permission for Dinicol to "go for it," and the reliance of each actor on decentered attention to the other, supports a potent overall intersubjective empathetic bond.

A theoretical complication arises, however, with the accounting for the self–other distinctions in Dinicol's Jazz: how does the actor decenter herself *and* continue to perceive herself as a distinct self from the person with whom she empathizes? In this case, the intersubjective self–other distinction is largely an extension of the intrasubjective self–other distinction, which is established during the intensive preparatory work that Dinicol describes. The actor's script analysis is geared towards supporting the actor in making her own creative contributions that feed the iterative on-set collaboration; even improvisatory jazz musicians still need to know what song that they are playing, what key they will play it in, and how the melody generally relates to the supporting harmonic structure. The imperative of "leave yourself alone" reminds the Dinicol's Jazz actor to let the iterative performed relationship play out spontaneously, rather than willing a particular performed moment to play out in a pre-determined way. It is the quotidian actor's self that must "leave alone" the actor-as-character's situational self, at least while the camera is rolling. Between takes, however, the quotidian self may return to seek collaborative refinements from her on-set colleagues. This underscores the situational-ness of the situational actor-as-character: the only selves that the actor must oscillate between during film production are her quotidian and situational selves. Therefore, the actor must self-organize into a sufficiently developed intrasubjective situational self that the situational character alone pilots the actor's bodymind once the director calls "action!" The predication of situational difference in the intrasubjective bond translates directly into the intersubjective self–other distinction. Besides, the industrial practicality of the actor only needing to play the role for which she has been hired should be sufficient to prevent her from intersubjectively losing herself to her scene partner. "Decentering," in Dinicol's Jazz, is therefore not synonymous with "self-erasure," "carelessness," or "passivity"; rather, it is an amplified and ecumenical attention to the scene partner explicitly to motivate appropriately matching actions and reactions in oneself.

Ultimately, the comparative weakness of a distinctly intersubjective self–other distinction is more of a theoretical than a practical problem. In practice, the risk of the intersubjective self–other distinction failing while shooting is that the actor is so excessively enworlded that she loses the ability to recall her lines since her decentered focus has counter-intuitively pulled her out of the iterative rapport. If this were to happen, the director would likely shoot another take,[43] and thereby move production along.

Habits of Comedic Screen Acting: Tennis Matches and McCarthy's Symphony

Although many actors would describe the freedom to experiment creatively with their scene partners as beneficial and would embrace the jazz analogy, not all bestow the same trust on the semi-improvisatory nature of Dinicol's Jazz. Sheila McCarthy also describes her on-set habits as an intense collaboration with her scene partners, even likening her performances alongside skilled star actors to a jazz improvisation: "every take is entirely different than the one before, and yet we're saying the same words. It's really something great."[44] However, where McCarthy differs from Dinicol is her embrace of premeditated tactical decisions and her close attention to the rhythms and paces of the sides' dialogue. This is particularly true for McCarthy when working on comedic film and television, in which the intersubjective enworlding relies heavily on the technical anticipation of the performative solicitation of the audience. For comedy shoots, McCarthy insists actors constrain their intersubjective connections within the often fast-paced dialogue by focusing on the necessary plot points and marks to be hit:

> Comedy demands a dexterity and speed and kind of a quicker muscle, and so the preparation to do a very high comedy is in rehearsal. Get that tennis game going. It's very difficult to practice alone. You need your partner. You need however many people are in the scene. [. . .] There's a rhythm to comedy which must be honored, and you can't do that alone, so it really is getting your scene partner in your dressing room—or wherever the hell you are, by the craft table—and force them to work with you.[45]

Although McCarthy is quick to insist that actors can and should inspire creative discoveries through spontaneous reactions to each other's work, the enactment of the sides' comedic rhythm often requires the precise performance of predetermined moments. The performative athleticism of McCarthy's tennis analogy, with its implicit likening of comedic screen acting to a fast-paced energetic sport based on technical bravado and calculated tactical responses, is an apt metaphor for inter-actor working conditions on set. Given comedy's tremendous reliance on pace, rhythm, and timing, and the often close relationship between comedic dialogue and the screenwriter's script, a more appropriate musical metaphor for comedic screen acting than loosely scripted jazz is the symphony. Both musical metaphors stress the collaborations among performers, but present different tactical goals for the performers' preparations.

Actor Jamie Spilchuk embraces the symphonic metaphor while explaining that comedic scriptwriting is so tightly structured that comedic acting becomes as much about realizing the jokes as bringing creative personal insights to a character:

> Sitcoms and film comedies have a different cadence [from melodramatic scripts]. Sitcom scripts are almost as tightly written as a symphony. If you miss a joke or you miss part of the rhythm, it's like hearing a violin string break. You can tell! You have to search the script properly [for the jokes].[46]

For comedies, Spilchuk willingly defers a great deal of creative agency to screenwriters on the understanding that his performance will be stronger—and funnier—if he trusts in their text, especially if he appears regularly on a sitcom:

> Writers on the big sitcoms are at the top of their game. Don't change a word because they know more than you do. So, when the sides say, "take a beat," you take a beat. You don't say, "I don't feel like it." It's there for a reason. [. . .] If you're a series

regular, the writers know you inside and out. They start writing for *you*, and they know what will hit the best.⁴⁷

The creative agency here is more about activating than originating the scripted source. Just as a symphonic violinist must master the difficult passages of his portion of the orchestral score in the anticipation of blending his performance with his colleagues, a comedic screen actor must prepare for the technical challenges of setting up and telling her jokes by understanding the narrative flow in which her comedic timings occur, which in turn allows her to refine her timings in collaboration with her fellow performers.

For example, McCarthy describes her collaborative experiences on set in a starring role in the CBC comedic series *Little Mosque On The Prairie* (2007–12) like an orchestra rehearsal, balancing the cast's mastery of precise comedic rhythms with the director's conductor-like sense of tempo: "we would rehearse and rehearse and rehearse, so that once we were rolling, the director would say, 'let's go faster, take the air out of it,' and we had to be ready".⁴⁸ Like Dinicol's Jazz, the performers of McCarthy's Symphony must have expert control of their instrument. However, unlike Dinicol's Jazz, the performer's proficiency with precise moments that further tax the actor's working memory shifts the priorities of the empathetic solicitations closer to explicit performative concerns so that comedic moments will fit the industrially determined length of the episode and, frankly, be funnier. This does not imply that McCarthy's Symphony requires less intrasubjective or intersubjective work than Dinicol's Jazz: McCarthy vehemently insists that comedic screen acting relies primarily on the intersubjective connection. The key difference lies in how the Jazz or Symphony actor constructs the character's cognitive scaffolding during script analysis.

The Dinicol's Jazz actor establishes an intrasubjective bond that lets her "leave her [quotidian] self alone" by letting performance choices happen in the moment on set. The McCarthy's Symphony actor intrasubjectively bonds with her character while identifying comedic moments and timings in anticipation of performing. The McCarthy's Symphony actor will then use these moments as clues towards the character's cognitive scaffolding to inform future appresentations about the character's experiences of the situational world. Since many comedic moments involve a character's reaction to a situational conflict, comedic actors have the opportunity to construct their character's cognitive scaffolding from the jokes upwards as clues towards how their character engages with their narrative world. This practice positions the comedic screen actor to engage her performative athleticism with her scene partner in order to collaborate in making the comedic moments work in performance.

"Make it Work": Habits for Breaking Creative Mismatches

In an ideal day on set, screen actors arrive at the shoot where they are greeted by fellow performers with whom they can easily establish a productive and compelling intersubjective collaboration. As any actor will report, however, all of the industrial, creative, and financial incentives in the world will not ensure that two actors will immediately—or even ever—connect with each other. Simply put, some intersubjective connections require concerted external habits to either ease or force connections into existence.

These habits forcibly manipulate both the quotidian and situational relationships between the actors, while also provoking an enworlding response from one's scene partner. In some situations, this provocation is shaped as a benign offering of one actor's intentional pull to another. Actor Chris Baker explains how day-players[49] on longstanding television shows often rely on enworlding cues from the series' lead actors to enworld them within the show's narrative circumstances and performance style as quickly as possible. When Baker appeared as a featured day player on the CBC television series *Murdoch Mysteries* (2008–present), he felt supported creatively by the series' lead, Yannick Bisson. Bisson's longstanding immersion in the *Murdoch Mysteries* world provided Baker with ample cues as to how their scenes together should look and feel. Moreover, Baker's pre-existing familiarity with *Murdoch Mysteries* and its characters guided his preparatory work because Baker could accurately inform his character's cognitive scaffolding with his sense of the show's style, thereby anticipating intersubjective and performative solicitations within his intrasubjective preparations:

> As soon as the camera started rolling, it's not [Bisson]: it's Murdoch. You get in to it pretty quickly because it's not like there's another just actor up there acting; it's the character in front of me, and he's just doing his thing. Then you think "okay, now I know who I am, because that's who they are," even if, as an actor, you're also thinking "what can I do that will be interesting?"[50]

For Baker, Bisson was so adeptly and instantaneously in character that the guesswork for how to engage with Bisson-as-Murdoch was eliminated. Baker could focus on playing the scene with a solid intrasubjective and intersubjective understanding of who Bisson-as-Murdoch was and what his own character's relationship to Murdoch should be for the scene to be compelling. Empathetically, Bisson's performative stylistic consistency supported Baker's enworlding of his situational character, which greatly benefitted all three of Baker's empathetic connections.

On many film and television shoots, however, even the best of intentions and the industrial culture's insistence on a productive, efficient, and compelling actorly collaboration simply does not happen. In these instances, the ecumenical nature of film production—the openness to getting the job done any way possible—prompts the actors to find new ways to solve their interpersonal connections.[51]

The majority of actors responded that their most common habit for solving intersubjective blockages was to drop any aspirations towards Dinicol's Jazz and to instead focus on their intrasubjective connection with their character. An efficient way to accommodate the performative solicitation to the camera amidst creative mismatches is to prioritize the McCarthy's Symphony affordances of the sides. The combined plan here is to stay immersed in one's character and prioritize the script's rhythm and tempo so that their performance will be as intrasubjectively grounded and appropriately paced as possible under sub-optimal creative circumstances. At the end of the day, most actors in these situations are resigned to hoping that the editors can turn their footage into something more compelling than what the actor recalls of her work.[52]

As a last-ditch resort, Natalie Lisinska describes a particularly forceful habit for soliciting a disconnected scene partner's empathetic connection. Lisinska was once frustrated during a film shoot[53] where she could not easily create and sustain what she felt to a be a compelling creative collaboration with the actor who was playing her character's husband. The narrative positioned Lisinska's character and her scene partner's character as being happily married, and yet Lisinska felt that the other actor was either creatively or personally uncomfortable around her. As such, the interpersonal connection during the initial blocking rehearsals of the scene felt awkward and cold when it ought to have been genial and warm: Lisinska explains that they "were both dancing to different music, so to speak." Rather than abandon hope that she would be able to meaningfully connect with her scene partner, Lisinska attempted to jolt her scene partner in the hopes of breaking the inexplicably blocked connection:

> I thought, "okay, I have to do something because we're supposed to be so in love." We're blocking the first scene, and it's just that I'm about to get in the car and I realize that I've forgotten my cellphone and he runs out to give it to me. And so, in the first take, I kissed him. He didn't know it was coming. He had this shocked look on his face. Sometimes you have to pull out little tricks like that on the other actor, just to create something.[54]

With the unexpected kiss diffusing the scene partner's awkward boundary, Lisinska and the other actor were able to proceed with a productive and compelling filming process.

This need to remove a creative blockage among the actors locates the problem in both the primary intersubjective connection between the actors, and the secondary intersubjective connection between the actor and her fellow actor-as-character. Lisinska's description of the initial collaboration as "dancing to different music" presumes that both actors were confident in their intrasubjective preparations but were having trouble making sense of the scene-partner-as-character's cognitive scaffolding.

Lisinska and her scene partner's inabilities to read each other's intersubjective and performative solicitations quickly escalated into a creative blockage between the quotidian actors themselves, exacerbated by the industrial pressures of needing to make their scenes work as quickly and compellingly as possible. The initial inability to connect to each other is not the intrusion of a hypothetical anti-appresentation: a bodymind phenomenon that would prevent or inhibit the development of empathy-inducing appresentations. The very notion of an anti-appresentation is dubious at best: if an appresentation is the imagined but likely perception from another hypothetical subjectivity,[55] an anti-appresentation implies either an objective perception or an intrusive, distracting, and antagonistic perception that takes up the same bodymind attention as a creative appresentation otherwise would. Instead, the problem rested in reorganizing their individual preparations to align with the surprises presented by each other's cognitive scaffolding, and to thereby intersubjectively enworld each other within the same situational space. The surprise of Lisinska's kiss capitalized on the lack of empathetic connection between them by disrupting the other actor's immersion in the performance choices that prevented him from connecting with Lisinska. The genuineness of his surprised reaction afforded the actors something to work with, which became the framework for the remainder of their creative collaboration.

As an attentively opposite but equally effective habit as Dinicol's Jazz for soliciting an intersubjective empathetic connection among actors on set, forcible habits of immersion like Lisinska's kiss certainly reify the ecumenical impulses of film production. The forcible habits, however, are often considered a tactic of last resort. After all, not all actors appreciate being spontaneously kissed or otherwise intruded upon by a co-star, and screen actors always have the option of playing primarily to the camera in the hopes that the post-production team will be able to compensate for the lack of interpersonal chemistry on set. As one actor explained, "on some sets, it's just a job. I clock my hours, I know what to do, I do it, and

I go home." The technical skills needed to refine this audition-like style of acting into a verisimilar performance, as well as those that compensate for the many adjustments for auteurist shot compositions and complicated eye-line matches, require the actor to expand her empathetic efforts to fit within the greater—and literal—frame of the camera.

Real Fake Tears, and Talking to Tennis Balls: Incorporating Production Conditions into Acting Choices

As an alternative tactic to the on-set practices that privilege the intersubjective connection, actors with strong understandings of the collaborative camera's affordances may prioritize their performative solicitations to the camera as a way of grounding themselves on set. This approach typically focuses on inviting the spectator into the actor's intrasubjective connection. More specifically, the actor self-organizes the performative articulation of her intrasubjective work to make herself-as-character lucid and compelling to the spectator by consciously incorporating the formal affordances of the film shoot into her acting work.

This tactic for producing the actorly raw materials of a screen-specific performance raises the inevitable critical issue of the actor's very agency in creating screen performances. Some screen acting habits are easily considered technical tricks, easily reproduced stock reactions that may generate a compelling performance of that reaction without any meaningful empathetic underpinnings from the actor. The wealth of apocryphal examples of non-empathetic-yet-compelling performance moments make allusions to the Kuleshov effect unavoidable. Alfred Hitchcock, for example, surprised Janet Leigh with ice-cold water to produce the scream at the beginning of *Psycho*'s (1960) shower sequence. Michael Curtiz directed Humphrey Bogart to look over his shoulder and nod in an unmotivated and isolated take in *Casablanca* (1942), only to use that disjointed take as the profound character development when Bogart-as-Rick cues the band to play *La Marseillaise*.

These kinds of technical performance tricks are sometimes passed off as industrial wisdom. For example, British screen acting instructor Bill Britten suggests that stage actors who hope to transition into screen work should experiment with the amount of performed thinking that can happen when an actor filmed in a close-up moves her eyes before speaking.[56] Britten prudently cautions actors to not rely on eye movements alone to express a character's emotional state, and he insists that the actor must be feeling something behind the eyes for the narrative moment to be compelling.[57] Still, the implication is that the camera will do most of the narrative work for the actor, so better to use a simple trick than risk overworking the moment. On one hand, these performance tricks are an ecumenical use of film editing's affordances for working the raw material from the actor, such as Leigh's scream or Bogart's nod, into a compelling performance. These moments represent a style of on-set collaboration that opts to solve a narrative moment with the versatility of the post-production process rather than give the moment in question unnecessary—and expensive— time on set. It would be naïve, after all, to presume that every moment performed by every screen actor is the result of carefully considered and painstakingly empathetic creative processes.

It is equally fruitless, however, to presume that the possibility for simple Kuleshovian tricks exists means that no screen actor ever engages with her character, her fellow actors-as-characters, or her on-set production conditions with the intensity of her theatrical counterparts. Again, this critical problem of throwing out the actor with the theoretical bathwater comes down to presuming that all screen acting is synonymous with the performance assembled in the final cut of the film. The actors interviewed for this study described several habits for not only using the on-set affordances to create deeply compelling raw material for the post-production performance, but how their habits for empathetic solicitation and sustenance actively overcome on-set anti-verisimilar working conditions. If anything, the practices described here present actors as active collaborators with their fellow on-set personnel, from DOPs to make-up artists to other actors and more, in their contribution to creating compelling screen performances.[58]

Lisinska's Tears: Acting with Set-specific Affordances

As a fierce counterpoint to the Kuleshovian technological determinism of unmotivated performances constructed primarily in editing rooms, many actors assert control over their performances by incorporating the industrial circumstances of the production process into their creative work on set. This habit places the affordances of formal "trickery," which are often the result of a greater environmental or narrative constraint, at the service of the actor's creative intuitions and sincere attempts to solicit empathetic relationships on set.

For example, Lisinska found herself working within a set of harsh narrative and environmental circumstances while shooting the post-affair confrontation sequence for an episode of *Orphan Black*. Ainsley, Lisinska's character, has been standing in the middle of her suburban street during a heavy rainstorm in early winter, furious and heartbroken that her neighbor and best friend Alison (Tatiana Maslany) has seduced Ainsley's husband. The scene was shot outdoors on a cold Toronto evening and Lisinska had to enter the scene already soaking wet from the rain and with tears streaming down her face.

Lisinska actively incorporated her personal on-set discomfort from the rain and the cold into her intrasubjective preparation for Ainsley's violent emotional explosion. Moreover, alongside her emotional priming before walking on set had prepared her to cry during the take, Lisinska rapidly embraced the make-up team's suggestion that she wear tear-inducing cosmetics:

> I was so cold, and they were spraying me down with the rain. Just before we started shooting, the make-up artist, who is very experienced and very sweet, right before we started, just came up to me and said, "do you want some tears, darling?" I was unsure. I've always had a strong "that's cheating" disdain for that. But in that moment, I said, "Yeah! I'm so fucking cold. I don't know if I can do this, so . . . yeah, I want some tears!" [. . .] He put glycerine drops into my eyes, which triggers your own tears. It was fascinating because it was almost like doing it backwards: the physiological response of tears triggered the emotions, and then I started crying for real.[59]

Lisinska's Tears incorporated the on-set affordances into her performance, in the hopes that the incorporated material would catalyze the performative expression of intrasubjective understanding, and further reinforce the verisimilar illusion because the actor-as-character fits naturally within her environment. In a way, this habit is an on-set extension of Lisinska's object-oriented pre-shooting preparations, wherein she imbues likely set pieces, props, and costumes with enworlding appresentations. In this instance, Lisinska mobilized *Orphan Black*'s on-set working conditions, such as the cold weather, with the affective impetus provided by the initially artificial tears, to immerse herself within the dramatic action through the *mise-en-scène*'s affordances, explicitly connecting the distributed network of acting work to the wardrobe and make-up personnel. Lisinska's Tears therefore links her emotional preparations and appresentational investments to the specific constraints and affordances of the film shoot, thereby reinforcing her performative solicitation to the camera by instigating a fluctuation in the dynamic boundaries of the distributed cognition network that, in this example, realized Lisinska-as-Ainsley.

Empathetically, Lisinska's Tears makes the actor's intrasubjective "Magic If" appresentations lucid for the camera by focusing on the clarity, compellingness, and complexity with which the actor enacts her understanding of the character's lived world. In the *Orphan Black* example, Lisinska-as-Ainsley's ferocious attack on Maslany-as-Alison clearly demonstrates how Lisinska has answered Magic If questions like: "How would I react if my husband had an affair with a beloved neighbor?"; "How would my feelings of betrayal change if I stood in the cold winter rain to confront my neighbor?"; "How do I feel about my social status in my prudish community if my marriage falls apart?"; and so on.

The intersubjective strategy for Lisinska's Tears is predicated on the acceptance that the actor may have little to no rehearsal time to establish the bonding rapport upon which Dinicol's Jazz and McCarthy's Symphony rely. Instead of committing to the unpredictability of what the scene partner will bring on set, the actor needs only enough of an intersubjective bond with her scene partners to ensure that their narrative relationship is sufficiently enworlded within the *mise-en-scène* so that the solicitation to the camera can occupy the majority of the actor's attention. Before shooting their fight scene, Lisinska and Maslany had already worked together on the *Orphan Black* set for weeks in scenes that rewarded the intimacy they established between their characters. During the fight scene, Lisinska's primary intersubjective concern was ensuring her and Maslany's personal safety during the fight sequence, since the actors' creative and personal rapport was already firmly in place. Lisinska was therefore free to focus her efforts on soliciting the spectator's connection to Ainsley's heartbroken anger, with complete trust that Maslany's performance would support the emotional narrative moment.

This same impulse manifested very differently in Lisinska's previous example, wherein she found it difficult to connect with the previously unknown actor playing her husband. In that film, Lisinska felt compelled to manufacture enough of an intersubjective bond with her scene partner by spontaneously kissing him, thereby breaking their creative barriers and, as Lisinska describes, making sure they were in the same scene together. Once sufficiently co-enworlded together, Lisinska was free to focus her attention on collaborating with the camera and soliciting her connection with the anticipated audience.

Lisinska's Tears is therefore quite tactically opposite to Dinicol's Jazz: whereas Dinicol's Jazz makes the actor "leave herself alone" to attend to the scene partner, Lisinska's Tears makes sure that that actor can potentially "leave her scene partner alone" to focus on medium-specific storytelling. It would be an unfair over-simplification to suggest that Lisinska's Tears requires a diva-like disinterest in all other actors' work. If anything, Lisinska revels in the collaborative and communal nature of film production, and the incorporation of creative fodder from any of her on- and off-camera colleagues is always a welcome boon to any performance. Her insistence on communicating her character to the implied audience through the camera is an assertion of control and responsibility for her own performance, and that she will ecumenically use whatever resources are available on set to fulfill her professional obligations to the best of her ability. In this regard, Lisinska's Tears is the industrial bodymind framework within which the logic of audition performances becomes verisimilar acting: if a viable intersubjective rapport with a scene partner makes her performative solicitation more compelling, so much the better for everyone; if not, she will proceed with her performative solicitation with whatever inductive and ecumenical affordances present themselves.

Taken to its logical extreme, the alternative—for which Lisinska's Tears is well-prepared but is less enthusiastic to accommodate—is to fully leave the scene partner alone and perform to inanimate objects on set. This common working condition is rarely the direct result of an irreparable intersubjective failure between the actors; it is far more likely that the actor will need to speak to a dot on the wall, a tennis ball on a stick, or some other off-screen object to ensure a verisimilar eye-line match in a complicated shot composition. The imaginary and empathetic infrastructure behind this kind of technical acting is inevitable in film production,[60] and requires some particularly focused acting to make a compelling performative solicitation.

Performative Adjustments: Talking to Tennis Balls

During any given film shoot, the actor may have to perform emotive sequences to off-screen actor-surrogate props, such as the previously mentioned "tennis ball on a stick." These off-screen actor-surrogates give the on-screen actor a specific visual focal point for their performative address, which is a necessary technical adjustment in which the actor supports the editor's anticipated eye-line matches, shot-reverse-shot patterns shot from complicated angles, and so on. The actor must spontaneously imagine the neon green tennis ball as a diegetic object, such as a scene partner's face, an important object, or a meaningful off-screen event. Obviously, playing a dramatic moment with an impaled tennis ball as a focal point requires a stronger imaginary investment from the actor to create the verisimilar illusion. On a larger scale, productions with extensive use of green screens, CGI embellishments, and motion-capture ("mocap") performances practically necessitate that the actor work within an audition-like minimalist *mise-en-scène* that will only be dressed and completed in post-production.[61]

The bodymind self-organizations required to create compelling raw performative material for these kinds of shots are therefore a true test of the actor's trust in her own technical skills to collaborate with the camera, in the skilled professionalism of the rest of the production staff, and in her own ability to suspend the disbelief in the anti-realistic performance conditions to maintain the realist empathic bonds despite the technical hurdles. The performative solicitation to the spectator is not fundamentally changed when the actor must play a scene with an off-camera tennis ball on a stick, but the actor's imagination must work harder than usual to sustain the solicitation.

For example, McGarry describes the process of shooting the horseback riding scenes for *Heartland* as an exercise in collaborative trust and imaginative focus. In order to accommodate multiple sight lines and the complex audio recording setup during scenes where two characters appear to ride beside each other while engrossed in conversation, actors are often required to ride staggered, facing in opposite directions, and never look at each other. The occasional two-shot of the actors riding together belies the complicated staggered staging required to shoot the individual shots without catching the crew filming the other actor in the background. The imaginary investment required by each actor to sustain a verisimilar illusion, wherein each actor speaks to an off-camera tennis ball while their diegetic scene partner rides ten paces in front or behind them, is significant:

> There are twenty crew guys following you both around, you're already bracing for the ADR[62] session, and you never see the person you're supposed to be acting with while you pretend that it's just you [and your scene partner] out there. If you watch it like theater, it's the most awkward-looking thing you've ever seen. I don't think it messes with the storytelling, but you definitely have to use your imagination.[63]

As much as the formal setup for these scenes requires extra work from the actors, McGarry reports that shooting these scenes has taught him a great deal about how to collaborate with the camera and that shooting these sequences becomes easier with each episode. The technical adjustment that makes the necessary additional concentration possible is that McGarry uses the inherent contradictions in realist acting's suspension of disbelief to reinforce a deep empathetic immersion in the dramatic moment; the only bodymind resources being used outside of the performative solicitation are the ones that buttress him against anti-verisimilar disruption:

> You just have to have that constant concentration. You have to train yourself to say "wait there: I'm going to black everything out like a little [iris lens]" and you just focus. It's weird because even on stage, you can't say you totally lose yourself. You're always aware of what's going on, and where you have to be facing so that everyone [in the audience] sitting around can see you. When you really focus on the story you

have to tell through that little blacked out [iris lens], it just becomes second nature and nothing is going to throw you off.[64]

By allotting as many bodymind resources as possible to the empathetic immersion in the situational moment—while maintaining the essential self–other distinctions that prevent realist acting from slipping into hallucination—veteran actors can trust that their deeply encultured technical training will support a verisimilar performance despite the rough terrain of the shoot's cognitive ecology.

Spilchuk asserts that one of the worst things a screen actor can do is to overthink the technical constraints instead of focusing on the storytelling task at hand:

Acting with tennis balls is weird, I'm not going to lie. At the same time, it's mind over matter. All you have to do is tap into your things and play the scene with a tennis ball, and if I can't hear [my scene partner's] voice, then I'll make-believe. We make-believe. Stop worrying about it and go do it.[65]

The screen actor is far from alone on set in her efforts to create a verisimilar performance in a complex shot composition. Rather than an actor worrying herself into performative paralysis, the formal complexity of some film shots also forces the screen actor to trust in the production crew's collaboration in a similar way that a stage actor must trust in the affordances of their performance space to be adequately seen and heard. The performative self–other distinction, by which actors learn to perform for the camera by watching their own work and making future adjustments based on their limited technical ability to self-monitor, is extremely difficult for the screen actor to establish on her own for these shots, since the complex performance demands impede any easy self-monitoring and the actor cannot allot so many bodymind resources to that self-monitoring without empathetically under-investing in the dramatic action. Instead, and more so than in straightforward shoots, formally intricate sequences like *Heartland*'s horseback riding conversations demand that the actor think along with the rest of the production crew to collectively create the verisimilar illusion.

For many screen actors, the inevitable deferral of some personal control over one's performance to the collaborative resources of the production crew is simply an industrial fact of life.[66] This is not to say that actors lack any creative agency in accommodating production conditions like complex shot compositions beyond, as McGarry and Spilchuk insist, focusing intently while pretending that the complication does not exist.

Figure 6.4 Kevin McGarry (left) and Shaun Johnston (right) in *Heartland*, season 7, episode 10, "Riding Shotgun" (Chris Potter, CBC, 2016)

Cayonne argues that, in some circumstances, the actor can incorporate the technical complexities of a given shot into the diegetic action:

> I don't have a lot of difficulty [making technical adjustments] and still being able to play in truth. I once had to deliver an entire monologue to a speck on the wall while the actor was behind me. It was fine because, before the set-up, he and I ran the lines, connected with each other, and had a real conversation. I know he's behind me and, if I had to create some sort of premise, I'm getting ready with the mirror while having a conversation with my brother, so what's the difference? I don't look at people all the time when I speak to them everyday. The set-up didn't feel unnatural at all.[67]

In this situation, Cayonne reorganized his situational bodymind to transform the formal constraints of the staging into a performative appresentation, playing the scene as if he could see his scene partner in a mirror. This appresentation allowed Cayonne to minimize the distraction-preventing imaginary buffers, and thereby allocate more of his bodymind resources to empathetic solicitations. The empathetic solicitations remained unchanged in nature, and required less of an investment in the distraction-preventing imaginary buffer.

This opportunity to layer additional appresentations into the actor's bodymind schema based on on-set affordances and constraints is a natural extension of the Cayonne's Minotaur metaphor[68]—the free blending of imagined and recalled creative fodder to support immersive intrasubjective appresentations—from Cayonne's own script-based intrasubjective preparations. Cayonne's Minotaur is already predicated on committing the bodymind to a situational reorganization, so it is not too far of a leap to extend the merged memory and imagination metaphor with the suspension of disbelief buttress against anti-verisimilar performance conditions. This connection between Cayonne's Minotaur and Lisinska's Tears—in that the actor incorporates on-set conditions into her constantly self-organizing situational body schema—further underscores the importance of trust in the co-collaborative filtering camera, the deferral of trust in the production team, and the ecumenical assertion of creative control through spontaneous and compelling adaptations to onset conditions. Cayonne can only accommodate last-minute performative appresentations, like the implied mirror shot of the previous example, if he understands how the camera will filter his performance so that he can make the strongest performative solicitation possible. This trust in the co-collaborative camera is only possible if Cayonne can think along with the production team to solve onset production issues with a competent and collaborative production crew. Finally, Cayonne must be in sufficient command of his bodymind resources to identify the potential performative appresentations that will prompt the most compelling self-organizations based on the on-set creative constraints and affordances.

Conclusion

This chapter has strived to show two fundamental sets of strategies for how actors establish and enact their three empathetic relationships on set: the Dinicol's Jazz and McCarthy's Symphony tactics for focusing all on-set work around the intersubjective bond, in the hopes that a potent connection with one's fellow actors will support the performative solicitation and enact the intrasubjective connection through interpersonal interaction; inversely, the Lisinska's Tears tactic prioritizes the performative solicitation to the audience through the camera, in the hopes that the scene partners will provide enough intersubjective bonding to present the actor-as-character as more-fully enworlded within the narrative moment. In both sets of general tactics, the one constant is the actor's understanding that she must somehow communicate her intrasubjective bond with her fellow actors and the spectator alike. The only question is which of the intersubjective or performative bond to establish first to contextualize the other.

If audition acting's cognitive ecology hamstrings the totality of an actor's work because it does not showcase all the connections that the actor will use on set, then the actor's work on set is to coordinate just one set of distributed cognition nodes within film and television production's greater cognitive ecology. This coordination prioritizes the actor's creative bodymind movement towards other nodes in that ecology: the ways in which the actor's embodied cognition navigates the distributed cognition network of character creation with the camera and other on-set constraints and affordances.

The portrait presented here of how actors work on set does not neatly align with any particular school of Method acting or other training regimen, even if components of each tactic may be particularly well-served by techniques advocated by a specific practitioner. Rather than make a proclamation about the general viability of one acting style over another, what I hope to show here is the fluid and ecumenical nature of a practice as amorphous as screen acting. If the principles of a famous practitioner must be bent, revised, or broken to produce a compelling performance within the industrial circumstances of a particular film shoot, so be it.

That which persists across all of these acting approaches, however, is a tacit understanding that each actor must navigate her relationships with her character, her fellow actors-as-characters, and the anticipated audience behind the surrogate camera. Without a connection to her character, the actor is an inanimate and glorified prop. Without a connection to another actor-as-character, the actor can pass an audition but will likely fail to produce compelling raw material for the final performance. Without an understanding of how the camera will record the performance and how to perform with the audience in mind, the actor's work is an illegible mess. The connections that the actor seeks with each of these three targets combine and reinforce each other's place in the creation of the verisimilar illusion to which realist acting aspires.

Notes

1. Caldwell, *Production Culture: Industrial Reflexivity and Critical Practice in Film and Television*, p. 18.
2. Lindsey Middleton (actor), in discussion with the author, August 2016.
3. Caldwell, *Production Culture: Industrial Reflexivity and Critical Practice in Film and Television*, p. 19.
4. See Chapter 6.
5. This manifestation of the ecumenical impulse will be covered more extensively in the Lisinska's Tears section of this chapter.
6. Warburton, "Becoming elsewhere: ArtsCross and the (re)location of performer cognition," pp. 94–6.
7. See Chapter 5.

8. Matthew MacFadzean (actor), in discussion with the author, August 2016.
9. Matthew MacFadzean (actor), in discussion with the author, August 2016.
10. Caldwell, *Production Culture: Industrial Reflexivity and Critical Practice in Film and Television*, pp. 20–1.
11. Ibid. p. 21.
12. Ibid.
13. Jamie Spilchuk (actor), in discussion with the author, August 2016.
14. That said, Lisa Bode's insightful analysis of computer-generated performances based on recordings of deceased actors draws attention to the recyclability of performances by actors who never set foot on the set of the film in which they appear. The digital animation of posthumous performances creates the illusion that the deceased actor themselves is acting on set, rather than being virtually revived during post-production. For better or worse, this book confines itself to performances that actors give while they are still alive. See Lisa Bode's "No longer themselves?: Framing digitally enabled posthumous 'performance'" (2010) for details.
15. Lutterbie, *Toward a General Theory of Acting: Cognitive Science and Performance*, p. 217.
16. Matthew MacFadzean (actor), in discussion with the author, August 2016.
17. See Chapter 4.
18. Julian DeZotti (actor/writer), in discussion with the author, July 2016.
19. Joe Dinicol (actor), in discussion with the author, June 2016.
20. This comment has been made anonymous at the actor's request.
21. Jamie Spilchuk (actor), in discussion with the author, August 2016.
22. This comment has been made anonymous at the actor's request.
23. Sheila McCarthy (actor), in discussion with the author, September 2016.
24. Joe Dinicol (actor), in discussion with the author, June 2016.
25. Joe Dinicol (actor), in discussion with the author, June 2016.
26. Kevin McGarry (actor), in discussion with the author, August 2016.
27. Kevin McGarry (actor), in discussion with the author, August 2016.
28. Antonio Cayonne (actor), in discussion with the author, August 2016.
29. Jamie Spilchuk (actor), in discussion with the author, August 2016.
30. Sheila McCarthy (actor), in discussion with the author, September 2016.
31. Sheila McCarthy (actor), in discussion with the author, September 2016.
32. McConachie, *Theatre and Mind*, p. 38.
33. Beaty and Jung, "Interacting brain networks underlying creative cognition and artistic performance," p. 280.
34. Kemp, "Devising—Embodied Creativity in Distributed Systems," pp. 50–2.
35. Caldwell, *Production Culture: Industrial Reflexivity and Critical Practice in Film and Television*, p. 21.
36. Joe Dinicol (actor), in discussion with the author, June 2016.
37. Vuust and Roepstorff, "Listen up! Polyrhythms in brain and music"; Wesolowski, "Cognition and the assessment of interaction episodes in jazz improvisation."

38. Seddon, "Modes of communication during jazz improvisation," p. 58.
39. Joe Dinicol (actor), in discussion with the author, June 2016.
40. Bruce Clayton, masterclass at Professional Actors Lab, Toronto, Canada, October 2006.
41. Joe Dinicol (actor), in discussion with the author, June 2016.
42. Joe Dinicol (actor), in discussion with the author, June 2016.
43. Joe Dinicol (actor), in discussion with the author, June 2016.
44. Sheila McCarthy (actor), in discussion with the author, September 2016.
45. Sheila McCarthy (actor), in discussion with the author, September 2016.
46. Jamie Spilchuk (actor), in discussion with the author, August 2016.
47. Jamie Spilchuk (actor), in discussion with the author, August 2016.
48. Sheila McCarthy (actor), in discussion with the author, September 2016.
49. "Day-player" is an industrial term for an actor who is hired for a small but featured role on a film or television shoot. Day-players rarely appear in more than one or two scenes, which are often shot on the same day to avoid hiring an actor for small role for two days of shooting (and therefore paying twice as much for the same performance).
50. Chris Baker (actor), in discussion with the author, August 2016.
51. Not surprisingly, even though many actors have been in film and television shoots where they did not feel they worked well with their scene partners, very few were willing to discuss the specifics of what went wrong, who they were unable to work with, the name of the casting director who mistakenly put them on set together, etc. The competitive and inherently gossipy nature of screen acting culture allows very little space to be seen as incompetent, and can easily hinder the ongoing careers of actors who "know better" than casting directors, producers, directors, co-stars, production companies, and so on. Every actor interviewed for this study was given the opportunity to take any of their responses "off the record," either at the time of the interview or retroactively in the weeks and months afterwards. Some actors were willing to share anecdotes about their on-set experiences on the condition that the title of the production and names of key production staff remained anonymous. I have strived, where possible, in this study to provide as much critical detail as possible while honoring my interviewees' requests for selective anonymity.
52. Jamie Spilchuk (actor), in discussion with the author, August 2016.
53. This film and the name of the other actor have been anonymized at Lisinska's request.
54. Natalie Lisinska (actor), in discussion with the author, October 2016.
55. Thompson, *Mind In Life: Biology, Phenomenology, and the Sciences of the Mind*, p. 383.
56. Britten, *From Stage to Screen: A Theatre Actor's Guide to Working on Camera*, pp. 124–7, 144.
57. Ibid. p. 118.
58. As a final thought before proceeding with an analysis of common on-set habits that prioritize soliciting performative empathetic connections with the

camera, it is important to note that an exhaustive list of every way that a screen actor connects to her audience is impossible within the scope of this study. The implications of genre, narrative specificities, personal style, popular tastes at the historical moment of production, and the intensity of technological collaboration (animation, CGI- and motion-capture filmmaking, etc.) for actorly empathetic solicitations will make for excellent future studies. What I strive to qualify in this study are general trends in how contemporary western realist screen actors self-organize their performances to solicit compelling connections from their anticipated audiences. I do so by placing their habits for empathetic solicitation in the formal industrial culture in which they take place.

59. Natalie Lisinska (actor), in discussion with the author, October 2016.
60. Natalie Lisinska (actor), in discussion with the author, October 2016.
61. Leberg, "Digital drapery and body schema-tics."
62. Automated Dialogue Replacement (ADR) is a post-production process in which the actor re-records their dialogue in a controlled studio setting to overcompensate for any flubbed lines or on-set background noise which obscured the initial audio recording. The actor watches the recorded scene and synchronizes her new performance of the dialogue with her mouth and lip movements on screen. Although some actors relish the opportunity for another day of paid work on set, many actors see ADR work as tedious and time-consuming.
63. Kevin McGarry (actor), in discussion with the author, August 2016.
64. Kevin McGarry (actor), in discussion with the author, August 2016.
65. Jamie Spilchuk (actor), in discussion with the author, August 2016.
66. Natalie Lisinska (actor), in discussion with the author, October 2016.
67. Antonio Cayonne (actor), in discussion with the author, August 2016.
68. See Chapter 5.

CHAPTER 7

Conclusion
"Ready for my Close-up"

This book argues that the screen actor's solicitation of three simultaneous empathetic relationships creates the verisimilar illusion before the camera upon which realist film and television acting depends. These solicitations take place within a diverse community of collaborative targets: from the situational center of intentionality in the sides who is attributed to all of the eventual actor-as-character's dialogue and actions; to the community of actors who often meet for the first time hours before shooting scenes in which the actors-as-characters have known each other their entire lives; to the audience of one that transcribes the performed actor-as-character into a diegetic center of intentionality to be reconstructed by an anticipated spectator—not to mention all the casting directors, producers, acting coaches, DOPs, audition readers, screenwriters, and directorial teams encountered along the way. That the actor is able to make these solicitations at all is predicated on the bodymind's capacity to link action to imagination in an iterative loop of self-organizing action and reaction. Even if empathy is more of an ideal than a guaranteed relationship for some actors in some roles, empathy as a framework provides a constructive place for discussing and comparing actorly creative processes.

My initial draw to theorizing the practice of screen acting as soliciting empathy was the ubiquity of the motif of "connections" in how actors talk about their work. I extend this motif to the various connections solicited by the actor while she works, and also the prospect of connecting actors and scholars through a potential common critical vocabulary for the actor's creative process. This concluding chapter proposes three potential further connections that this research could make between various researchers, critical fields, actors, and other screen media production personnel. First, I sketch the possibilities for connecting my model of screen acting as empathetic solicitations to star studies as a companion to historical performance analysis, using Jared Leto's performance in *Suicide Squad* (David Ayer, 2016) and Diane Keaton's Oscar-winning performance in *Annie Hall* (Woody Allen, 1977) as case studies. Second, I suggest that actorly empathy could be a starting point for productively incorporating distributed cognition, imagination, and improvisation into production studies and broader notions of collective authorship on set. Third, I propose that screen acting's ever-changing physical presence in its performance space prompts an examination of how modern filmmaking technologies re-contextualize the actor's empathetic solicitations in terms of collaborative cognition and computable geometry.

Histories of Force and Eloquence

Jorg Sternagel, Deborah Levitt, and Dieter Mersch's definition of screen acting as "force" and performances as "eloquence"[1] calls attention to the crucial differences between the process of acting work and its artistic results. At the risk of being pedantic, the word "force" works equally well as a verb or a noun, whereas "eloquence" is a noun or an adjective: both terms name a thing or an idea, which makes sense since acting and performances do indeed exist. However, "force" describes acting as a practice of moving, doing, becoming; Sternagel, Levitt, and Mensch's use of "eloquence" leans towards a completed articulation or a named quality thereof.

One of the conceptual origins of this book is the question of unpacking the verb-like nature of acting to contextualize how it culminates in its adjective-laden results. James Naremore, for example, characterizes the problem of analyzing acting through performances alone as an overreliance on "fuzzy adjectival language"[2] when analyzing the degrees of subtlety in an actor's performance. At the same time, Naremore compounds the problem of identifying acting as the force behind an eloquent performance by framing the film actor's process within only its manifestation in single roles: "the actor hardly exists but as an agent of narrative, and movie performers cannot be discussed apart from the many crafts that surround and construct them."[3] This dramatically shrinks the conceptual space that my book gives to the entire meaning-making process by which acting's force crystalizes into eloquent performances.

For all of their articulate historicization, Naremore's historical case studies of well-chosen screen performances demonstrate the struggle to account the verb-like force of acting amidst the adjectival specificities of a given performance. For example, Naremore's take on Marlon Brando's performance in *On The Waterfront* (Elia Kazan, 1954) presents a convincing short history of Brando's relationship with various Method acting movements with a specific focus on the famous "glove" scene between

Brando and co-star Eva Marie Saint. In this scene, the awkward budding romance between Brando-as-Terry and Saint-as-Edie reaches a memorable peak when Kazan continued to shoot the scene despite an accident within the staging. When Saint inadvertently drops her glove and Brando unexpectedly picks it up, continues to play the scene while caressing the glove, and ignores Saint's requests to give it back, Saint is caught between the professional code of continuing to perform until the director calls cut and her uncertainty as to why Kazan refuses to call cut when expected.

Naremore stops explicitly short of reading Method acting's force into the eloquence of the "glove" scene because the realist illusion created in this scene is not categorically different from that of non-Method performances in classical Hollywood films.[4] The missed opportunity here does not so much lie in the description of Brando and Saint's performances but rather the inductive and ecumenical rationales that spontaneously motivated the acting work behind those performances. The issue is not that the dropped glove is a performance choice which fosters a distinct sense of realism from that of contemporaneous Hollywood films. The glove scene's demonstration of Method acting principles is fundamentally about process rather than result. Brando and Saint's navigation of the dropped glove's affordances disarms any pretense of adhering to the sides and instead fosters the sincere and, spontaneous intersubjective relationships between actors that Brando and his contemporary Method practitioners cherished. Moreover, the Lisinska's Tears-like effect of the dropped glove

Figure 7.1 Marlon Brando (left) and Eva Marie Saint (right) in *On The Waterfront* (Elia Kazan, 1954)

inadvertently created a productively awkward experience for Saint, whose performance of romantic uncertainty was suddenly being informed by her actorly confusion about how to proceed with the scene.

Nevertheless, Naremore's impulse to historicize acting practices makes sense in that the standards of acceptable realist screen acting change over time. Moreover, the notion that actors will often work some aspect within their social, cultural, and historical moment into their performances is uncontroversial. Cynthia Baron and Yannis Tzioumakis's analyses of actors in American independent cinema, for example, productively integrate a given actor's other roles on professional film sets, such as their directorial or screenwriting work, into their actorly performances.[5] These additional historically-specific contexts for an actor's work still beg the question of process over result.

I therefore suggest that an empathetic model of acting can historicize acting practices within performance styles in part by presenting Coplan and Decety's criteria as common denominators for what actors are doing and how they are doing it across historical circumstances. On one hand, this application of the empathetic solicitation framework complements existing research on the influence of an actor's contemporary moment on her acting, such as Julie Levinson's articulate treatment of 1970s neo-Strasbergian Method acting amidst its discourses of celebrity culture and the era's emerging self-help pop psychology movement.[6] I described a preliminary study of this sort in Chapter 3 in direct reference to Levinson and neo-Strasbergian Method acting in my sketches of Robert de Niro and Daniel Day-Lewis's radical intrasubjective practices of editing their bodies to fit the character's memories. On the other hand, the ways in which realist actors over time have prioritized and configured Coplan's criteria and Decety's criteria of care within the three empathetic solicitations provides a preliminary framework and vocabulary for historical comparisons of screen acting practices.

Jared Leto's "package pranks"

During the interviews for this book, an article in *The Atlantic* on Jared Leto's on-set bahavior during the production of *Suicide Squad* and the "demise" of American Method acting, was very much on the mind of many of my respondents. Bastién argues that Leto's harassment of his co-stars, such as mailing them packages of dead animals and used condoms, replaces the traditionally "feminine" aspects of Method preparations associated with emotional access with cruel and destructive hyper-masculine behaviors.[7] The outrageousness of these hyper-masculine preparations taps into the marketable martyrdom that propelled the celebrity status of radically intrasubjective Method actors of the 1970s, such as Robert De Niro and Jack Nicholson.[8] For Bastién, not only do on-set pranks like Leto's marginalize the creative experiments of contemporary female actors as de-beautifying "liabilities",[9] but they also perpetuate the narrative that self-harm and depraved indifference to the well-being of others are viable paths to producing compelling art.

Many of my interviewees[10] echoed Bastién's disapproval of Leto's creative process by embellishing on related critiques of professionalism, consent, health and safety concerns, and even insurance liability. Of all the interviewees, Kevin McGarry's relatively even-handed take on both Bastién's article and Leto's process drew attention to the disconnect between the way that critics write about "good" acting and the work that actors do to produce their performances. While still dubious of whether Leto's co-stars were willing participants in Leto's off-camera creative experiments, McGarry suggested that the equation of acceptable acting with Brando's process, and the moralistic value judgments of non-actors about creative experimentation, leads to professional standards for actors set by people who have never worked as actors themselves.[11] The critical or journalistic impulses to label acting's creative processes without firsthand experience of those processes risks making some acting practices sound like a set of sanctified, approved "assembly instructions". McGarry's response to Bastién stresses the need for a critical vocabulary on acting that is grounded in the firsthand experience of the actor that can also be mobilized to make practice-based historical comparisons of acting processes.

I therefore suggest that investigating the empathetic underpinnings of screen acting practices and traditions can clarify and historicize the key differences within their creative processes. The framework of tactics for empathetic solicitations could provide a useful comparative template for evaluating how on-screen Method acting practices, in this instance, have changed since the prime days of Brando. Furthermore, I argue that the general disapproval among my interviewees of Leto's on-set antics is symptomatic of preferential practices in contemporary screen acting culture, and that these preferential practices can be partially identified through an empathetic analysis of Leto's process.

Presuming that Bastién's article faithfully represents Leto's creative experiment with mailing repulsive objects to his co-stars, Leto sought a firsthand experience of how Leto-as-Joker could make people feel vulnerable and threatened. He therefore attempted to develop compelling intrasubjective appresentations primarily finding an intrasubjective affective match for the Joker's cruelty and depraved unpredictability. Specifically,

Leto linked his intrasubjective affective match with the primary intersubjective other-oriented perspective-taking, while simultaneously diminishing the intrasubjective self–other distinction to presumably feel more vividly as Joker. The result of this experiment was that Leto-as-Joker performed an action in the quotidian world intended to help Leto generate an experience to be extrapolated as an intrasubjective appresentation for Leto-as-Joker's sadism. This intrasubjective appresentation would ideally help ensnare Leto within Leto-as-Joker's intentional pull and thereby inform the process of soliciting useful intersubjective and performative connections once on set. Using part of one empathetic relationship to bolster another—following one target's intentional pull temporarily towards another target—is common practice for many actors. Leto's pattern of solicitations, however, obscured the situational and quotidian boundaries of performance locations by forcing other quotidian actors to engage with Leto-as-Joker's intentional pulls outside of the situational narrative realm. This means that the empathetic solicitations become inherently skewed because of the severely compromised self–other distinctions.

The key difference between Leto's prank packages and the 1970s radical intrasubjective practices is that Leto diminishes the self–other distinctions across all three empathetic solicitations, rather than only the obvious intrasubjective version. The packages prank severely complicates the intersubjective self–other distinction because the targeted quotidian co-stars could not accurately respond to perpetuate the iterative exchange: if the package was from quotidian Leto, then the abuse of his colleagues unnecessarily complicates and endangers the set's social climate; if the package was from Leto-as-Joker, then Leto-as-Joker is targeting the other actor's quotidian selves who cannot adequately reply without risking their own intrasubjective self–other distinctions and thereby compromising their own acting work. This difficulty in responding is compounded by an obscured performative self–other distinction: by positioning himself as the spectator of his co-stars' reaction to the package prank, Leto abdicates responsibility for his co-stars' suffering because they owe him a response for Leto's experiment to produce Leto's appresentation-fostering experiences. Moreover, while the wanton grotesqueness of these preparations is plausibly useful in establishing an intrasubjective affective match with Leto-as-Joker, they invert the intersubjective criterion of care into Leto seeking community with his colleagues by antagonizing and revolting them. The commitment to enworlding the narrative with his fellow actors is present but the terms of that showing of care depends on giving unrequested permission for Leto to harass his co-stars off-set. The solicitation of reciprocated care for Leto becomes constricted within the discourses of repulsion, dominance, and entitlement, regardless of what empathy-inducing questions his co-stars may be asking about their actor-as-character's relationship with Leto-as-Joker.

This forced involvement of one's co-stars is a significant step beyond Robert De Niro's radical intrasubjective experiments with the self–other distinction on films like *Raging Bull* and *Taxi Driver*, wherein De Niro not only immersed himself in his characters' lives but also changed his physical quotidian body to better remember as his characters. De Niro's weight fluctuations, skill acquisitions, and self-mutilations were largely confined to his own body for the exclusive purpose of supporting the actor's reorganization of his bodymind schema as a situational self.

In contrast, Leto crosses a boundary within acting culture by pushing his creative experiments with his scene partners off-camera, where the normal framework of the intersubjective connection must work at a disadvantage without the goal of producing verisimilar fiction. This level of confusion, repulsion, and uneasiness may indeed have provided Leto with the experience and appresentations that he desired to better connect with Leto-as-Joker. The cost, however, seems to have outweighed its benefits in the eyes of many fellow screen actors: the general disapproval of Leto's package prank among my interviewees reflects a contemporary attitude about intersubjective solicitations, at least in Canadian screen acting culture, that each actor is responsible for her own work, and must consent to be part of someone else's off-camera experiments. The often highly individual nature of pre-filming preparations anticipates a great deal of hope and trust in the talents of one's scene partners that, on the day of shooting, the actors will creatively support each other in front of the camera. By relying on on-set off-camera pranks that risk antagonizing one's scene partners, Leto not only broke the trusting professionalism at the core of on-set tactics like Dinicol's Jazz, but potentially obscured the intersubjective connections to a point where the cast's only remaining option was to revert to audition-style performances in lieu of acting work.

In the absence of some insight into the actor's creative process, such as Bastién's report on Leto, an analysis of a given performance's empathetic underpinnings is a limited and convoluted approach to performance studies. Many actors freely blend techniques from across acting styles, and may not necessarily attribute the components of this blend to any particular major practitioners. Conflicts among practitioners and masochistic radical intrasubjectivity, however, need not be the only contexts for reading acting practices into histories of performance style.

Diane Keaton, Meisner, and Annie Hall

In instances where a contemporary acting technique is immediately ascribable to a performance, an analysis of how the actor's empathetic solicitations intersect with the performances of cultural paradigms like race, gender, and class can provide valuable nuance to the intentional foundations of the performed cultural paradigm. In fact, the vigorous inclusion of acting practices and their empathetic solicitations within star studies can lead to a more holistic analysis of an actor's performance because it positions the actor as creative agent who produces meanings, rather than just an over-determined semiotic specimen: what the actor *does* alongside what her performance *represents*.

For example, Diane Keaton's Oscar-winning performance in *Annie Hall* (Woody Allen, 1977) is often analyzed in terms of its gender representation. Structural and auteurist analyses often position Keaton-as-Annie within a series of tensions between second-wave feminist politics and the narrational agency of Allen as the director and Allen-as-Alvie.[12] Keaton-as-Annie is also frequently invoked in commentary on contemporary women's fashion. Journalist Ruth La Ferla, for example, cites *Newsweek*'s contemporary review of *Annie Hall* that connects Keaton's performance, Keaton-as-Annie's wardrobe, and contemporary discourse on femininity: "[Keaton's] throwaway verbal style and her thrown-together dress style became symbols of the free, friendly, gracefully puzzled young women who were busy creating identities out of the epic miscellany of materials swirling in the American cultural centrifuge."[13] What is not often read into analyses of Keaton-as-Annie is that, as a young actor and prior to shooting *Annie Hall*, Keaton studied intensively with Meisner for two years at New York's Neighborhood Playhouse.[14] When viewing the film with this in mind, the intersubjective solicitations upon which Meisner's Method depends are clearly informing Keaton's performance choices and the ensuing significations.

As discussed in Chapter 2, Meisner's Method prioritizes the connection among actors "living under imaginary circumstances" by encouraging truthful and spontaneous reactions to one's scene partner, thereby creating the situational verisimilar world of those imaginary circumstances. Meisner-based acting is therefore far more invested in paying attention to the subtext of the scene partner's communications than it is in recalling one's lines perfectly or hitting a pre-determined emotional mark at a set point in the drama. Whereas Keaton and Allen appear to be telling jokes in their slapstick-laden previous collaborations on *Sleeper* (1973) and *Love and Death* (1975), their non-fantastical performances in

Annie Hall generate the impression that Keaton-as-Annie and Allen-as-Alvie are actually listening to each other. Their many long-take conversations showcase how Keaton's "throwaway verbal style" goes hand-in-hand with her close attention to Allen-as-Alvie's reactions.

I therefore suggest that Keaton plays a high-level version of Meisner's Repetition Game to connect Keaton-as-Annie with Allen-as-Alvie. The naturalistic ease of Keaton's performance in the tennis and post-tennis sequences, for example, stems from the iterative loop of responses that she establishes by playing off Allen's intention-laden dialogue and body language. In their conversations at the tennis club and on Annie's balcony, Keaton-as-Annie constantly probes Allen-as-Alvie's intersubjective intentional pull for cues towards his cognitive scaffolding—especially for narrative cues that he may also fancy her. Keaton-as-Annie immediately latches on to any indication that he wishes to continue talking to her while actively trying to continue the conversation despite her verbal clumsiness. At the same time, Keaton seems to defer her performative address to her co-collaborators, especially Allen as her director and co-star, trusting that her prioritized connection with Allen-as-Alvie will be transcribed by the camera in a way that faithfully pushes her intentionality towards the spectator.

Keaton-as-Annie's giddy post-tennis flirtations screen like a Meisnerian monologue exercise. Meisner instructed his actors to treat monologues as a conversation where only one person has the impetus to speak, on the

Figure 7.2 Diane Keaton in *Annie Hall* (Woody Allen, 1977)

presumption that the actor communicates her cognitive scaffolding and extends her intentional pull—or, what Meisner would simply call her "character"—through how she uses that impetus to speak.[15] Whether the post-tennis dialogue was scripted by Allen from the beginning or grew out of an onset improvisation between the two actors, the Meisnerian effect of the indirectly repeated text and the directly sustained subtext becomes a spontaneous reciprocation of their amorous connection. Keaton's most likely appresentational Magic If for this sequence of "If I was Annie, how would I speak with this man if I wanted to impress him?" not only gives her narrational license to include all of Annie's anxieties about her intelligence in her flirting but to use the answer to that Magic If to present Annie's cognitive scaffolding as an intentional snare to pull Allen-as-Alvie and the anticipated spectator towards her compelling character.

Keaton's acting is not necessarily the only manifestation of Meisner's Method in *Annie Hall*. After the tennis match, Keaton-as-Annie and Allen-as-Alvie discuss Annie's photography while superimposed subtitles comically reveal the romantic and sexual subtexts of their conversation. This impulse to explicate each character's intentions, and to recode their desires as the subtext of a pseudo-intellectual conversation about art, playfully deconstructs the Repetition Game's emphasis on sincerity and spontaneity. Moreover, the importance of the highbrow language that Keaton-as-Annie and Allen-as-Alvie use in their efforts to impress each other—often accompanied by their insecurities about whether they sound as smart as they hope—reflexively appropriates Meisner's disdain for precious and premeditated dialogue. By recoding their flirtation as detached and distracted intellectualism, Allen's narrational device pits the sincerity of the Repetition Game against itself: Keaton-as-Annie and Allen-as-Alvie must pay great attention to each other to project that they are not expressing too much interest in each other. Keaton and Allen are also complicit in the performative aspects of the gag, since they both know from the screenplay that the subtitles will be added later. They are both therefore free to play the scene as dry as possible, knowing that the scene's comedy emerges in the contrast between the dry performances and the emotionally loaded subtitles. Keaton and Allen therefore adjust their performances to collaborate with the subtext-laden subtitles in a meta-textual joke about Meisnerian acting, interpersonal communication, and the banality of flirtation.

Keaton's Meisner-based intersubjective connections were likely bolstered by readily accessible intrasubjective appresentations from her contemporary romantic relationship with Allen. In this case, Keaton's performance presents an interesting overlap of Keaton's primary and secondary intersubjective relationships: Keaton's personal and professional synchronicity with Allen mirrors the dynamics of their characters' rapport on-screen. This is not to suggest that the self–other distinctions across Keaton's solicitations are diminished or flawed; rather, the compelling appresentations that encouraged Keaton's affective matches and other-oriented perspective takings were evidently enough to ensnare Keaton in Annie's intentional pulls and pushes. By establishing a compelling continuity between her intrasubjective and intersubjective solicitations, Keaton is able to let Keaton-as-Annie be herself, firm in her trust that her lover, co-star, and director's camera would capture the raw materials of her performance.

The possibilities for connecting the context of Keaton's acting work to the ongoing conversation on *Annie Hall*'s gender politics force a more clear distinction between performance and acting. Christopher J. Knight convincingly argues that *Annie Hall*'s narration constructs Keaton-as-Annie exclusively in terms of how Allen-as-Alvie remembers their romantic relationship, and that Annie's presence primarily catalyzes Alvie's development as a character.[16] It would be too reductive, however, to claim that the intersubjective focus of Meisner's technique predisposed Keaton to make her performance subservient to that of Allen.

First of all, Meisner-based screen acting is by no means a gender-exclusive practice. To claim that Meisnerian intersubjectivity in *Annie Hall* positions Keaton as a mirror for Allen's auteurist genius conflates Keaton-as-Annie's narrative affordances with Keaton's capacity to perform that narrative. *Annie Hall*'s narration provides relatively few biographical details on Annie's life prior to meeting Alvie. The personal cognitive scaffolding that Keaton-as-Annie intentionally pushes towards the spectator—that Annie is an insecure, unpretentious Midwestern woman who struggles to acclimatize to life in New York—only manifests on screen because Keaton uses her Meisnerian training to make those imaginary circumstances real and compelling through her spontaneous and sincere performance choices. In *Annie Hall*'s specific narrative and industrial circumstances, an actor with Keaton's repository of bodymind resources and Method-specific training as an actor could not help but signify the socio-cultural gender politics that she does. Given that Keaton-as-Annie's breezy spontaneity is as much a character choice by Keaton as it is a reflection of Keaton's professional training, the complicity of Keaton's intersubjective connections in *Annie Hall* with her performative solicitation warrants further research. By including Keaton's creative technique and capacity for reorganizing her bodymind as the situational self of Annie, Keaton's creative agency signifies, among other things, "white,"

"Midwestern woman," "modestly educated," "aloof and insecure," by reacting to her key collaborators to realize the goals of her situational self in the drama's imaginary circumstances. Keaton-as-Annie's ensuing cultural significations for the spectator are certainly a valid topic of study, but there is no reason to marginalize Keaton's creative agency in the process. If anything, by enriching studies on specific performances with the context of the actor's creative process, this type of research can challenge and reinvigorate problematic presumptions in, among other things, auteurist film criticism.

Despite Allen's significant auteurist control over *Annie Hall* as its writer, director, and leading man, Keaton had considerable creative freedom throughout the filming process. Annie's iconic necktie and vest costume, for example was Keaton's idea: Allen reportedly dismissed the wardrobe department's protests against the necktie and vest by telling them that Keaton was a "genius" and should be given creative license to work as such.[17] Allen's general reliance on long-take cinematography for scenes with Allen-as-Alvie and Keaton-as-Annie shows a great degree of trust in Keaton as a highly skilled co-collaborator. Although Knight accurately positions *Annie Hall*'s narrative structure as privileging Annie's narrational subservience to Alvie's recollection of their relationship,[18] Keaton's actorly contributions to *Annie Hall* demonstrate a highly proficient application of inductive creativity that capitalized on the film's set-specific affordances.

At the same time, any claim about Allen's treatment of women on- and off-camera is inherently problematic: his marriage to Soon-Yi Previn has been heavily criticized, and numerous women within the #MeToo movement have accused Allen of abuse, exploitation, and performative victimhood.[19] The inclusion of Keaton's approach to acting to a performance analysis of *Annie Hall* does not exonerate Allen. Instead, I suggest that Keaton's considerable skill with Meisnerian acting technique nuances the criticism of Keaton-as-Annie as Allen's misogynist accomplice by stressing Keaton's creative agency in generating a compelling, if culturally problematic, performance.

Collective Cognition and Production Studies

A critical vocabulary for the bodymind processes that give screen actors creative agency presents at least two major challenges to auteurist criticism.

First, acknowledging that actors make artistic contributions during filmmaking is a direct challenge to the creative autonomy often ascribed to directors by classical auteur theory. Infamous auteur critic Andrew Sarris, for example, praises Elia Kazan as an "actor's director" and insists that Marlon Brando, one of Kazan's most prolific collaborators, is an auteur in his own right.[20] Sarris, however, refuses to elevate Kazan into his pantheon of cinematic auteurs despite Kazan's considerable skill in assembling highly skilled casts and drawing compelling screen performances from them.[21] The problem of the monolithic director-auteur is more of a historicized concept than an industrial reality. In her book *Directing Actors*, filmmaking instructor Judith Weston insists that directors learn to treat actors as talented creative agents whose approach to their filmmaking responsibilities is significantly different than the director but is no less valuable: screen actors and directors must collaborate and synthesize, rather than compromise, to create compelling screen performances.[22] This discrepancy between concepts of authorship and the industrial nature of on-set collaborations leads to the second major challenge that actorly creative agency presents to classical auteurism.

One of the foundational premises of John Caldwell's production studies is that screen media production is inherently collaborative, and that each member of a film or television show's production staff practices skillful crafts towards the project's completion.[23] Caldwell positions the practices of the entire production team as working towards the same greater goal of producing an aesthetically compelling and commercially viable media text. This mobilization of a professional community of media-producing specialists implies not only a chain of command, but also a mostly common vision of the final project towards which each member of the production team directs their efforts.

Caldwell's studies of film and television production teams as practice-driven professionals intersects productively with Colin MacCabe's theory of collective film authorship. In response to Michel Foucault's dismissal of the author as a side effect of how a text is read,[24] MacCabe argues that film is not only collectively authored by the entire production team but that this production team further comprises the film's first audience.[25] The collective vision for the completed production therefore draws on the imagination and expertise of the entire production staff, since it stands to reason, after all, that films are made with attention to how the final version should eventually look, sound, and feel. In this light, filmmaking is a practice of collaborators sharing appresentations for how each shot ought to look. These shared appresentations are then realized through a strategic combination of specialized professional contributions from all of the on-set collaborators.

As members of the community of authors and of the film's first audience, MacCabe's model of collective authorship is consistent with my suggestions for the actor's performative solicitation. Screen actors study their craft in part by watching their recorded performances to gain a stronger idea of how their performing body schema communicates to the audience. Moreover, by appresenting herself as part of the film's anticipated audience, the actor adjusts her performances in ways that she presumes will best solicit the desired connections from that anticipated audience. To build upon MacCabe with my theory of empathetic solicitations, I suggest that the actor's greater creative collaboration with the rest of the production personnel comprises a form of industrialized thinking-together: the collective production of a media text guided by a shared set of professional goals and imaginary constructions of what the final filmed production should be. Nearly every actor interviewed for this book remarked that the sense of community and common purpose on set among film production staff impacts the ways in which actors can collaborate during production. This does not suggest that these on-set collaborations are free from conflict, disagreement, power struggles, or miscommunication. It does suggest, however, that the performative solicitation is one actor-specific aspect of an industrial thinking-together within film and television production.

The prospect of creative individuals thinking together is hardly new: even if the term "empathy" is misapplied in Ribeiro and Fonseca's model of kinesthetic empathy in modern dance,[26] the dance practices that they analyze could certainly qualify as a form of kinesthetic thinking-together through dance. One of the challenges presented by applying collective cognition to film production, however, is the diversity of professions and the industrial hierarchy that in part coordinates their efforts. It is one thing for Ribeiro and Fonseca analyze the relationships among dancers and choreographers, who are presumably also competent dancers; it is another to draw this equivalency between screen actors and cinematographers, neither of whom may have ever worked in the other's specialization.

To this end, I suggest that Hung's model of collective cognition and team-based problem solving (TBPS) could serve as a useful conceptual intermediary between cognitive science and production studies because of the ways in which it accounts for individual specializations, group dynamics, and multiple hypothetical solutions to the same problem. In film production, for example, there is rarely only one way to shoot, stage, and dramatize a scene. Following Hung, the way in which a scene is eventually shot and staged is not an aggregate of all the thought put towards producing the scene; rather, the way the scene is realized is the resulting meeting place of many individuals who coordinate their professional skills, knowledge, insight, and focused efforts towards realizing a "shared mental model" of what the scene could be.[27]

The inherently collaborative nature of filmmaking means that many highly-skilled specialized workers, from actors and directors to lighting technicians to production assistants, all make their best contribution to the as-yet-unrealized final product. Wanda Orlikowski's use of a jazz metaphor for creative constraints and affordances is helpful here: an improvisational jazz performance is what ensues when specialized musicians agree upon a melody, a musical key, and a tempo, and leave the rest up to how it plays out in action.[28] No screenplay is the finished film, so what the actor and her on-set collaborators do with the constraints and affordances of that screenplay based on their best intuitions about what makes for a compelling film is what ultimately forms the final edit, even if the narrative and production roles of all staff are largely agreed upon before shooting begins. Affordances and their constraining counterparts address the subject's adaptation to the situation-specific possibilities for action; the process of realizing a goal through informed improvisation and best guesses, rather than an analysis of the goal itself. Although empathy is likely too strong and specific of a term to describe the entire professional thinking-together among all production staff on set, the actor's performative solicitation and collaboration with the camera might be her specialized contribution to the TBPS project of film and television production.

Sympathy for Kuleshov: (Re-)Introducing Acting to Film Form

In looking across the phases of screen acting from the initial audition to the final take filmed on set, the most significant variation in overall empathetic solicitations takes place in the actor's relationships with her core co-collaborators: the camera and her fellow actors. In particular, the consistency of empathetic prioritization between audition acting and Lisinska's Tears asserts the actor's creative agency in, and contributing potential towards, the finished performance. Screen actors use what they have on set, both in terms of bodymind resources and the set's physical conditions, to communicate a narrative moment to the camera without the necessary accommodation of another actor. This is not to suggest that Lisinska's Tears forces the actor to work against or despite her scene partner: whereas audition readers tend to be non-actors, Lisinska and Maslany already had a productive, genial professional relationship by the time they filmed the Lisinska's Tears scene. Lisinska was able to include the onset affordances of the weather and her physical discomfort with her intrasubjective preparations, and was thereby able to trust that Maslany would intersubjectively support her performance without the constant "checking in" of Dinicol's Jazz, for example. Lisinska was able to immerse herself in the narrative moment and intentionally push that immersion towards the camera, regardless of Maslany's presence in the shooting of a given take. As a screen-specific acting practice, Lisinska's Tears represents the point where the performance leaves the audition performances' empathetic constraints behind: when the intersubjective connection is so firmly in place that she can leave it alone and focus on performatively communicating her intrasubjective understanding to the spectator.

Although the intrasubjective connection remains consistently important across the various phases of acting work, the differences in empathetic priority between Dinicol's Jazz, Lisinska's Tears, and McCarthy's Symphony, and even audition acting demonstrate the changeable potential of the intersubjective and performative connections in screen-specific acting. Although Lutterbie argues persuasively that theater actors are connected to the situation-specific conditions availed by the performance venue, realist theatrical acting simply does not let the actor marginalize the rest of the cast to project her character at the audience, nor does it permit the actor to ignore those venue-determined conditions. The shifting position of the camera in the eventual intersubjective and performative solicitations reflects praxis attitudes of how the actor ought to fill the space before the camera and, more specifically, her space within that camera's lens.

Ideas about how screen-specific acting practices should fill performance spaces not only go far back in film history but also resonate in contemporary scholarship on-screen performance. Kuleshov's little-known Metric Web experiments, for example, are a fascinating historical counterpoint to Stanislavsky's system because of its medium specificity and its contemporaneity with Stanislavsky's theatrical work. Kuleshov was exclusively interested in developing a performance method for screen actors, deeming the emotional excesses of the stage actors from Stanislavsky's Moscow Art Theater to be unintelligible on screen.[29] What was necessary, then, were meticulously calculated performances that were crafted around communicative clarity rather than emotional verisimilitude. Embracing Delsartian ideas about acting through refined gestures, poses, and facial expressions,[30] Kuleshov insisted that a character's emotions were to be demonstrated through codified external motions, rather than implied by psychological realism. The actor's motions were to be scripted and fixed in duration like musical notes in an orchestral score[31] to make them as understandable and recordable as possible.

Kuleshov related the actor's external performance to the actor's location in an imaginary geometric prism extending from the camera's lens called the Metric Web. An actor's gestures and motions across the screen could presumably be measured and charted within the Metric Web for optimal communicability based on their angle of presentation to the camera and orientation within the frame.[32] Although Kuleshov noted that movements along straight lines on ninety- and forty-five-degree angles from the camera are the easiest for the audience to follow,[33] a particularly articulate actor can make all motions clear provided he understands and internalizes his place within these planes of motion.[34] Actors and director must therefore construct the film's performances with the rest of the film's form already in mind. Despite Kuleshov's close association with Soviet montage theory, the Metric Web process positions acting as an active force and primary formal concern in the greater vision of the film, rather than an auteurist relegation of acting as an unpredictable sub-aspect of the *mise-en-scène*.

To reframe Kuleshov's questions about screen actors, performance spaces, and technological over-determinations in terms of acting as a practice of soliciting empathetic connections, I suggest a comparative historical approach to how actors worked with the filmmaking technologies of their day. Subsequent generations of screen actors have stylistically moved beyond the technological accommodations required for acting in front of early Soviet film technology. Whereas Kuleshov was prepared to sacrifice psychological realism in realist acting for communicative clarity, mainstream contemporary screen acting now draws so readily on the common realist practices for intrasubjective and intersubjective work for screen and stage alike to ensure psychological realism. At the same time, contemporary screen actors often find themselves navigating a new series of technological developments that make different demands of the verisimilar forces latent with a performance's—increasingly computational—geometry.

As if talking to tennis balls and acting in front of green-screens did not place enough medium-specific demands on actors, the increasing use of motion-capture suits for CGI-animated "synthespians"[35] in large-budget film production forces actors to come up with ways for including post-production animators within the greater industrial collaboration that completes the actor's performance. Although it would be easy to see these technological interventions as a further nail in screen acting's formal coffin, it could be more productive to explore how the physicality of screen acting is changing to accommodate the actor's empathetic solicitations within the creative industrial collaboration.[36] Comparing the technological innovations to screen acting's physicality by actors like Andy Serkis with the creative practices of voice actors in traditional animation films could lead to new insights about creative collaboration and appresentational sharing, since both sets of actors must defer a significant percentage of their physical appearance on screen to other artists and craftspeople, such as animators and computer programmers. These colleagues must also think along with the creative raw material of the recorded actor's performance, which raises interesting questions of technological intervention in collaborative creative cognition. As potentially the most screen-specific acting and performance styles possible,[37] CGI acting and animation voice acting present a compelling reminder that acting's empathetic solicitations have never been formally or technologically neutral.[38]

Acting Studies and Resets

If a director wishes to get a second take of the scene that he is shooting, he may order his cast and crew to reset for another take with the phrase, "back to 1s". The "1" in question here is an abbreviation of "Position 1", referring to the starting place of every actor and crew member for the upcoming take. The request to make another attempt at producing something meaningful, laden with the possibilities of new discoveries, means going back to the start.

Beyond the critical vocabulary for analyzing screen acting that his book introduces, what is needed to launch a new realm of studies into screen acting practices is a comparable and fundamental reset of how film, television, and media scholars approach actors and acting in the first place. On some level, this whole project began from a desire for a book that connects the professional acting practices from my decades of work as an actor with the critical insights possible through academic research. Actors and scholars can look at each other's skills and expertise with a respectful common interest in cinema and artistry, but also with more than a little conversation-muffling mystique. I remain convinced that actors and scholars stand to learn a great deal from each other on many topics: art and aesthetics, media industries, creativity and embodiment, imagination and memory, exploitative and alienated labor, and more. It seems counterintuitive, after all, to obscure the common boundary of cinema as art to two communities whose interest in that boundary stems from inspiration, insight, professional ambition, and cinephilia.

The point of this book has never been to transform realist screen acting into a critical practice, or to advocate for intellectual art, or to call for the neuroscience of acting that Rhonda Blair and Amy Cook caution against.[39] Instead, this common critical vocabulary provides scholars with a point of access to the notoriously amorphous creative bodymind practices of screen actors. At the same time, this same common critical vocabulary gives actors a way to faithfully represent their craft to scholars without fear of losing sight of it within scholarly language. Cook suggests that the point of interdisciplinary research is not to use one discipline to validate another but to invigorate critical debates by posing new questions and starting new conversations:

> While I cannot use Shakespeare's poetry to prove a question in cognitive linguistics and cognitive linguistics cannot prove the value of Shakespeare, integrating the two enriches both and ignoring the knowledge and research across the disciplines imperils the work in our own. My means are interdisciplinary, but my goals are disciplinary.[40]

Ultimately, I hope that this research can put intelligent and creative people with similar interests into direct conversation, encouraging them to imagine themselves in someone else's shoes, connect with another who aspires to a reciprocated connection, and then sharing their collaboration. Rick Kemp's argues that devised theater is an improvisatory process wherein the end result is unknown but the practitioners can trust that the creative collaboration process will lead them somewhere interesting, innovative, and ultimately worthwhile.[41] So too with the critical study of screen acting: by going back to 1s and giving actors and practitioners room to express themselves, we open ourselves to the unpredictable movements of the selves who create the film and television productions that we spend so much time reading about.

The study of screen acting, either while training as an actor or analyzing its empathetic solicitations, means dealing with other people. The notion of film critics and scholars speaking directly with filmmakers and actors is far from new, despite the logistical hurdles that such research presents. The preface and introduction to François Truffaut's venerable interview-based book on Alfred Hitchcock describes the years of transcription, translation, and transportation required to complete such a study.[42] Carole Zucker's most recent book of interviews with screen actors plainly identifies the challenges faced by the need to coordinate with modern actors' agents, personal assistants, and publicists in order to conduct this kind of research.[43] Logistical challenges are far from being practical impossibilities: the ongoing research of Aaron Taylor's film acting research group at the University of Lethbridge embraces modern film actors' descriptions of their creative habits and processes, and I eagerly look forward to learning more about their findings. Despite the logistical inconveniences involved to contact the artists one wishes to write about, an analysis of screen acting that begins and ends with watching a finished film or television episode will ultimately fall into the robust and compelling traditions of performance analysis which, as this book has shown, should not be construed as studying the force of acting. In other words, the pragmatic and ecumenical impulses behind academia and acting alike suggest that the potential discoveries of resetting back to 1s for an extra take could be worth it.

Notes

1. Sternagel et al., "Etymological uncoveries, creative displays: acting as force and performance as eloquence in moving image culture," p. 53.
2. Naremore, *Acting in the Cinema*, pp. 2–3.
3. Naremore, "Introduction," p. 2.
4. Naremore, "Marlon Brando in 'On The Waterfront' (1954)."
5. Baron and Tzioumakis, *Acting Indie: Industry, Aesthetics, and Performance*.
6. Levinson, "The auteur renaissance, 1968–1980."
7. Bastién, "Hollywood has ruined Method acting."
8. Levinson, "The auteur renaissance, 1968–1980."
9. Bastién, "Hollywood has ruined Method acting."
10. As per the privacy clauses in the interview release agreements, I have chosen to make many of my respondents' reactions to Leto's creative process anonymous.
11. Kevin McGarry (actor), in discussion with the author, August 2016.
12. Knight, "Woody Allen's Annie Hall: Galatea's triumph over Pygmalion"; Schatz, "Annie Hall and the issue of modernism"; Brenneman, "Play it again, Diane."
13. La Ferla, "Unbuttoning Annie Hall: Diane Keaton, 58, comes of age."
14. Mitchell, *Diane Keaton: Artist and Icon*, p. 9.
15. Meisner and Longwell, *On Acting*, pp. 148–50, 156.
16. Knight, "Woody Allen's Annie Hall: Galatea's triumph over Pygmalion."
17. Mitchell, *Diane Keaton: Artist and Icon*, p. 40.
18. Knight, "Woody Allen's Annie Hall: Galatea's triumph over Pygmalion."
19. Lee, "Woody Allen: 'I should be the poster boy for the #MeToo Movement.'"
20. Sarris, "Notes on the auteur theory (1962)," p. 43.
21. Sarris, *The American Cinema*, pp. 158–9.
22. Weston, *Directing Actors*, p. 9.
23. Caldwell, *Production Culture: Industrial Reflexivity and Critical Practice in Film and Television*.
24. Foucault, "What is an author? [Extract]."
25. MacCabe, "The revenge of the author," p. 36.
26. See Chapter 1.
27. Hung, "Team-based complex problem solving: a collective cognition perspective," pp. 368–71.
28. Orlikowski and Hofman, "An improvisational model for change management: the case of Groupware Technologies."
29. Kuleshov, "Art of the Cinema (1929)," p. 99.
30. Levaco, "Introduction," p. 9.

31. Kuleshov, "Art of the Cinema (1929)," p. 105.
32. Ibid. p. 111.
33. Ibid. p. 109.
34. Ibid. p. 113.
35. Burston, "Synthespians among us: rethinking the actor in media work and media theory."
36. Leberg, "Digital drapery and body schema-tics."
37. I acknowledge that some traditions of theatrical puppet performance require actors to speak as-puppet/character in ways that may resemble how voice actors perform for animated films. In the same vein, the close collaborations between puppeteers and voice actors in children's television production represent a complicated blend of screen and theatrical performance conventions. Although this could make for an interesting future project, I simply do not have time to "Muppet-proof" this book without further research funding.
38. Baron, "The Modern Entertainment Complex," pp. 143–4.
39. Blair and Cook, "Introduction," p. 2.
40. Cook, "Emergence, meaning, and presence: an interdisciplinary approach to a disciplinary question," p. 226.
41. Kemp, "Devising—embodied creativity in distributed systems."
42. Truffaut, *Hitchcock*, pp. 12–14.
43. Zucker, *Don't Think. Be. 20 Actors Talk about Training, Technique, and Process*, p. 2.

Bibliography

Adamou, Christina, "Postfeminist portrayals of masculinity and femininity in action films: Mr. and Mrs. Smith," in Jörg Sternagel, Deborah Levitt, and Dieter Mersch (eds), *Acting and Performance in Moving Image Culture* (Bielefeld: transcript Verlag, 2012), pp. 101–13.

Adler, Stella, *The Art of Acting*, ed. Howard Kissel (New York: Applause Books, 2000).

Alford, C. Fred, "Mirror neurons, psychoanalysis, and the age of empathy," *International Journal of Applied Psychoanalytic Studies* 13, no. 1 (2016): 7–23, <https://doi.org/10.1002/aps.1411>.

Arévalo, Analía, Juliana Baldo, Fernando González-Perilli, and Agustín Ibáñez, "What can we make of theories of embodiment and the role of the human mirror neuron system?", *Frontiers in Human Neuroscience* 9, September (2015): 1–3, <https://doi.org/10.3389/fnhum.2015.00500>.

Bal, P. Matthijs and Martijn Veltkamp, "How does fiction reading influence empathy? An experimental investigation on the role of emotional transportation," *PLoS ONE* 8, no. 1 (2013): 1–12, <https://doi.org/10.1371/journal.pone.0055341>.

Bandelj, Nina, "How method actors create character roles," *Sociological Forum* 18, no. 3 (2003): 387–416.

Baron, Cynthia, "The modern entertainment complex," in Claudia Springer and Julie Levinson (eds), *Acting* (London and New York: I. B. Tauris, 2015), pp. 143–67.

Baron, Cynthia, Diane Carson, and Frank P. Tomasulo, "More than the Method, more than one Method," in Cynthia Baron, Diane Carson, and Frank P. Tomasulo (eds), *More Than a Method: Trends and Traditions in Contemporary Film Performance* (Detroit, MI: Wayne State University Press, 2004).

Baron, Cynthia, and Yannis Tzioumakis, *Acting Indie: Industry, Aesthetics, and Performance* (London: Palgrave Macmillan, 2020).

Barthes, Roland, "The death of the author," in Keith Barry Grant (ed.), *Auteurs and Authorship: A Film Reader* (Malden, MA: Blackwell Publishing, 2008), pp. 97–100.

Bastién, Angelica Jade, "Hollywood has ruined Method acting," *The Atlantic*, August 2016, <https://www.theatlantic.com/entertainment/archive/2016/08/hollywood-has-ruined-method-acting/494777/>.

Beaty, Roger E. and Rex E. Jung, "Interacting brain networks underlying creative cognition and artistic performance," in Kalina Christoff and Kieran C. R. Fox (eds) *The Oxford Handbook of Spontaneous Thought: Mind-Wandering, Creativity, and Dreaming* (Oxford: Oxford University Press, 2018), pp. 275–84, <https://doi.org/10.1093/oxfordhb/9780190464745.013.10>.

Bella, Robert, "Practical aesthetics: an overview," in Arthur Bartow (ed.), *Training of The American Actor* (New York: Theatre Communications Group, 2006), pp. 223–50.

Blair, Rhonda, "Cognitive neuroscience and acting: imagination, conceptual blending, and empathy," *TDR: The Drama Review* 53, no. 4 (2009): 92–103, <https://www.jstor.org/stable/25599520>.

Blair, Rhonda, *The Actor, Image, and Action: Acting and Cognitive Neuroscience* (London and New York: Routledge, 2008).

Blair, Rhonda and Amy Cook, "Bodies in performance," in Blair and Cook (eds), *Theatre, Performance, and Cognition* (London: Bloomsbury, 2016), pp. 75–7.

Blair, Rhonda and Amy Cook, "Introduction," in Blair and Cook (eds), *Theatre, Performance, and Cognition* (London: Bloomsbury, 2016), pp. 1–15.

Blair, Rhonda and Amy Cook, "Situated cognition and dynamic systems: cognitive ecologies," in Blair and Cook (eds), *Theatre, Performance, and Cognition* (London: Bloomsbury, 2016), pp. 128–32.

Bode, Lisa, "No longer themselves?: framing digitally enabled posthumous 'performance'," *Cinema Journal* 49, no. 4 (2010), pp. 46–70.

Brenneman, Brianne Jewett, "Play it again, Diane," *Film International* 14, no. 1 (2016): 24–34.

Britten, Bill, *From Stage to Screen: A Theatre Actor's Guide to Working on Camera* (London: Bloomsbury Methuen Drama, 2015).

Buckner, Randy L. and Daniel C. Carroll, "Self-projection and the brain," *Trends in Cognitive Sciences* 11 (2007): 49–57.

Burston, Jonathan, "Synthespians among us: rethinking the actor in media work and media theory," in James Curran and David Morley (eds), *Media and Cultural Theory* (London: Routledge, 2006), pp. 251–62.

Butler, Judith, "Gender is burning: questions of appropriation and subversion," in Sue Thornham (ed.), *Feminist Film Theory: A Reader* (New York: New York University Press, 1999), pp. 336–49.

Butler, Judith, "Performative acts and gender constitution: an essay in phenomenology and feminist theory," *Theatre Journal* 40, no. 4 (1988): 519–31.

Caldwell, John Thorton, *Production Culture: Industrial Reflexivity and Critical Practice in Film and Television* (Durham, NC: Duke University Press, 2008).

Cantrell, Tom and Christopher Hogg, "Returning to an old question: what do television actors do when they act?" *Critical Studies in Television: The*

International Journal of Television Studies 11, no. 3 (2016): 283–98, <https://doi.org/10.1177/1749602016662430>.

Carnicke, Sharon Marie, *Stanislavsky in Focus: An Acting Master for the Twenty-First Century*, 2nd edn (New York and London: Routledge, 2009).

Cassidy, Gary and Simone Knox, "Phil Davis: the process of acting," *Critical Studies in Television* 13, no. 3 (2018): 315–32, <https://doi.org/10.1177/1749602018785833>.

Cavell, Stanley, "Reflections on the ontology of film," in Pamela Robertson Wojcik (ed.), *Movie Acting, The Film Reader* (London and New York: Routledge, 2004), pp. 29–37.

Chubbuck, Ivana, *The Power of the Actor* (New York: Gotham Books, 2004).

Clurman, Harold, *The Fervent Years: The Group Theatre And The Thirties* (New York: Harcourt Brace Jovanovich, 1975).

Collard, Christophe, "Living truthfully: David Mamet's practical aesthetics," *New Theatre Quarterly* 26, no. 4 (2010): 329–39, <https://doi.org/doi:10.1017/S0266464X10000631>.

Cook, Amy, *Building Character: The Art and Science of Casting* (Ann Arbor: University of Michigan Press, 2018).

Cook, Amy, "Emergence, meaning, and presence: an interdisciplinary approach to a disciplinary question," in Rick Kemp and Bruce McConachie (eds), *The Routledge Companion to Theatre, Performance, and Cognitive Science* (London: Routledge, 2019), pp. 225–34.

Coplan, Amy, "Understanding empathy: its features and effects," in Amy Coplan and Peter Goldie (eds), *Empathy: Philosophical and Psychological Perspectives* (Oxford: Oxford University Press, 2011), pp. 3–18.

Coplan, Amy and Peter Goldie, "Introduction," in *Empathy: Philosophical and Psychological Perspectives* (Oxford: Oxford University Press, 2011), pp. ix–xlvii.

Corradini, Antonella and Alessandro Antonietti, "Mirror neurons and their function in cognitively understood empathy," *Consciousness and Cognition* 22, no. 3 (2013): 1152–61, <https://doi.org/10.1016/j.concog.2013.03.003>.

Croft, David G., "Acting on Film with Michael Caine" (London: BBC Television, 1987).

Csikzentmihalyi, Mihaly, *Creativity: Flow and the Psychology and Discovery of Invention* (New York: Harper Perennial, 1997).

de Valck, M. "Film festivals, Bourdieu, and the economization of culture," *Canadian Journal of Film Studies* 23, no. 1 (2014): 74–89.

Decety, Jean, "The neural pathways, development and functions of empathy," *Current Opinion in Behavioral Sciences*, 3 (2015): 1–6, <https://doi.org/10.1016/j.cobeha.2014.12.001>.

Decety, Jean, Inbal Ben Ami Bartal, Florina Uzefovsky, and Ariel Knafo-Noam, "Empathy as a driver of prosocial behaviour: highly conserved neuro-behavioural mechanisms across species," *Philosophical Transactions of the Royal Society* B 371, no. 1686 (2016): 1–11, <https://doi.org/10.1098/rstb.2015.0077>.

Decety, Jean and Jason M. Cowell, "Friends or foes: is empathy necessary for moral behavior?" *Perspectives on Psychological Science* 9, no. 5 (2014): 525–37, <https://doi.org/10.1177/1745691614545130>.

Drummond, John J., "Imagination and appresentation, sympathy and empathy in Smith and Husserl," in Christel Fricke and Dagfinn Føllesdal (eds), *Intersubjectivity and Objectivity in Adam Smith and Edmund Husserl*, 8th edn (Frankfurt: Ontos Verlag, 2012), pp. 117–37.

Dyer, Richard, *Stars*, new edition with a supplementary chapter, 1998 (London: British Film Institute, [1979]).

Dyer, Richard, "White," *Screen* 29, no. 4 (1988): 44–65, <https://doi.org/10.1093/screen/29.4.44>.

Ebert, Roger, "The Silence of the Lambs movie review (1991) | Roger Ebert," www.rogerebert.com, 2001, <http://www.rogerebert.com/reviews/great-movie-the-silence-of-the-lambs-1991>.

Fauconnier, Gilles and Mark Turner, *The Way We Think: Conceptual Blending and the Mind's Hidden Complexities* (New York: Basic Books, 2002).

Feagin, Susan L., "Empathizing as simulating," in Amy Coplan and Peter Goldie (eds), *Empathy: Philosophical and Psychological Perspectives* (Oxford: Oxford University Press, 2011), pp. 149–61.

Feinstein, David, "Archetypes," *Encyclopedia of Psychology*, vol. 1 (American Psychological Association and Oxford University Press, 2000).

Fife Donaldson, Lucy and James Walters, "Inter(acting): television, performance and synthesis," *Critical Studies in Television: The International Journal of Television Studies* 13, no. 3 (2018): 352–69, <https://doi.org/10.1177/1749602018781465>.

Foucault, Michel, "What is an author? [Extract]," in John Caughie (ed.), *Theories of Authorship* (London and New York: Routledge, 1981), pp. 282–91.

Frome, Shelley, *The Actors Studio: A History* (Jefferson, NC: McFarland, 2001).

Gallagher, Shaun and Julia Gallagher, "Acting oneself as another: an actor's empathy for her character," *Topoi* 2019 <https://doi.org/10.1007/s11245-018-9624-7>.

Gallese, Vittorio, "Visions of the body: embodied simulation and aesthetic experience," *Humanities Futures* June (2017): 1–25, <https://doi.org/10.13128/Aisthesis-20902>.

Gallese, Vittorio and Valentina Cuccio, "The paradigmatic body—embodied simulation, intersubjectivity, the bodily self, and language," in Thomas Metzinger and Jennifer M. Windt (eds), *Open MIND* 14: 1–22, Frankfurt am Main, Germany, 2015, <https://doi.org/10.15502/9783958570269>.

Gallese, Vittorio and Michele Guerra, *The Empathic Screen*, translated by Frances Anderson (Oxford: Oxford University Press, 2020).

Goldman, Alvin, *Simulating Minds: The Philosophy, Psychology, and Neuroscience of Mindreading* (Oxford: Oxford University Press, 2006).

Greeno, James G., "Gibson's affordances," *Psychological Review* 101, no. 2 (1994): 336–42.

Hagen, Uta, *A Challenge for the Actor* (New York: Scribner, 1991).

Hart, Victoria, "Meisner technique: teaching the work of Sanford Meisner," in Arthur Bartow (ed.), *Training of The American Actor* (New York: Theatre Communications Group, 2006), pp. 51–96.

Hill, John Wesley and Rhonda Blair, "Stanislavsky and cognitive science," *TDR – The Drama Review – A Journal of Performance Studies* 54, no. 3 (2010): 9–11, <https://doi.org/10.1162/DRAM_c_00002>.

Hirsch, Foster, *A Method to Their Madness: The History of the Actors Studio* (New York: W. W. Norton, 1984).

Hung, Woei, "Team-based complex problem solving: a collective cognition perspective," *Educational Technology Research and Development* 61, no. 3 (2013): 365–84.

Hutchins, Edwin, "The cultural ecosystem of human cognition," *Philosophical Philosophy* 27, no. 1 (2014): 34–49.

Jackman, Christopher J., "Training, insight and intuition in creative flow," in Rhonda Blair and Amy Cook (eds), *Theatre, Performance, and Cognition* (London: Bloomsbury, 2016), pp. 107–21.

Johnston, Daniel, "Stanislavskian acting as phenomenology in practice," *Journal of Dramatic Theory and Criticism* 26, no. 1 (2011): 65–84.

Kelso, J. A. Scott, *Dynamic Patterns: The Self-Organizations of Brain and Behavior* (Cambridge, MA, and London: MIT Press, 1995).

Kemp, Rick, "Acting technique, Jacques Lecoq and embodied meaning," in Rick Kemp and Bruce McConachie (eds), *The Routledge Companion to Theatre, Performance, and Cognitive Science* (London: Routledge, 2019), pp. 177–90, <https://doi.org/10.4324/9781315169927-19>.

Kemp, Rick, "Devising—embodied creativity in distributed systems," in Rick Kemp and Bruce McConachie (eds), *The Routledge Companion to Theatre, Performance, and Cognitive Science* (London: Routledge, 2019), pp. 48–57, <https://doi.org/10.4324/9781315169927-5>.

Kemp, Rick, *Embodied Acting: What Neuroscience Tells Us about Performance* (London and New York: Routledge, 2012).

Klevan, Andrew, *Film Performance: From Achievement to Appreciation* (London: Wallflower, 2005).

Knight, Christopher J., "Woody Allen's Annie Hall: Galatea's triumph over Pygmalion," *Literature/Film Quarterly* 32, no. 3 (2004): 213–21.

Kuleshov, Lev, "Art of the cinema (1929)," in Ronald Levaco (eds), *Kuleshov on Film: Writings of Lev Kuleshov* (Los Angeles: University of California Press, 1974), pp. 41–123.

La Ferla, Ruth, "Unbuttoning Annie Hall: Diane Keaton, 58, comes of age," *New York Times*, February 22, 2004, < https://www.nytimes.com/2004/02/22/style/unbuttoning-annie-hall.html>.

Lamm, Claus and Jasminka Majdandžić, "The role of shared neural activations, mirror neurons, and morality in empathy—a critical comment," *Neuroscience Research* 90 (2014): 15–24, <https://doi.org/10.1016/j.neures.2014.10.008>.

Leberg, Dan, "Digital drapery and body schema-tics," *Public*, no. 60 (2020): 237–49.

Lee, Benjamin, "Woody Allen: 'I Should Be the Poster Boy for the #MeToo Movement'," *The Guardian*, June 4, 2018, <https://www.theguardian.com/film/2018/jun/04/woody-allen-dylan-farrow-metoo-movement-poster-boy>.

Levaco, Ronald, "Introduction," in Ronald Levaco (ed.), *Kuleshov on Film: Writings of Lev Kuleshov* (Los Angeles, USA: University of California Press, 1974), pp. 1–37.

Levinson, Julie, "The auteur renaissance, 1968–1980," in Claudia Springer and Julie Levinson (eds), *Acting* (London and New York: I. B. Tauris, 2015), pp. 95–119.

Lutterbie, John, *Toward a General Theory of Acting: Cognitive Science and Performance* (New York: Palgrave Macmillan, 2011), <https://doi.org/10.1057/9780230119468>.

Lyall, Sarah, "The Daniel Day-Lewis Method: a kind of vanishing Act," *New York Times*, March 9, 2003.

MacCabe, Colin, "The revenge of the author," in Virginia Wright Wexman (ed.), *Film and Authorship* (New Brunswick, NJ: Rutgers University Press, 2003), pp. 30–41.

Mamet, David, *True and False: Heresy and Common Sense for the Actor* (New York: Vintage Books, 1997).

McCarroll, Sarah E., "The historical body map: cultural pressures on embodied cognition," in Rhonda Blair and Amy Cook (eds), *Theatre, Performance, and Cognition* (London: Bloomsbury, 2016), pp. 141–58.

McConachie, Bruce, *Theatre and Mind* (New York: Palgrave Macmillan, 2013).

Meisner, Sanford and Dennis Longwell, *On Acting* (New York: Random House, 1987).

Mikulan, Ezequiel P., Lucila Reynaldo, and Agustín Ibáñez, "Homuncular mirrors: misunderstanding causality in embodied cognition," *Frontiers in Human Neuroscience* 8, May (2014): 8–11, <https://doi.org/10.3389/fnhum.2014.00299>.

Mirodan, Vladimir, "Acting and emotion," in Rick Kemp and Bruce McConachie (eds), *The Routledge Companion to Theatre, Performance, and Cognitive Science* (London: Routledge, 2019), pp. 100–114.

Mirodan, Vladimir, *The Actor and The Character* (London and New York: Routledge, 2019).

Mitchell, Deborah C., *Diane Keaton: Artist and Icon* (Jefferson, NC: McFarland, 2001).

Naremore, James, *Acting in the Cinema* (Berkeley and Los Angeles: University of California Press, 1988).

Naremore, James, "Introduction," in *Acting in the Cinema* (Berkeley and Los Angeles: University of California Press, 1988), pp. 1–6.

Naremore, James, "Marlon Brando in 'On The Waterfront' (1954)," in *Acting in the Cinema* (Berkeley and Los Angeles: University of California Press, 1988), pp. 193–212.

Newhouse, Miriam and Peter Messaline, "Some career problems: gloomy reality," in *The Actor's Survival Guide*, 5th edn (Toronto: Dundurn Press, 2010), pp. 17–32.

O'Toole, Fintan, "Step by step toward creating 'My Left Foot'," *New York Times*, November 5, 1989.

Oppenheim, Tom, "Stella Adler Technique," in Arthur Bartow (ed.), *Training of The American Actor* (New York: Theatre Communications Group, 2006), pp. 29–50.

Orban, Guy A., "The mirror system in human and nonhuman primates," *Behavioral and Brain Sciences* 37, no. 2 (2014): 215–16.

Orlikowski, Wanda J. and J. Debra Hofman, "An improvisational model for change management: the case of groupware technologies," *Sloan Management Review* 38, no. 2 (1997).

Pierce, Nev, "Portfolio 20: Anthony Hopkins and Jodie Foster: 'The Silence of the Lambs' (1991)," *Empire* 240, June 2009 (2009): 105–8.

Plantinga, Carl, "The scene of empathy and the human face on film," in Carl Plantinga and Greg M. Smith (eds), *Passionate Views: Film Cognition, and Emotion* (Baltimore: Johns Hopkins University Press, 1999), pp. 235–55.

Rosenfeld, Carol, "Uta Hagen's Technique," in Arthur Bartow (ed.), *Training of The American Actor* (New York: Theatre Communications Group, 2006), pp. 127–68.

Sarris, Andrew, "Notes on the auteur theory (1962)," in Keith Barry Grant (ed.), *Authors and Authorship* (Malden, MA: Blackwell Publishing, 2008), pp. 35–45.

Sarris, Andrew, *The American Cinema* (New York: E. P. Dutton, 1968).

Sayad, Cecilia, *Performing Authorship: Self-Inscription and Corporeality in the Cinema* (London and New York: I. B. Tauris, 2012).

Schatz, Thomas, "Annie Hall and the issue of modernism," *Literature/Film Quarterly* 10, no. 3 (1982): 180–87.

Seddon, Frederick A., "Modes of communication during jazz improvisation," *British Journal of Music Education* 22, no. 1 (March 2005): 47–61, <https://doi.org/10.1017/S0265051704005984>.

Smith, Murray, "Empathy, expansionism, and the extended mind," in Amy Coplan and Peter Goldie (eds), *Empathy: Philosophical and Psychological Perspectives* (Oxford: Oxford University Press, 2011), pp. 99–118.

Sobchak, Vivian, "What my fingers knew," in *Carnal Thoughts: Embodiment and Moving Image Culture* (Berkeley and Los Angeles: University of California Press, 2004), pp. 53–84.

Stanislavsky, Konstantin, *An Actor Prepares*, ed. Elizabeth Reynolds Hapgood (London: Routledge, 1964).

Sternagel, Jörg, Deborah Levitt, and Dieter Mersch, "Etymological uncoveries, creative displays: acting as force and performance as eloquence in moving image culture," in Jörg Sternagel, Deborah Levitt, and Dieter Mersch (eds), *Acting and Performance in Moving Image Culture* (Bielefeld: transcript Verlag, 2012), pp. 51–60.

Strasberg, Anna, "Lee Strasberg Technique," in Arthur Bartow (ed.), *Training of The American Actor* (New York: Theatre Communications Group, 2006), pp. 17–28.

Strasberg, Lee, *A Dream of Passion: The Development of the Method* (Boston: Little Brown and Company, 1987).

Strasberg, Lee, *The Lee Strasberg Notes*, ed. Lola Cohen (London and New York: Routledge, 2010).

Taylor, Aaron, "Thinking through acting: performative indices and philosophical assertions," in Jörg Sternagel, Deborah Levitt, and Dieter Mersch (eds), *Acting and Performance in Moving Image Culture* (Bielefeld: transcript Verlag, 2012), pp. 395–412.

Thompson, David, *Why Acting Matters* (New Haven and London: Yale University Press, 2015).

Thompson, Evan, *Mind In Life: Biology, Phenomenology, and the Sciences of the Mind* (Cambridge, MA: Harvard University Press, 2007).

Tribble, Evelyn, *Cognition in the Globe: Attention and Memory in Shakespeare's Theatre* (New York: Palgrave Macmillan, 2011).

Tribble, Evelyn, "Distributed cognition, mindful bodies, and the arts of acting," in Rhonda Blair and Amy Cook (eds), *Theatre, Performance, and Cognition* (London: Bloomsbury, 2016), pp. 133–40.

Tribble, Evelyn, "Distributing cognition in the Globe," *Shakespeare Quarterly* 56, no. 2 (2005): 135–55, <https://doi.org/10.1353/shq.2005.0065>.

Tribble, Evelyn and Robin Dixon, "Distributed cognition: studying theatre in the wild," in Rick Kemp and Bruce McConachie (eds), *The Routledge Companion to Theatre, Performance, and Cognitive Science* (London: Routledge, 2019), pp. 264–75.

Truffaut, François, *Hitchcock*, revised edn (New York: Simon and Schuster, 1984).

Utterback, Neil, "The Olympic actor: improving actor training and performance through sports psychology," in Rhonda Blair and Amy Cook (eds), *Theatre, Performance, and Cognition* (London: Bloomsbury, 2016), pp. 79–92.

Varela, Francisco, "Organism, cognitive science and the emergence of selfless selves," *Revue Europeenne Des Sciences Sociales* 29, no. 89 (1991): 173–98.

Vervaeke, John, Leo Ferraro, and Arianne Herrera-Bennett, "Flow as spontaneous thought: insight and implicit learning," in Kalina Christoff and Kieran C. R. Fox (eds), *The Oxford Handbook of Spontaneous Thought: Mind-Wandering, Creativity, and Dreaming* (Oxford: Oxford University Press, 2018), pp. 309–26, <https://doi.org/10.1093/oxfordhb/9780190464745.013.8>.

Vignemont, Frederique de, "Body schema and body image—pros and cons," *Neuropsychologia* 48, no. 3 (2010): 669–80, <https://doi.org/10.1016/j.neuropsychologia.2009.09.022>.

Vuust, P. and A. Roepstorff. "Listen up! Polyrhythms in brain and music," *Cognitive Semiotics* 2008, no. 3 (2008): 134–58, <https://doi.org/10.3726/81606_134>.

Warburton, Edward, "Becoming elsewhere: ArtsCross and the (re)location of performer cognition," in Rhonda Blair and Amy Cook (eds), *Theatre, Performance, and Cognition* (London: Bloomsbury, 2016), pp. 93–106.

Weber, Bruce, "Cozying up to the psychopath that lurks deep within," *The New York Times*, February 10, 1991.

Wesolowski, Brian C., "Cognition and the assessment of interaction episodes in jazz improvisation," *Psychomusicology: Music, Mind, and Brain* 23, no. 4 (2013): 236–42, <https://doi.org/10.1037/pmu0000016>.

Weston, Judith, *Directing Actors* (Los Angeles: Michael Wiese Productions, 1996).

Wojciehowski, Hannah and Vittorio Gallese, "How stories make us feel: toward an embodied narratology," *California Italian Studies* 2, no. 1 (2011): non-paginated, <http://escholarship.org/uc/item/3jg726c2#main>.

Yoder, Keith J. and Jean Decety, "The neuroscience of morality and social decision-making," *Psychology, Crime & Law* 24, no. 3 (March 16, 2018): 279–95, <https://doi.org/10.1080/1068316X.2017.1414817>.

Young, Paul, "The other side of Viggo Mortensen," *Variety Magazine*, 2003.

Zahavi, Dan, "Empathy and other-directed intentionality," *Topoi* 33, no. 1 (2014): 129–42, <https://doi.org/10.1007/s11245-013-9197-4>.

Zahavi, Dan, "Self and other: from pure ego to co-constituted we," *Continental Philosophy Review*, no. April (2015): 143–60, <https://doi.org/10.1007/s11007-015-9328-2>.

Zarrilli, Phillip B., *(Toward) A Phenomenology of Acting* (London and New York: Routledge, 2019).

Zucker, Carole, *Don't Think. Be. 20 Actors Talk about Training, Technique, and Process* (published independently, 2018).

Index

Note: **bold** indicates illustrations

abstraction, 117–19, 121–5, 129
acting
   distinction from performance, 3, 22, 159, 172–3, 181
   force of, 3, 172–3, 187, 190
   as practice, 2, 7, 24
   as process, 2, 3, 6, 172–4
action, 11, 12–14, 19, 29, 35, 70–1, 91, 147–8, 152, 171
Actors Studio, 57, 59, 60, 68
ACTRA, 88–9
Adamou, Christina, 4–5
Adler, Stella, 13, 36, 40, 51, 52, 53, 57, 59–60, 62, 74, 75, 77, 85, 126, 129
affective congruence, 39
affective match, 39–41, 50, 55, 57, 59, 63–5, 70–1, 79, 101–2, 111–17, 124, 128, 130, 148, 151, 175–6, 181
affective memory, 57–61, 68–9, 81, 126
affective sharing, 41
affordances, 5, 6, 22–4, 44, 71, 75–7, 86–8, 92, 100, 109, 118, 133, 136–40, 144, 147, 158–67, 173, 181–2, 185
agency, 5, 6, 7, 9–10, 17, 85–6, 126, 137, 150, 153–4, 158, 164–5, 178, 181–3, 185
Albee, Edward, 66
Allen, Woody, 178–82
American Pie (1999), 18
Aniston, Jennifer, 22
animation, 187–8
anti-appresentations, 157
Annie Hall (1977), 172, 178–82, **179**
appresentations, 32–4, 38, 40, 49–52, 59, 62–8, 70, 71, 74, 76–81, 94–5, 99, 103, 109–13, 122, 125, 128–31, 140–5, 147, 151, 154, 157, 160, 165–6, 175–7, 180–81, 183, 187
archetypes, 118–19, 121–5, 126
Atlantic, 61, 174

attention, 20, 31, 65, 68, 69–70, 74–80, 126, 148–51, 179, 180
audience feedback, 43–4, 76, 80
audition costumes, 90, 96
audition preparation, 94, 97–102, 109
audition readers, 96, 102, 171, 185
audition sides, 92, 94, 96, 97–101, 103, 128
auditions, 21, 87–105, 109, 128, 144, 166–7, 185, 186; *see also* casting
auteurist criticism, 2, 178, 182–3
authorship, 172, 183–4
autonomy, 12, 33
Awful Truth, The (1937), 5

Baker, Chris, 24, 95, 120, 155–6
Bal, Matthjis, 36
balanced script analysis, 110, 111, 116, 125–31
Baron, Cynthia, 174
Barthes, Roland, 4
Bastién, Angelica, 174–5, 177
Beaty, Roger E., 126
Bellows, Gil, **149**, 149–51
Bisson, Yannick, 155–6
Blair, Rhonda, 7, 10, 16, 18–20, 21, 30, 58, 59–60, 188
Bleak House (2005), 23
bodymind
   bodymind experience, 13, 35, 39, 99, 116
   bodymind interconnection, 10, 11, 56, 60
   bodymind resources, 14, 23, 29, 40, 52, 76, 131, 163–6, 181, 185
   movement of, 7, 11, 18, 45, 50, 167
   reorganization of, 7, 11–14, 23–4, 29–34, 42, 45, 49–51, 79, 87, 94, 99, 110, 116, 117, 122–3, 125, 139, 144–5, 162–3, 166, 177, 181–2
Bogart, Humphrey, 158

Boleslavsky, Richard, 55, 57, 59
bottom-up script analysis, 110, 111–17, 122, 124–8
Brand, Phoebe, 59
Brando, Marlon, 172–4, **173**, 175, 183
Britten, Bill, 53, 158
Brown, Blair, 123
Burton, Richard, 64, 66
Butler, Judith, 3

Caine, Michael, 77
Caldwell, John, 133–4, 135, 137, 183
call-backs, 103–4, 128
camera, collaboration with, 9, 75, 76–7, 133, 138–45, 158, 163, 164, 166, 185
Cantrell, Tom, 21–2
care, 41–4, 65, 174, 176–7
Carnicke, Sharon, 55
Carnovsky, Morris, 59
Casablanca (1942), 158
Cassidy, Gary, 23
casting, 17–18, 34, 88–105, 183; *see also* auditions
catachresis, 62–3, 67, 100–1, 112–13, 117, 127
Cavell, Stanley, 123
Cayonne, Antonio, 16–17, 24, 30, 98, 101–2, 111, 120, 127–9, 130–1, 165–6
Cayonne's Minotaur, 16–17, 30, 111, 127–9, 131, 134, 165–6
celebrity, 18, 89, 112, 174, 175
Chekhov, Michael, 16, 32, 55
Chubbuck, Ivanna, 43, 67–8, 72
cinematography, 1, 80, 90, 99, 137, 182
circular causality, 63, 64, 65, 66, 69
class, 4, 73, 178
Clayton, Bruce, 43, 53, 65, 118–21, 148
close-ups, 17, 116, 120, 158
Clurman, Harold, 57
cognitive blending, 16, 88
cognitive ecologies, 20–1, 28, 41, 45, 79–80, 86–7, 92, 97–9, 110, 126, 133, 137–8, 164, 166–7
cognitive scaffolding, 35–6, 42–5, 51–5, 59, 60, 64, 68–70, 75, 78, 94, 97, 99, 104, 109–12, 115, 118–19, 124, 127–9, 145, 147, 154–5, 157, 179–81
collaboration, 9, 18, 52, 66–7, 70, 72–80, 85–7, 90–1, 94–9, 103–4, 110, 116, 122, 130–1, 133–4, 137–67, 171, 178–85, 187–9
collective authorship, 172, 183–4

collective cognition, 72, 172, 182–5
comedic acting, 152–5
community formation, 41
compression, 16, 17, 19
computable geometry, 172, 187
computer-generated imagery (CGI), 162, 187–8
conceptual blending, 15–20, 122
conditioning, 58, 94–5
constraints, 5, 6, 22, 24, 76, 86–8, 92, 93, 118, 133, 135–40, 160, 164–7, 185, 186
Cook, Amy, 7, 16, 17–18, 75, 88, 188–9
Coplan, Amy, 16, 28, 34, 37, 39–42, 43, 50, 54–7, 58–9, 70, 76, 101, 111, 123–4, 174
costume designers, 52, 99, 130
costumes, 22, 54, 77, 90, 96, 178, 182
Cowell, Jason M., 42
creative agency, 4, 5, 7, 9, 153–4, 181–3, 185
creative blockages, 156, 157
creative cognition, 10, 138
creative mismatches, 155–8
Cuccio, Valentina, 35
Curtiz, Michael, 158

Damasio, Antonio, 30, 60–1
Dance, Charles, 22
Davis, Phil, 23, 24
Day-Lewis, Daniel, 18, 56–7, 174
de Niro, Robert, **39**, 50, 54, 61, 174, 175, 177
decentering, 148–52
Decety, Jean, 16, 34, 40–4, 65, 174
default network, 126–7, 146
Delsart, François, 186
DeZotti, Julian, 24, 94
DiCaprio, Leonardo, 56
Dinicol, Joe, 23–4, 51, 120, 137, 143, 146–52, **149**
Dinicol's Jazz, 23–4, 146–52, 154, 156, 161, 166, 177, 186
directors, 2, 18, 21, 44, 52, 65, 79–80, 90, 99, 134–8, 150, 154, 171, 182–3, 185, 188
directors of photography (DOPs), 79, 116, 150, 159, 171
disconnection, 55
distributed cognition, 14, 20–1, 28, 45, 137–8, 160, 167, 172
Donaldson, Lucy Fife, 22, 87–8
Duse's Blush, 111

Dyer, Richard, 3–4, 6
dynamic systems theory (DST), 11–12, 31

economic pressures, 88–9
ecumenical practices, 134–6, 143, 147, 152, 156, 157, 159, 162, 166, 167, 173
editing, 90, 158, 159, 185; *see also* post-production
eloquence, 3, 172–3
embodied cognition, 10, 14, 16, 20, 21, 45, 167
embodied dynamicism, 11–13, 31
embodied imagination, 10, 18–19
embodied simulation, 34–7
emotion, 10–13, 17, 36, 39, 41, 52–3, 55–63, 67–8, 71–3, 93, 94, 111–18, 121, 126, 129, 134, 136, 142–4, 160–1, 186–7
emotional common denominators, 111–17, 122, 129
emotional contagion, 41
emotional preparation, 71, 73, 160
emotional recall, 57–61, 68, 111–14, 126
empathy
  intersubjective empathy, 9, 22–4, 43, 49–50, 63–75, 77–81, 92, 96–7, 102–5, 110, 131, 133, 140–2, 145–58, 161–2, 166, 173, 176–81, 185–7
  intrasubjective empathy, 9, 22, 42–3, 49–63, 75, 77–81, 94, 96–7, 99–103, 105, 110–25, 128–31, 133, 140–3, 145–58, 160, 165–6, 174–7, 180–1, 185–7
  kinesthetic empathy, 184
  Lipps on, 37–8
  performative empathy, 9, 17, 22, 43–5, 49–50, 54, 74–81, 96–7, 101–3, 105, 110, 131, 133, 140–3, 145, 152–8, 160, 162–6, 176, 180–2, 184–6
  phenomenological empathy, 37–9
  solicitation of, 9, 10–11, 17, 19, 21–2, 24, 28, 36, 38, 40–5, 49–52, 63, 69, 73–81, 85–6, 94, 97, 101–2, 116, 133, 138, 140–8, 150–66, 171–8, 181, 184–9
  Stein on, 34, 37–8, 40
enculturation, 14, 34, 86, 138, 164
enworlding, 30, 33, 49, 54–5, 57, 63–74, 78, 80–1, 147, 151–2, 155–6, 161, 176
essential self, 14, 29, 61
ethnicity, 3, 90
evolutionary biology, 41, 44

executive control network, 126–8, 130, 146
experimentation, 1, 50, 51, 54, 55, 56, 59–60, 66, 92, 100, 110, 149, 152, 174–7
extended mind, 20
extrapolation, 15, 16, 19, 62, 97, 100, 112
eye-line matches, 77, 158, 162
Eyre, Richard, 56

facial expressions, 79, 186
family archetypes, 118–19, 125
Fargo (2014–21), 18
Fassbender, Michael, 61
Fauconnier, Gilles, 15
Feagin, Susan, 34, 35–6, 64, 112
feminism, 178
Ferraro, Leo, 31
film sets, 5, 20, 21, 77, 79–80, 87
film studies, 1–4, 25
filtering camera, 143–4, 166
flow states, 31
Fonseca, Agar, 184
force, 3, 172–3, 187, 190
forcible habits, 157
Foucault, Michel, 183
fourth wall, 77–8, 98
Freeman, Martin, 18
Freud, Sigmund, 58
Friends (1994–2004), 22

Gallagher, Julia, 9
Gallagher, Shawn, 9
Gallese, Vittorio, 34, 35
Game of Thrones (2011–19), 22
Gandolfini, James, 87–8
Gangs of New York (2002), 18, 56
gender, 3, 4, 73, 90, 118, 174–5, 178, 181–2
Gerold, Sebastian, 43
gesture, 4, 11, 75, 79, 98, 186, 187
Gibson, J. J., 86–7
Glazer, Eugene Robert, 142, **142**
Globe Theater, 20–1
Goldie, Peter, 37
Grant, Cary, 5
green screens, 162, 187
Greeno, James, 86–7
Gross, Paul, 150
Guerra, Michele, 35
guesswork, 100–1, 104, 109

Hagen, Uta, 51, 77–8, 112
Hamlet (Shakespeare), 56

Heartland (2007–), **115**, 115–16, 163, 164, **165**
Herrera-Bennett, Arianne, 31
Hill, John Wesley, 19
Hitchcock, Alfred, 158, 189
Hobbit films (2012–14), 18
Hoffman, Dustin, 61
Hogg, Christopher, 21–2
Hollywood, 3, 5, 16, 89, 142, 173
Hopkins, Sir Anthony, 123
Hung, Woei, 184
Hunger (2008), 61
Husserl, Edmund, 32
hyper-masculinity, 174–5

imagination, 10–14, 18–19, 24, 29, 32, 37–40, 45, 52–7, 59–61, 77–8, 96, 100–1, 112–13, 116, 123–31, 162–6, 171, 172, 178, 183
immersion, 13, 16, 18, 31, 36, 54, 56, 59, 61, 68, 77, 95, 99, 101, 117, 125, 156–7, 163–4, 177, 186
improvisation, 68, 71, 74, 146–52, 172, 180, 185, 189
In the Name of the Father (1993), 56
inductive practices, 134–5, 162, 173, 182
industrial culture, 21, 24, 40, 42, 45, 80–1, 85–6, 92, 95–6, 104–5, 133–4, 137–8, 150, 156–7
inner monologue, 52, 53, 64
integration, 12–13, 15, 17, 19
intentionality, 4, 5–6, 12, 14, 29, 30–8, 40, 45, 50–4, 57–8, 62–80, 94–101, 110–12, 116–17, 124, 140, 145, 147–8, 150, 155, 171, 176, 178–81, 186
  intentional pull, 9, 34, 37–8, 40, 45, 50–4, 57, 64, 69–70, 72, 75, 78, 94, 97, 99, 101, 110–12, 147–8, 150, 155, 176, 179–81
  intentional push, 73, 75, 76, 77, 116, 140, 145, 181, 186
intersubjective empathy, 9, 22–4, 43, 49–50, 63–75, 77–81, 92, 96–7, 102–5, 110, 131, 133, 140–2, 145–58, 161–2, 166, 173, 176–81, 185–7
intimacy, 139, 141, 145
intrasubjective empathy, 9, 22, 42–3, 49–63, 75, 77–81, 94, 96–7, 99–103, 105, 110–25, 128–31, 133, 140–3, 145–58, 160, 165–6, 174–7, 180–1, 185–7

jazz, 23–4, 146–52, 154, 156, 185
Johnston, Daniel, 33

Johnston, Shaun, **165**
Jolie, Angelina, 4
Jung, Carl, 118–19, 125
Jung, Rex E., 126

Kazan, Elia, 172–4, 183
Keaton, Diane, 50, 171–2, 178–82, **179**
Keitel, Harvey, 38–9, **39**, 54
Kemp, Rick, 1, 14, 16–17, 18, 29, 55, 56–7, 60–1, 189
kinesthetic empathy, 184
Klevan, Andrew, 5
Knight, Christopher J., 181
Knox, Simone, 23
Kubrick, Stanley, 123
Kuleshov, Lev, 158–9, 186–7
Kuleshov effect, 158–9

La Ferla, Ruth, 178
layering, 114–15, 122–3, 124, 165
LeDoux, Joseph, 61
Leigh, Janet, 158
Leto, Jared, 61, 171, 174–7
Levey, Jon, 17
Levinson, Julie, 61, 174
Levitt, Deborah, 3, 172
Levy, Brian, 90
Levy, Eugene, 17–18
Lewis, Robert, 59
lines, memorization of, 21, 53, 94, 95, 100, 110, 121, 145, 147
Lipps, Theodor, 37–8
Lisinska, Natalie, 22–4, 51, 88–9, 93, 95, 113–17, **114**, 120, 122, 124, 129–31, 136–7, 156–62, 185–6
Lisinska's Tears, 22–3, 113–14, 136, 159–62, 166, 173–4, 185–6
literary characters, 34, 35–6
Little Mosque on the Prairie (2007–12), 154
Lord of the Rings films (2001–3), 54
Love and Death (1975), 178
Lutterbie, John, 11, 12–13, 34, 139, 186

MacCabe, Colin, 183–4
McCarthy, Sheila, 24, 91, 112, 120, **142**, 142–3, 146, 152–5
McCarthy's Symphony, 153–4, 156, 161, 166, 186
McConachie, Bruce, 16, 17
MacFadzean, Matthew, 24, 91–2, 93, 97, 103–4, 120, 134, 136, 137, 139, 146
McGarry, Kevin, 92, 111, 114–18, **115**, 122, 124, 125, 143–4, 163–5, **165**, 175

McGarry's Relatability, 111, 114–16, 117–18, 124, 143–4
MacKinlay, Lauren, 24, 93, 109
Macy, William H., 73–4
Magic If, 13, 19, 32–4, 37, 40, 55–6, 58, 62, 64, 67, 71–2, 91, 94–5, 99, 110, 160–1, 180
make-up artists, 138, 159, 160
malleability, 14, 29–30, 63, 110
Mamet, David, 73–4
Marathon Man (1976), 61
marking, 136, 178
Mary Kills People (2017–19), 113, 136
Maslany, Tatiana, 23, 103, **114**, 159–61, 185–6
meaning-making, 5, 9, 10, 11, 13, 172, 178
Meisner, Sanford, 13, 23, 24, 32, 40, 43, 50–1, 62–3, 68–74, 75, 81, 85, 102, 127, 147–8, 178–82
memory, 10, 11, 13–14, 20, 24, 33, 37–8, 40, 52, 57–63, 68–9, 81, 111–14, 125–31, 154, 165–6
Merleau-Ponty, Maurice, 11, 62
Mersch, Dieter, 3, 172
Method acting, 13–14, 23, 36, 40, 49–63, 68–74, 75, 85, 147–8, 167, 172–5, 178–82
Method of Physical Actions, 59–60
Metric Web, 186–7
Middleton, Lindsey, 134–5, **135**
Minelli, Liza, 142–3
mirror mechanism (MM), 34–5, 37
mirroring, 34–5, 37, 65, 145, 148
moment, being in the, 31, 42, 64, 73, 80, 95, 99, 146, 150
monologues, 179–80
Monster (2003), 61
Mortensen, Viggo, 54
Moscow Art Theater, 57, 186
motion capture (mocap), 162, 187
motivation, 4, 29, 35, 43–4
Mr. and Mrs. Smith (2005), 4
Murdoch Mysteries (2008–), 155–6
My Left Foot (1989), 56

naming, 117–18
Naremore, James, 5, 172–4
National Theatre, London, 56
Neighborhood Playhouse, 74, 178
neo-Strasbergian Method acting, 67, 174
neurophenomenology, 10–15, 29, 34, 35, 37, 45

neuroscience, 10, 11, 18, 28, 29, 34–5, 60, 61, 126–8, 188
Nicholson, Jack, 175

objects, 22, 30, 54, 77–8, 129–30, 162
observation, 13–14, 36, 52, 63, 69–70, 71–2
Office, The (2001), 18
O'Flynn, Danelene, 24, 121–3, 125, 126
Olivier, Laurence, 54, 61
on-set practices, 3, 22–4, 77, 80, 133–67
On the Waterfront (1954), 172–4, **173**
Orlikowski, Wanda, 185
Orphan Black (2013–17), 22–3, 103, 113–14, **114**, 159–61
other-oriented perspective taking, 40–2, 50, 55, 57, 59, 65–6, 70–2, 79, 99, 101, 111, 124, 128, 130, 148, 150, 176, 181
Ouspenskya, Maria, 57, 59
out-of-sequence shooting, 109–10, 117, 136
Out With Dad (2010–17), 134–5, **135**

particularization, 62, 71–2
Passchendaele (2008), **149**, 149–51
Pavlov, Ivan, 58
payment, 88–9
perception, 11, 12, 20, 86, 157
performance
    distinction from acting, 3, 22, 159, 172–3, 181
    eloquence of, 3, 172–3
    as focus of critical analysis, 2–6, 189–90
performance scores, 62, 65–6, 67, 79
performance studies, 2, 6, 177, 189–90
performative continuity, 99, 117, 156
performative empathy, 9, 17, 22, 43–5, 49–50, 54, 74–81, 96–7, 101–3, 105, 110, 131, 133, 140–3, 145, 152–8, 160, 162–6, 176, 180–2, 184–6
permission, 148–51
persona acting, 18
personal references, 4, 10, 23, 30, 33, 111–13, 116–17, 121–5, 128–9
personal visibility, 18
phenomenological empathy, 37–9
phenomenology, 7, 10, 11, 28, 29, 37–9
Philadelphia Story, The (1940), 5
physical transformations, 61, 174, 177
"pinch and the ouch, the," 69, 70
Pitt, Brad, 4
Plantinga, Carl, 17
popular psychology, 61, 174

post-feminism, 4
post-production, 92, 145, 157, 159, 187
post-traumatic stress disorder (PTSD), 61, 115–16
posture, 4, 11, 79, 186
power dynamics, 117–19
practical aesthetics, 73–4
precarity, 42, 88–91, 105, 138
pre-shoot preparation, 109–31, 147, 151, 154, 155, 160, 177
Previn, Soon-Yi, 182
problem-solving, 137, 184–5
production budgets, 73, 133, 135
production schedules *see* shooting schedules
production studies, 172, 182–5
production team, 18, 21, 44, 79–80, 87, 90–1, 99, 110, 116, 122, 130–4, 137–8, 150, 163–6, 183–5
Professional Actors Lab, 43, 118–21, 125
proprioceptive self, 14–15, 29
props, 2, 22, 54, 77, 78, 129–30, 162
Psycho (1960), 158

quotidian self, 6–7, 9, 10, 15, 18–19, 29–30, 36, 40–3, 49–53, 56, 62–3, 68, 74, 75, 79, 110, 113, 117, 145, 151–2, 176–7

race, 3–4, 73, 178
Raging Bull (1980), 54, 61, 177
Rain, Douglas, 123
reaction, 13–14, 19, 23–4, 65, 67, 68–72, 74, 91, 147–54, 157–8, 178–9
reactive emotions, 39
Rear Window (1954), 6
reciprocated care, 43, 176–7
rehearsal, 22, 52, 55, 65–6, 92, 136, 145–6, 153, 154, 161
relatability, 111, 114–16, 117–18, 124, 143–4
Repetition Exercise, 74
Repetition Game, 69–71, 73–4, 81, 127, 179, 180
representational politics, 90–2
rhythm, 152–4, 156
Ribeiro, Mônica M., 184
Romeo and Juliet (Shakespeare), 14–15, 67, 134
Rotenberg, David, 118
Ryerson University, Toronto, 130

Saint, Eva Marie, **173**, 173–4
Sarris, Andrew, 182–3

Schiff, Richard, 17–18
screenwriters, 53, 134, 153–4, 171
script analysis, 34, 37, 52–4, 74, 90, 92, 94, 97–101, 110–31, 145, 147, 151, 154
Seddon, Frederick, 148
self-effacing practices, 134, 136–7
self–other distinction, 40–3, 50, 55–7, 59, 61, 62, 66–7, 70–3, 79, 102, 112, 117, 124, 128, 151–2, 164, 176–7, 181
selfhood models, 11, 14, 29–30, 35, 45
selfless self, 29–30
semiotics, 3–4, 6, 9, 13, 178
Serkis, Andy, 187
Shakespeare, William, 15, 20–1, 56, 67, 120, 134, 189
Sherlock (2010), 23
shooting schedules, 21, 73, 80, 90, 92, 93–4, 104, 109–10, 133, 135–7, 149, 151
Silence of the Lambs (1991), 123
situational self, 6–7, 14–15, 20, 21, 28–32, 36, 38, 40–3, 45, 49–52, 54, 56, 58–9, 69, 73, 77, 79, 94, 98–9, 101–2, 110, 113, 117, 124–31, 145–7, 150–1, 176–7, 181–2
skill acquisition, 54, 89, 177
Sleeper (1973), 178
Smith, Murray, 20
Sobchak, Vivian, 62
Sopranos, The (1999–2007), 87–8
sound recording, 79, 138, 163
Soviet montage theory, 187
spatiality, 5, 139, 186–7
spectatorial approaches, 2–6
Spilchuk, Jamie, 24, 94, 95, 96–7, 99, 104, 120, 138, 141, 153–4, 164–5
spontaneity, 62–3, 68–9, 72, 81, 94–5, 146–52, 166, 173, 178, 180, 181
stage acting, 7, 13, 43–4, 65, 76, 92, 120–1, 123, 139, 186
Stanislavsky, Konstantin, 18–19, 30, 32–4, 40, 50–1, 55–60, 71, 74, 186
star studies, 3–4, 6, 171–2, 178
Stein, Edith, 34, 37–8, 40
Stepping Out (1991), **142**, 142–3
Sternagel, Jörg, 3, 172
Stewart, Jimmy, 6
Strasberg, Anna, 52, 57–8
Strasberg, Lee, 13, 40, 50–1, 52, 55, 57–63, 67–9, 74, 75, 81, 85, 126, 134–5
substitutions, 67–8, 72, 113–16, 117, 118, 122, 124, 125, 128

subtexts, 5, 69–70, 71, 74, 119, 121, 127, 149, 178, 180
subtitles, 180
Suicide Squad (2016), 61, 171, 174–7
supporting roles, 23
suspension of disbelief, 16, 19, 73, 79, 163–6

Taxi Driver (1976), 38–9, **39**, 54, 61, 177
Taylor, Aaron, 6, 189
Taylor, Elizabeth, 64, 66
theater acting *see* stage acting
Theron, Charlize, 61
thinking-together, 184–5; *see also* collective cognition
Thompson, Evan, 11–13, 31, 32, 34
team-based problem solving (TBPS), 184–5
tears, 22–3, 113, 134, 159–62
technical adjustments, 162–6
technical tricks, 158–9
technicians *see* production team
technology, 162, 172, 187–8
television studies, 3, 7, 21–5
tennis balls, 162–4, 187
tennis metaphor, 153
theater studies, 7, 10–21, 24
timing, 153–4, 156
top-down script analysis, 110, 111, 117–28
training, 10, 12–14, 16, 20–1, 36, 42–5, 49, 51, 57–8, 69–78, 85–6, 111, 118–21, 123, 130, 138, 139, 145, 147, 164, 167, 181, 189
transformative acting, 18

trauma, 59, 61, 115–16
Tribble, Evelyn, 20–1
Truffaut, François, 189
trust, 43–4, 63–5, 122, 131, 140–3, 145, 148–9, 152, 163, 166, 177, 181, 182
Turner, Mark, 15
2001: A Space Odyssey (1968), 123
typecasting, 89
Tzioumakis, Yannis, 174

Varela, Francisco, 11, 29, 31
Veltkamp, Martijn, 36
Vervaeke, John, 31
vocal intonation, 4, 79
voice acting, 187–8

Waiting for Guffman (1996), 18
Walker, James, 87–8
Walters, James, 22
Warburton, Edward, 136
watching own performances, 75–6, 77, 78–9, 144, 164, 184
West Wing, The (1999–2006), 17–18
Weston, Judith, 183
Who's Afraid of Virginia Woolf? (1966), 64, 66
working memory, 42, 126–7, 128, 130, 154
writers *see* screenwriters

Zahavi, Dan, 37
Zarrilli, Philip, 11, 12–13
Zirodan, Vladimir, 18
Zucker, Carole, 189

EU representative:
Easy Access System Europe
Mustamäe tee 50, 10621 Tallinn, Estonia
Gpsr.requests@easproject.com

www.ingramcontent.com/pod-product-compliance
Lightning Source LLC
Chambersburg PA
CBHW071841230426
43671CB00012B/2036